About the Author

Craig Sim Webb is an author, dream analyst/researcher, singer-songwriter, award-winning filmmaker, and inventor. His life path was set in motion in 1986 when he nearly drowned on a rafting trip and suddenly began having powerful lucid and vision dreams. A McGill University graduate with pioneering lucid dream research at Stanford University and Montreal's Sacré-Coeur Hospital, he has designed personal development and biofeedback tools with worldwide distribution, written music for TV/film/radio/online, and helped found/produce *Making Contact* (a respected international radio show that has aired weekly on 100-250 stations since 1995). Mr. Webb has also had the honor to be an invited expert for major motion pictures, Fortune 500 corporations, various universities, and over a thousand international media, presenting about dreams and creativity with a refreshing style that blends science, soul, heart and (hopefully!) humor. It's been his privilege to empower CEO's, world-class athletes, top celebrities, best-selling authors, and many others, helping them make profound breakthroughs while having plenty of fun in the process. He has also performed and presented at benefit concerts and events, and served as a volunteer for Children's hospitals and environmental organizations, Montreal's suicide hotline, 3rd world development programs, non-profit organizations, and various other humanitarian causes.

www.CraigWebb.ca

The Dreams Behind the Music

Learn Creative Dreaming as 100+ Top Artists Reveal their Breakthrough Inspirations

by Craig Sim Webb

~

www.**DreamsBehindTheMusic**.com

~

Copyright © 2016-2025 Craig Sim Webb

All rights respectfully reserved.

Print edition 2.05

ISBN: 0973428228
ISBN-13: 978-0-9734282-2-3

Table of Contents

Little-Known Musical Dreams that Rocked the Modern World

Paul McCartney • Billy Joel • Sting • Paul Simon • Ladysmith Black Mambazo • Billie Eilish • Michael Jackson • The Rolling Stones • Taylor Swift • Ed Sheeran • Lady Gaga • Teddy Swims • Shawn Mendes • Jimi Hendrix • Peter Gabriel • Bobby Braddock • Carl Perkins • David Crosby • Neil Young • The Mamas and the Papas • The Beach Boys • Fleetwood Mac & Stevie Nicks • Dave Grohl (Nirvana/Foo Fighters) • Pharrell Williams • Black Eyed Peas • Fergie • Train • Lorde • LL Cool J • Drake • Katy Perry • Meghan Trainor • Miley Cyrus • Madonna • Blake Shelton • Dolly Parton • R.E.M. • Bruce Springsteen • The Fray • Queen • The Kinks • David Bowie • Donovan • Van Morrison • Rush • Radiohead • Deep Purple • The Cure • Iron Maiden • Black Sabbath • The Muse

Stevie Wonder • Marc Anthony & Jennifer Lopez • Stevie Ray Vaughan • The Allman Brothers • Ziggy Marley • Rachmaninoff: Dream Coach for Olga Kern • Musical Prodigy Downloads Dream Gift from Mozart • The Grateful Dead • Sammy Hagar & Eddie Van Halen • Sinéad O'Connor • Barenaked Ladies • Rodney Crowell • Florence Welch (Florence & the Machine) • The Killers • Dr. John • Rory Block • Joe Hill Visitation • Elsiane • Tegan and Sara • Megadeth • Timbaland & Aaliyah

Richard Wagner • George Frideric Händel • Ludwig van Beethoven • Franz Schubert • Robert Schumann • Johannes Brahms • Sir Arthur Sullivan • Igor Stravinsky • Giuseppi Tartini • Anton Bruckner • Hector Berlioz • André Grétry & Daughter Lucile • Edvard Grieg • Gustav Mahler • Carl Jung – Music Archetypes & Healing • John Coolidge Adams • Rev. C.E. Hutchison and Alice in Wonderland's Lewis Carroll • Samuel Taylor Coleridge & Charles Tomlinson Griffes • Jacob Druckman • Gunther Schuller • Bright Sheng • William Grant Still

"Any artist who ignores their dreams is ignoring half of their creative potential." –**Sting**[1]

"The best songs are the ones that come to you in the middle of the night, out of a creative space, and you have to get up and write them down." –**John Lennon**[2]

"When you're dozing, that's when the creative ideas come."
–**folk music legend Pete Seeger**[3]

"I wake up with a melody in my head in the morning and I have to write it down. I don't have to write it down because we need another song for the record. I write it down because I'm excited by the idea of making music." –**Bono**[4]

"You must learn the way to follow the dream."
–**seventeen-time nominated and five-time Grammy-winning singer-songwriter Joseph Shabalala**[5]

"All great musical composers have been connected, consciously or unconsciously, with this [inner] source of music—a fact that enabled them to become masters of their art. Their compositions contain specific messages brought through from high realms for the definite purpose of bettering world conditions and bestowing upon mankind greater illumination." –**Corinne Heline**[6]

"If a man could pass through Paradise in a dream, and have a flower presented to him as a pledge that his soul had really been there, and found that flower in his hand when he awoke—Ay!— and what then?" –**poet Samuel Taylor Coleridge**[7]

"When a really great dream shows up, grab it!" –**Larry Page, founding CEO, Google (a company sparked by a dream)**[8]

Applied Dreaming Adventures

I am fortunate to have the opportunity to guide individuals and also embark alongside enthusiastic teams of dreamers on *Dream Mastery and Lucid Living* teleclass adventures. Each journey brings amazing insights and major breakthroughs as intrepid explorers experiment with weekly 'homeplay' techniques to help remember and understand their dreams, become more lucid, overcome tough challenges, and harvest many other highly valuable waking life benefits. To learn more or hop aboard, please email: ***dreamclass@craigwebb.ca***

Whether you are interested in cultivating dreams filled with music, enjoying exciting lucid explorations, or experiencing other adventures in dreamland, I wish you many fascinating and powerful experiences. I hope that such dreams contribute to your best life and also deeply benefit those around you.

From the web site below, you can also click through to **www.CraigWebb.ca** to learn free techniques for understanding dreams, including how to resolve common recurring nightmare themes such as being chased, falling, or being unprepared for an exam. There are also tips for boosting dream recall and having more lucid dreams, as well as updates about special events related to dreams, creativity, and music. Owners of this book can also get discounts on training, products, and events:

www. Applied Dreaming .com

ACKNOWLEDGMENTS

First of all, my appreciation to you for the trust you offer sharing your time to read this book. I have devoted a great deal of time and energy towards the goal of making the journey you are now embarking upon insightful, inspiring, and valuable for your life in practical ways. I genuinely hope you enjoy the adventure.

A grateful nod to the team at Google who offer us all tremendous search tools at no charge, which have helped immeasurably while researching this book. This includes a special recognition of Google's founding CEO, Larry Page, for acting on the dream he awoke from that showed him how to design a better search engine. In doing so, he thereby not only birthed the multi-trillion dollar company most people benefit from regularly, he also proved to us through his concrete actions and described in words the important truth that underlies this entire book: "When a really great dream shows up, grab it!"[9]

Many thanks to the artists and producers who personally responded to my questions about their dreams. Special gratitude to other artists, both living and beyond the veil who graciously shared their creative process and dreams, and who devoted so much time to share inspired music with us all. Without you having revealed such dreams, and in many cases personal details about your lives, this book would not have been possible. It is my genuine hope that all such stories and contributions will serve to inspire and help others cultivate and harvest valuable insights from their own dreams—for music and other arts, as well as for health, relationships, business, learning, and spiritual growth.

Thanks also to the many radio and TV hosts, authors, anthropologists and scientists who have shared interviews and research, or written about dreams and music. Sources far too numerous to detail here helped while researching this book. I offer gratitude to all, though I wish to acknowledge friends and colleagues Nancy Grace, Patricia Garfield, Stephen LaBerge, Deirdre Barrett, as well as other colleagues such as Hans Prokop, Irving Massey, Paul Zollo, Ryan Smith, and many more. Much gratitude also to the proofreaders who kindly helped edit and polish this manuscript.

I offer the greatest appreciation of all to the amazing Dream Weaver and Muse who continue to bring me so many powerful dreams and creative insights, including many beautiful original melodies, lyrics, and soundscapes, as well as regular song title- and lyric-based intuitive guidance for this unparalleled learning adventure we call life.

Introduction

You will find on these pages fascinating, true accounts of *over two hundred dream-inspired musicians, composers, producers, and others*, including plenty of well-known artists. The anecdotes reveal private dream inspirations that grew into a wide variety of incredible creative and career successes. In some cases, the dreams actually saved lives! I also show powerful dream principles, offer proven dreaming tips and techniques, and share intriguing music dream examples from over fifteen thousand recorded dreams of mine, which include many hundreds that offered musical inspirations and over a thousand lucid (i.e. conscious) dreams.

As I gathered story after intriguing story for this book, I grew increasingly amazed at the huge extent to which little-known dreams of major artists have had a tremendous yet mostly invisible influence on the music we know. **Seen together, this unique collection of individual experiences shapes an impressive and perhaps even surprising picture that shows how dreams have played a significant role in weaving the musical, if not overall fabric of our culture.**

Alongside other factors, the dream-inspired successes in this book add to my sense that we are experiencing a culture-wide, and perhaps even global expansion from head to include more heart. This shift is expanding the focus from mental reasoning and intellectual analysis to include more intuition and empathy, and from honoring thinking as paramount to include more respect for and more of a connection with feelings, our bodies, other people, and nature. One way this is showing up is through increasing environmental awareness and greater respect for the shared global body we call Earth. Another way is with increased creative expression such as the popularity of music and video-sharing websites, crowdfunding campaigns, and as exemplified by the recent success of singing, dancing, and talent-competition shows. Another facet of this shift is increasing trends in personal development and spirituality as demonstrated by growing worldwide interest in yoga,[10] and related pursuits such as lucid dreaming. I have been fortunate enough to have lucid dreaming as an integral part of my personal journey for four decades and professional path for over three decades since my involvement in the pioneering lucid dream research at Stanford University. I therefore foresee more and more people, including recovering 'think-a-holics' like me, developing a deeper connection with their dreams, intuition, feelings, and artistic selves in order to inspire and help express their creative gifts.

"Intuition is the father of new knowledge...Intuition, not intellect, is the 'open sesame' of yourself." –**Einstein**[11]

Considering this global shift alongside the renowned quote from 17th-century thought pioneer René Descartes,[i] "*I think, therefore I am*", I would like to respectfully offer a newer and more open-ended perspective for consideration that will hopefully be a seed for our modern era from which fresh insights and valuable new experiences can grow:

I dream, therefore Who am I?

Making the Most of This Book

As you read the various true-life anecdotes, I encourage you to view the dream inspiration process I share here not just as a creative tool for musical artists, but as a universal key that can unlock the doors behind which lie answers to any question as well as potential solutions for any problem you ever face in life. Put simply,

Creative solutions to life's toughest challenges are but one dream or insight away.

---

[i] I feel that it is wise for us individually and collectively to develop both reasoning and intuition and honor both thoughts and feelings, and thereby, over time, bridge head and heart. This is why I wish to bring attention to the fact that although Descartes was a forefather of modern science, his revolutionary contemplations that helped form the foundation of the scientific method and boosted the importance of the reasoning mind were confirmed, if not conceived of, during 3 dreams he had on November 10, 1619. Descartes claimed that the dreams, especially the third one, revealed to him his calling to develop a new philosophical system, and he described the dream(s) as "the most important thing in my life." (A. Baillet, La Vie de Des-Cartes, Paris: Daniel Horthemels (1691), pp. 82-85).

I hope you find the stories in these pages interesting and inspiring, and I encourage you to experiment with the dream principles spread throughout the book and the techniques offered near the end—they show how anyone from musicians to parents to inventors to farmers to athletes to business executives can cultivate and harvest dreams for surprisingly powerful creative insights that offer significant benefits for work, relationships, health, spiritual growth, and all other aspects of life.

Enjoying the Reader Journey

How you might like to read this book depends a good deal on your interests. Perhaps you are most interested in popular mainstream or folk artists who dreamt up some of their greatest hits, or maybe you are most interested in classical, soundtrack, or electronic composers, or even indigenous shamans including how their nocturnal musical experiences serve their communities. Or you might be particularly fascinated, as I am, by how dreams offer a portal through which others can visit us, including the deceased. Possibly, you wish to learn about dreams that guide us in life either as nightmares that warn us away from dark possible futures or as beautiful visions that call us towards bright, joyful ones. Perhaps lucid dreams intrigue you, including how they can benefit songwriting, among many other pursuits. Maybe you are an artist yourself and wish to learn right away how to cultivate and harvest your own dreams, which I am quite sure from experience, are waiting to offer you artistic inspiration, important career guidance, and plenty of other benefits too. If any of the above topics strongly call you, I encourage you to trust your enthusiasm and follow what inspires you. This book is structured so that you can jump to any chapter at any time without missing a beat since there are sections that highlight each of the above topics. However, if you do jump ahead, I still heartily encourage you to return to enjoy the rest of the book. I've highlighted important dream, consciousness, and life principles that appear in many of the artists' experiences so that they can be helpful for us all, since we are all creatives of one sort or another. If you skip sections of the book without ever returning, you will miss some of these valuable principles and tips since they are spread throughout the book alongside the inspired yet pragmatic dreamers that demonstrate them in action.

You may wish to enjoy the various dream inspiration stories a few at a time, ideally just before sleep. Contemplating the anecdotes in such a way can become a simple creative practice that offers your subconscious examples (and therefore suggestions) about what is possible, and that subtle yet important process may well inspire your own creative dream muse.

Craig Sim Webb

Chapter 1

Harvesting Music from Dreams

Perhaps it is more than coincidence that the first ever Grammys awarded for Song of the Year and Record of the Year were won by dream-inspired artists. It may come as a bit of a surprise, but you will learn in this book of at least twenty[ii] Grammys and scores of other major awards that have been won thanks to dream-inspired works, as well as many dreamland creations that resulted in nominations, including a dream that not only brought the potential song that would later be nominated for a Grammy, but

---

[ii] At least twenty Grammy wins can be directly attributed to dream-inspired works described in this book. The actual number is likely far above that, yet is hard to calculate since some Grammys were won for albums or artists with dream-inspired songs, and many were won by artists like Joni Mitchell or Dave Grohl whose career path was set in motion by a dream, or Beyoncé whose many song inspiration dreams and dream-inspired backup band Suga Mama likely contributed to her 35 Grammy wins, or 15-Grammy-winner Michael Jackson who claimed that many creative inspirations came in dreams even though few specifics are known, or 31-time Grammy winner Sir Georg Solti who won Grammys for conducting two dream-inspired works, including his most famous recording: Richard Wagner's dream-harvested *The Ring of Nibelung* opera, or 25-time Grammy winner Vladimir Horowitz whose dreams improved his piano playing, or the 1973 Grammy wins for both the audio book LP and the film adaptation soundtrack of Richard Bach's dream-inspired blockbuster novel *Jonathan Livingston Seagull*, etc.

also specifically predicted exactly that. Surely numerous Grammys and many other awards worldwide have also honored musicians and producers who chose to weave dreams into their work, even though the story of their creative process has not yet come to light. Without a doubt, dream-inspired works will also contribute to many future awards and other creative successes, including launching entire careers—perhaps even yours!

The rest of this chapter highlights a few examples of what you will learn more about in this book.

Long before Grammys and other modern awards were created, dream-inspired music brought impressive success to classical composers who tapped and acted on their muse's gifts, and for millennia to shamanic musical dreamers from many indigenous cultures worldwide who received great healing and teaching dream gifts for their tribes.

Perhaps modern composers and artists who tap dreams for their music, lyrics, and performing skills are like creative public shamans in this big world tribe that we call our society.

Mainstream musical icons **Beyoncé**, **Paul McCartney**, **Billy Joel**, and **Sting**, opera composer **Richard Wagner**, and African singer-composer and late **Ladysmith Black Mambazo** founder, **Joseph Shabalala**, are all documented as having been prolific at creating and sharing very successful dream-inspired music. In addition to other mainstream artists like **U2**, **Taylor Swift**, **Ed Sheeran**, **Billy Eilish**, **Drake**, **Shawn Mendes**, **Teddy Swims**, **The Rolling Stones**, **Lorde**, **Michael Jackson**, **Roy Orbison**, **Jimmy Hendrix**, **Lady Gaga**, and scores of others, numerous folk and electronic music artists, as well as composers and instrumentalists past and current have also tapped dreams for their creations, as you will soon learn. Even the melody for a well-known

Christmas carol came from a dream. A few composer examples among many include **Ludwig van Beethoven, Igor Stravinsky, Johannes Brahms**, **Frédéric Chopin**, and French composer **Maurice Ravel,** who claimed that he dreamt delightful melodies.[12]

You will also soon read amazing accounts of people whose life path has been radically changed literally overnight by dreaming about their new musical calling such as a revelatory vision dream by seventh-century Anglo-Saxon singer-poet **Cædmon**, a career-sparking dream by **Foo Fighters** and **Nirvana** rocker **Dave Grohl**, the dream that seeded classical composer **Giuseppi Tartini**'s best known work and later led to the violin school he created, and modern day surgeon and now pianist **Tony Cicoria**, whose musical muse came calling in dreams shortly after he was struck by lightning.

You will also find here fascinating accounts of music-related life and death warning dreams, such as Canadian folk composer and CBC radio host **Clary Croft**'s song *Black Sails* about a powerful warning dream that both saved a man from death by shipwreck and, unheeded by others, cost them their lives. A very similar scenario and dream is linked with the deaths of **Lynyrd Skynyrd** band and crew members, as you will soon discover. **John Lennon** had dreams which seem to have foretold his murder, **Stevie Ray Vaughan** had a portentous nightmare about his own funeral the day before he died, and artist **Patti Smith** seems to have had a premonition that predicted **Rolling Stones** founder **Brian Jones'** tragic drowning. Not only did **The Beatles' George Harrison** dream about his father saying goodbye the night before his dad passed on,[13] George's own son also dreamt of his deceased father visiting him in a dream. "Where have you been since I last saw you?" Dhani Harrison asked his father in the dream, and George answered, "Here the whole time."[14]

There are also a number of songs and tours by well-known artists such as **Stevie Wonder**, **Ziggy Marley**, **The Barenaked Ladies**, **David Bowie**, **The Grateful Dead**, **Sammy Hagar**, **Florence and The Machine**, and classical composers **Gustav Mahler**, **Robert Schumann**, **Anton Bruckner**, among others, that were inspired by dream visitations from deceased loved ones or colleagues. Both **Stevie Ray Vaughan** and **Duane Allman** were paid dream visits by the late dream-inspired rocker **Jimi Hendrix** who brought them performing and songwriting tips from 'the other side'. Deceased band leaders for **The Grateful Dead** and **Van Halen** appeared in the dreams of their living band mates offering musical inspirations for new songs. Late jazz-blues legend **Dr. John** also recorded an entire 13-song album of **Louis Armstrong** songs because the late Armstrong (also a dream-inspired artist), appeared in a dream and encouraged him to do so. Some deceasedVirtuoso pianist **Olga Kern** was helped in a dream by a deceased master pianist to win an important piano competition that lifted her budding career to international success, and iconic rock and roller **Prince** enjoyed lucid dreams where he connected with deceased friends and colleagues.

Dreams: Surprising Benefits Beyond Songwriting

"The musical dream is not merely a curiosity, but a potential source of valuable information." –**Irving Massey**[15]

It seems as though an entire unexpected level of communication and support transpires between various artists invisibly, at deeper levels. In addition to some of the cases mentioned above where living musicians are helped by deceased colleagues, as you will soon see, dreams have also sparked collaborations amongst various artists including **U2**'s **Bono** with **Roy Orbison** then later with **Bob Dylan**, **Arcade Fire** with **Neil Young**, **Barry Manilow** with **Bette Midler**, **Johnny Cash** with **Willie Nelson**, **Kris Kristofferson**, and **Waylon Jennings**, and quite possibly **Eric Clapton** with **B.B. King**. Singing icon **Diana Ross** seems to have dreamt herself into a motion picture lead role that also made possible **Michael Jackson**'s movie debut which deepened a bond between the two that endured throughout Jackson's life.[16]

Dreams also help in other ways. Superstar **Taylor Swift** claims that in addition to using dreams to inspire her music, she experiences a recurring nightmare that motivates her tour planning. Many visuals and storyline elements for **Billie Eilish**' hugely successful debut album music videos and live performances[17] are derived from her nightmares, night terrors, and lucid dreams. **Beyoncé** conceived of the concept for her all-female touring band Suga Mama in a dream. Among various bands like **Air Supply** whose names came from dreams, a series of dreams evolved into a new name and spiritual path for dream-inspired Grammy-winner **Maitreya** (formerly known as **Terence Trent D'Arby**). Instrumentalists also dream about their craft: blind multi-instrumentalist **Rahsaan Roland Kirk** not only twice tweaked his name thanks to dreams, he also dreamt how to play multiple instruments simultaneously, and thereafter pioneered an impressive new skill which was later picked up by others. Russian-born American pianist and 25-time Grammy-winner **Vladimir Horowitz** and his contemporary **Leonid Hambro**, staff pianist at The New York Times' classical station WXQR, both dreamt specific performance fingerings in order to play various difficult pieces of piano music,[18] as did esteemed Chilean pianist **Claudio Arrau**.[19] Not only composers dream about music—many writers, poets, and others do as well, including even famed poet **Edgar Allan Poe**,[20] who also used his dreams for poetic inspiration.

Insightful music-related dreams also come not just for crafting and performing music but for music producers, inventors, and other professionals as well. **Darren Higman**, Senior VP of Soundtracks for Warner Brothers, claims to have dreams that help him with important business decisions.[21] In 1790, **Dr. Ernst Chladni** dreamt up the 'Euphon' which used water-filled crystal glasses as its sound source,[22] an instrument similar to Benjamin Franklin's better-known glass harmonica. The Central Asian horse-head fiddle also seems to have originated in a dream. More recently, **Texas Tornadoes** singer and guitarist **Junior Brown** created his "guit-steel" double-necked, guitar-like instrument after having a dream in which he was playing both instruments,[23] and composer/inventor **Wendy Mae Chambers** created a 26-note "organ" from car horns thanks to a dream that incorporated honking from a nearby New York traffic jam.

Famed psychiatrist, psychotherapist, and master dream analyst **Carl Jung** even spoke about the transformational power of universal musical archetypes and music therapy to help clients heal psychological problems.

And the musical dreamer list goes on and on, and hopefully will soon include you, if you wish it so. Thoughts have their own momentum, so quite possibly just by reading about the various artists and contemplating their stories of inspiration, this book will inspire creative dreams of your own, perhaps even musical dreams. If you don't yet consider yourself a musical artist and yet start having musical dreams, perhaps consider partnering with a musician to create an inspired collaboration.

If that sounds interesting, then I wish it for you, and if such dreams come and you would like to share them with a like-minded community, please contact me via the website below. Readers of this book are also welcome to special discounts[24] on *Applied Dreaming and Lucid Living* team adventures:

www.DreamsBehindTheMusic.com

No book of this kind can be fully comprehensive. There are surely accounts of dream-inspired artists and music not included here, and there will hopefully be many more in the future. I plan to release updated future editions, so if you are aware of any such stories not included here, please do share them with me by email at: *music@craigwebb.ca*

Craig Sim Webb

Chapter 2

Dreams and Creativity

The cycle of being cared for as a young child, learning through childhood and teen years, and then refining our skills into and throughout adulthood in order to give back to the community, is as natural as any plant growing from a seed by taking in sun, earth, water and air eventually bearing flowers and fruit for other creatures to enjoy and survive on.

In the same way that (natural) fruits contain seeds to continue the growth cycle, the invisible seeds which are our dreams and creative inspirations, once actualized, can feed our community and inspire future generations. The following quote artfully expresses the profound universal nature of this cycle and the importance of serving others:

"My life is like a loan given from God, and [by serving others] I will give this loan back with interest." **–Andy Wimmer, 17-year volunteer, Mother Teresa's Calcutta Home for the Dying**[25]

Creative expression of our intrinsic talents (i.e. self-actualization) to inspire and help others is therefore one of our most profound and universal needs. For this to happen effectively, we want to find the best mentors and take the steps required to master the skills involved with our profession or art form, as well as stay connected as clearly and fully as possible to the _innernet_.

Connecting to the _Innernet_

'Innernet' is a word I playfully created many years ago to describe the inner source of information imperceptible to our physical senses, somewhat like the external internet that we know as the web, yet which each of us can connect to inside ourselves through dreams, meditation, and intuition. On this inner level, not only are we all interconnected like we are through the internet, it is also where the blueprint of our greatest potential lies, and is the source of the powerful intuitive guidance and creative inspirations that often come as 'dream downloads' to help us manifest this amazing potential into our lives. These insights are like seeds waiting to grow into the daylight of the physical world by our discovery of them, and by our choice to act upon them.

Our actions are simply thoughts in motion, so our most-inspired thoughts and dreams, acted upon, will allow us to become brilliant artists and magnificent individuals. It is therefore vital to develop our ability to receive important insights as clearly as possible, wisely prioritize them, and courageously move past fears and limitations to act on the best insights and thereby bring our unique creative gifts alive.

This process of living our deeply-inspired Truth is a recipe not just for bringing true our brightest dreams to inspire and help others, it is also how each of us can ultimately find the joy and peace that will become our individual piece in the greater mosaic of world Peace.

"If we can invoke Peace and then offer it to somebody else, we will see how Peace expands from one to two persons, and gradually to the world at large." –**Sri Chinmoy**[26]

As humans, we have free will, so we can live in alignment with the natural process of insight and creative expression—or not. It is quite possible to block the process unknowingly, via hidden limiting beliefs, fears, or habits. And while few people consciously resist the process and most artists happily embrace it, one example of conscious blocking is classical composer **Hector Berlioz** for what seemed at the time to be understandable reasons, but which may in retrospect have been an unfortunate acquiescence to a voice of fear that limited his creative expression and success.

So fear is one way we sometimes block the process, either consciously or unknowingly. However it is also possible to limit fulfillment of our creative goals and our life purpose by distraction or addiction. These three challenges—fear, distraction, and addiction—are central blocks that can limit our happiness and fulfillment in life. Surmounting these challenges, as well as consciously aligning with our inspired dreams and developing the skills, jewels of character, and relationships with others required to bring them to fruition, is a very worthwhile endeavor and a core element of what I call *Lucid Living*.

From the insights and lessons my life has offered, and from the examples in this book, it becomes clear therefore that a very key practice for any artist and anyone interested in fresh, creative solutions is to find ways to regularly connect within to the internal source spring where dreams, intuition, creative inspirations, hunches, gut feelings, and spontaneous impulses exist in infinite abundance. In a way, everyone is an 'artist' creatively expressing themselves in different forms, so I believe connecting regularly within is important for all of us. As we learn to connect to the *inner*net more regularly and more effectively, and also develop the skills of our respective craft to creatively express the ideas, feelings, and experiences from our journeys within, we master a universal creative process that allows us to share our unique gifts to inspire, entertain, and uplift others.

Chapter 3

The Experience of Musical Dreaming

"When you're dozing, that's when the creative ideas come."

–folk music legend Pete Seeger[27]

One study of 5000 dreams shows that less than 1.5% of dream reports mention sound or music.[28] Another 2005 study shows that musical dreams are twice as common for musicians, and that about half of all music dreamt is original to the dreamer.[29]

Considering that it is not common for the majority of people to remember dreams involving sound or music, I feel very grateful to enjoy such dreams on average once or twice a week[iii] with no effort, and more often when I focus on it. On some occasions, I am blessed with multiple music dreams per night. At other times, musical themes develop in multiple dreams spread over a period of nights. This is one of the main reasons why I am interested in the topic of dream-inspired creativity, especially musical dreams, and one of my motivations for writing this book.

[iii] On average, about 7% of my dreams contain sound or music, and the percentage has been growing.

My frequency of musical dreams has also been increasing over the years. Perhaps this increase is related to a powerful life-calling vision dream I had two decades ago in which I saw and felt the profound joy of a bright possible future where I could write, present, and teach about dreams to many people around the world. The second scene of that dream, also filled with deep joy, suggested that I could also share music as a singer-songwriter and performer. I have had the great privilege to write, present, teach extensively, and share films about dreams and their practical benefits. I have had the good fortune share such work in many countries, at universities, for Fortune 500 corporations, as a consultant for film and TV, and on numerous media to many millions of people worldwide. So the first part of the dream seems to have come true, thanks to grace and to my commitment to offer empowering information and tools to people. I have also had the good fortune to perform music internationally. If grace continues to smile upon my path, I hope the dream will continue coming true for years to come, including opportunities to compose, share, and perform songs inspired by my huge and growing collection of dream-inspired melodies and lyrics.

I sometimes dream music by other artists, but the majority is original music I have never heard before in waking life, although during the dream, it sometimes seems that someone else has composed it. In such cases, it is only after I awaken that I recognize the 'someone else' to be a deeper level of consciousness, usually my own. As you will soon learn, a fair number of composers and songwriters have experienced this interesting 'creatorship uncertainty' phenomenon in dreams. Such dreams are not unique to musical artists either. Any new creative idea that bubbles up from the subconscious in a dream can seem beyond our current identity until we accept and create it, which may be why we sometimes don't believe it could have come from us. Perhaps artists and creatives act as the conduits through which the mass psyche of the culture brings forth important insights and unspoken feelings that it needs to become aware of. Accordingly, it is not surprising that important revelations that can positively affect many people arrive in the dreams of those who are likely to act on such inspirations and bring them into the world.

After following a guidance dream that encouraged me to fly the next day to Los Angeles and meet Director **James Cameron** (which I did), he ended up sharing with me on national radio[30] the two dreams that directly inspired the film *Avatar*, the top-grossing film of all time which he wrote and directed. In one of the dreams, Cameron saw a breathtaking bioluminescent forest and glowing river, and as he awoke, he found himself wishing that he could create something that beautiful. Moments later, he laughed realizing that 'he' did create the lovely images, though at a deeper level—in his dreams. Cameron quickly sketched the images with pastels, and later decided to incorporate that visual theme into *Avatar*.

"I think [dreams] are an important part of a lot of people's creative process, and certainly have been for me."
–James Cameron[31]

Although art and film are different mediums than music, it is not uncommon for all types of creators to think during a dream, and even sometimes afterwards, that art or music or other new creative works were crafted by 'someone else'.

Bestselling author **Richard Bach** had a similar experience regarding a dreamlike event that came to him during waking hours. As a skin diver, he had spent a lot of time watching seagulls. "Once I was down in some boulders at the Corona Del Mar breakwaters," recalled Bach, "and I heard the sound of their wings fast and low…just a few feet over me. I never forgot that sound." Some days later, while out walking one night by the Belmont Shore canals near Long Beach, California, Bach "heard" a "voice" a few feet behind and to his right say directly to him: "Jonathan Livingston Seagull".[32] When he arrived home a short while later, he started "receiving" the images and scenes of the book's storyline almost faster than he could write them.[33] For quite some time afterward, he did not really feel that he personally created what became his best-selling inspirational novel *Jonathan Livingston Seagull.* The remarkable book remained #1 on the New York Times bestseller list for 38 weeks starting in 1970, has sold over 44 million copies, and won Grammy Awards for both its audio book version[34] and movie adaptation soundtrack by Neil Diamond as his sole Grammy win.[35]

Other artists also report similar experiences. **Sir Paul McCartney**, as you will learn shortly, for a little while after dreaming the melody for the Beatles' #1 hit *Yesterday*, didn't believe that the tune had originated with him. U2 singer-songwriter **Bono** divulged that, for him, "Lots of songs arrive in a dream state. At first you think it must be somebody else's song, because it's there, verse, chorus, melody."[36] In a dream, **Roy Orbison** heard a new song he understood to be created by a famous contemporary. Only upon awakening did he realize the song was his own creation. Classical composer **Anton Bruckner** described his *Te Deum in C major* as the work of another composer who revealed it to him in a dream. Since many other artists have experienced this same creator confusion in dreams, perhaps, as Bruckner suggests,[37] such works involve some sort of collaboration at deeper levels.

A dream of mine occurred the night after I had been working on an African-sounding melody that came in a dream a month or so before:

> *I hear this amazing African-sounding piece of music in its entirety. I am quite taken with it and think, 'Wow. I want to remember this!' In the dream, a woman comes and tells me*

*that the song was recorded by so-and-so already. Not
realizing that I am still dreaming, I feel a bit disappointed.*

Awakening, I couldn't remember any of the melody or lyrics,
which is rare for me. Although I felt a little disappointed, I mostly
find the experience amusing, since I am fairly confident I could
dream the melody again if I focused on it. Yet because I did not
realize that I was dreaming (i.e. I was not lucid in the dream), this
odd but not uncommon experience of thinking someone else had
created the music fooled me into forgetting it.

In another experience, I 'awaken' and tell someone to wait while I
record into my voice recorder a song I just dreamt. Only later do I
actually wake up (in my physical bed) and realize that I had
previously only dreamt that I had woken up (from a dream within
my dream), so I only recorded the dreamt melody into a 'dream
replica' of my voice recorder (i.e. not my physical recorder!) This
confusing experience is called a false awakening and is somewhat
common, especially for lucid dreamers.

These last couple of dream experiences show why it can be
valuable to set an intention before sleep to avoid such potential
problems, so I share a powerful exercise in the Techniques
chapter that has been proven to influence dream content and
recall.

According to French-Israeli ethnomusicologist Simha Arom, all
music is "an act of creation that actualizes intention."[38] It can be
surprisingly valuable then when the initial inspiration for a
waking intention and action arises from deep levels of our being
such as when we remember and then act on a dream. Perhaps we
can find a new word for such deeply-inspired artworks, such as
'*he*artworks', because by sharing such works, we express a deep
part of ourselves and grow into someone greater in the process.
Quite possibly we can also rise to a significantly new level of
professional success, as did so many of the artists discussed in this

book. This is the almost magical, perhaps alchemical, and yet quite pragmatic and empowering process of literally 'making our dreams come true'.

Although I have placed indigenous and shamanic dreamers who receive healing and teaching songs for their tribe in a different chapter than classical, electronic, and mainstream artists, it seems important to mention that the process of receiving music or music-related guidance in a dream that can benefit the dreamer's life and the wider community is universal to all of them. In native cultures, what is referred to as the larger tribe may well have as its modern equivalent what we call audiences at public concerts, operas, and on radio, TV, mobile devices, and Internet.

What is the source of such inspirations that seem to offer career breakthroughs for so many? Clearly the subconscious and unconscious mind have greater depth and wider reach than our conscious mind, so life-changing melodies and other treasures from the dream realm arise from some vast field of ideas and can help open doors to bright potential futures. Some such inspirations come as answers to problems our mind has been focusing on, like **Stravinsky**'s dream solution about using wind instruments as the arrangement for a composition where he had just finished the first part, yet had no idea what arrangement to use.

Help from the Deceased

In a number of dream-inspired pieces, there seems to be help from the deceased, a process apparently honored by **Train** lead singer Pat Monahan when he thanked his late mother in his Grammy-winning acceptance speech. Some artists in this book share stories about friends and musical colleagues who helped them in their dreams. **David Bowie**, **Jimi Hendrix**, and many other artists speak of late parents, siblings, and grandparents appearing in the dreams that inspired their creations. Since those we are close to in life are often glad to contribute to our well-being and success, it does not seem too surprising that a similar process continues after they graduate from earth (i.e. pass on). Many experiences working with my own and others' dreams have shown me that the deceased, from their more expansive vantage point, are indeed often able to help the living in significant ways.

Musical Dream Recall

Artists who dream music report varying ease of recall when it comes to dream melodies as compared to dream imagery, feelings, or plot. Research suggests that recall of music lasts longer than other elements of the dream,[39] which has also been my experience. Psychiatrist and frequent musical dreamer Heinz Prokop reported that, for him, "The musical element was almost always far stronger than the visual element of the dream."[40] American cognitive scientist and psychologist Roger Shepard, father of the fascinating audio illusion called the Shepard scale, reported a number of musical dreams, describing the instruments and sounds that he heard with crystal detail and specificity.[41] Other artists like **Sir Arthur Sullivan** or **Shawn Colvin**, who you will read about shortly, report dreamt music as being tougher to remember. French Composer Vincent d'Indy often awoke from musical dreams yet recalled them only vaguely and had to focus intensely to capture even a few measures.[42] Conversely, music prodigy **Mozart**'s remarkable 'hearing it all-at-once' musical 'imagining' process is an especially interesting case of extremely clear recall of inner musical perception.

I have noticed for myself that the duration of recalled melodies is generally about 10-30 seconds, a duration which may be due to a short-term brain mechanism called echoic memory. I generally interpret these shorter musical 'ideas' as the theme, potential chorus, or hook of a song, similar to how guitarist **Keith Richards** dreamt the guitar hook for the song that became **The Rolling Stones** first international #1 hit. I think of these short 'dream sound bites' as seeds or sprouts that I can then choose to actively grow and refine. Once I begin crafting the sound bite into a larger piece, other elements of the composition may come in another dream, as happened with my African dream melody mentioned previously.

This exemplifies a principle I have seen at work many times now whereby <u>the 'Dreamweaver' part of us who weaves creative inspiration dreams seems more likely to do so to help along the creation process once a commitment has been made to work on the song or other artistic work</u>. Such subsequent dream inspirations generally come only after action has been taken and time has been spent developing the initial inspiration. It is as though the muse at first goes on a date with us to learn if we might be open to the greater relationship that can bring additional creative flashes and joy, yet which also requires the greater commitment of actively completing and then publicly sharing the creative work.

Of the musical dreamers I have researched or spoken to, the majority seem to remember more of their dreamt music near the moment of waking rather than experiencing it as an intrinsic part of the dream, as though it were coming on a separate channel of information than the imagery of the dream. The same is also true for me. This interesting subjective separation seems to be supported by recent brain research evidence suggesting that music may well be processed by specialized neural networks in the brain which are distinct from those for processing other cognitive functions,[43],[44] including even speech and the recognition of non-musical sounds.[45],[46] Although both sides of the brain process sound, the distinction between perception of sounds, speech, and music extends even to the ears, with research showing that "the left ear is better at perceiving vocal nonverbal sounds, such as hummed melodies, laughing, and crying; the right ear is better at perceiving verbal sounds."[47]

Dreams and Music – Connections and Subjective Experiences

When I am feeling content, I often find myself spontaneously humming, or singing, or whistling some tune. Sometimes, the melodies are by other artists, and in such cases the moment I realize I am singing, the specific lyrics going through my mind (or mouth!) at that moment offer surprisingly insightful and important intuitive guidance about whatever situation I am facing. At other times, the melodies are original, and seem like joy and other feelings bubbling up from my deeper being in musical form.

So, I find it quite intriguing therefore that the simplified Chinese symbol ('lè') is the same for the English words 'happy' and 'music'.[48]

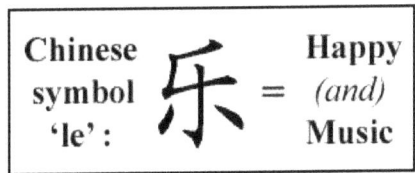

Chinese symbol 'le' :	乐 =	**Happy** *(and)* **Music**

This makes sense, since I know other people who sing or hum or whistle when they are in a light, happy mood, including children, who are generally more connected with the muse and the natural, spontaneous joy of our deeper being.

What came as quite a revelation to me, reinforcing the above point and even more so the theme of this book, are the multiple meanings of the Old English word *drēam*, which are the same as above: melody/music/song, joy/gladness (noun), and rejoicing (verb).[49]

Music as an experience is unlike the senses of sight and smell, in that certain types of music or rhythms seem to intrinsically have a motivating effect on the body, inspiring us to dance. It is perhaps not surprising then that, in several African languages, the same word refers to both music and dance.[50]

Melodies I experience during dreams are sometimes directly connected with the dream's plot. In such cases however, the dream's 'soundtrack' message may not always complement the plot imagery, as in one dream of mine where a violent fight dream was contrasted by a very happy and upbeat background melody. More often than not, the dreamt music continues 'playing' (in my mind) for a while past the moment of physically arising from bed, possibly due to a short-term memory brain mechanism akin to a musical version of what is called 'the phonological loop' from a memory model proposed by psychologists Alan Baddeley and Graham Hitch.[51] If such is true, a small region of the brain may then act a bit like a computer's cache memory allowing us to transfer dreamt sounds and music into waking memory independently from the memory of the dream's imagery or plot.

Musicians such as **Giuseppi Tartini** and **Billy Joel**, among others, agree that it can be difficult to fully reproduce not just the complete melody but also the arrangement or rich soundscape of the music they have heard in dreams, suggesting the inner faculty of hearing can sometimes be a more expansive experience than its outer counterpart of hearing with our physical ears. Like musical dreams author Hans Prokop, I also quite easily remember most dreamt melodies for some time after waking. However, the feelings from the dream often fade within a few days or even hours, as does, to some degree, the ease by which I can expand the dreamt melody or lyrics effortlessly into a full song that has the same feel as the original dream and sound bite. Some artists who you will read about shortly, therefore quite purposefully and rather wisely chose to start composing the same day they received their dream muse's inspiration in order to more clearly reproduce what they heard. A few artists like **Anton Bruckner**, **Julia Ward Howe**, **Robert Schumann**, **Jimmy Webb**, **Brian Eno**, and others, have been? motivated enough to compose or record the song immediately after waking—even in the middle of the night.

In my experience teaching thousands of people how to recall dreams, it is also wise to keep any physical sounds or music (like a wake-up alarm) to a minimum before a dream is captured, at least in rough form or as a basic recording. This is especially true for musical dreams since physical sound and music can quickly start to impinge on recall of the dreamt tune. Research shows that even something as simple as chewing can limit recall of melodies playing in our brains.[52] In Appendix 1, along with proven tips for recalling dreams, I describe how it is possible to intentionally awaken before or even without an alarm.

Artists vary in their reports of how much of the music they dream is original, which may depend on how much new music they have been composing recently since one studies suggests the quantity of new dreamt music is proportional to the amount of time spent creating new music while awake.[53] In my dreams, about four in five melodies are original, but that proportion has been increasing over time. Some people only remember dreaming of known music. Conversely, singer-songwriter and producer **Scott Mathews** admits, "I don't recall ever dreaming music that I've heard before."

Otherworldly Music During Near-Death Experiences

"Music…Is it the language of some other state [of being echoing in our memory]? For what can wake the soul's strong instinct of some other world like music?" –**Letitia Elizabeth Landon**[54]

An interesting related fact is that people who have had Near-Death Experiences (NDEs) also sometimes report hearing music whose beauty and richness is beyond anything heard on earth.

Don Piper's car was run over by an oncoming tractor trailer. He was pronounced dead, but was later revived. Piper claims that when the collision happened, he was immediately transported to heaven and "heard music I've never heard on earth." Piper added that he vividly remembers angels "all singing glory-to-God songs, hallelujah songs, and praise songs simultaneously, and there was no chaos."[55]

Although not a near death experience per se, music appeared in what seems to be the earliest ever recorded lucid dream, experienced by Roman physician Gennadius, who harbored fears regarding death and doubts about an afterlife. In his dream, Gennadius was visited by a youth of commanding presence who took him to a city where he heard, to his right, exquisitely beautiful and divine music. When he inquired about it, his dream guide called it "The Hymn of the Blessed and the Holy". Although Gennadius did not later compose the music he had heard, it is quite interesting to note that the same youth re-appeared in a following dream and led Gennadius through questioning to confirm that he was, at that moment, experiencing a dream, and that his physical body was asleep in bed with eyes closed. The youth explained that as Gennadius was still able to see and hear in the dream even though his physical body was asleep and his eyes closed, so it would be when he died. The youth counseled Gennadius to therefore hold no more fears of death or doubts about the afterlife.[56]

When Dreams May Come

I have noticed that musical dreams tend to come more the night before days on which I have already planned to work on music, perhaps as a result of subconscious preparation, yet almost as encouragement. As I mentioned before, based on many years working with dreams, I also see that creative inspiration dreams of any nature come in response to the time commitment made to develop and actively express the inspirations they offer.

The Dreamweaver also seems to know ahead of time whether I will follow through on such a commitment or not. One example of this is when a dream offered a catchy new song idea on a day I had committed to only creating music. However, the same dream also warned me that unless I really prioritized it that day, I would not find time to develop the dreamt melody into more of a song. Unfortunately, even though the warning was quite clear, I still somehow managed to get distracted with emails and other not-so-important tasks most of the day until it was too late to do much with the song. Following days were full with other commitments, so developing the song slipped down my to do list. Although likely not too serious in this case since I have the dreamt musical sound bite on file, the dream's warning did indeed prove accurate, and I share the scenario with you to offer a glimpse of how perceptive dreams can be about our lives and tendencies.

Dream melodies and musical motifs can return days, weeks, months, and perhaps even years later, just like dream characters, symbols, and plot themes do. I have re-dreamt almost-identical melodies on more than one occasion. One interesting case of a returning musical dream inspiration, as you will soon learn, was reported by popular artist **Billy Joel**, who re-dreamt the melody for *Just The Way You Are* while dozing two weeks after he originally awoke with it in the middle of the night.[57]

"I don't always remember what I dreamt," shares Joel, "but I know all of the music I've composed has come from a dream."[58] He also revealed that the majority of his musical dreams include melodies and arrangements rather than lyrics.

My experience is a little different. While some of my music-related dreams contain only melodies, some offer lyrics or title or instrumentation ideas, some reveal arrangements or soundscapes or audio effects, yet others bring new performance ideas or musical instrument inventions, and a few even train my performing skills. However, the majority contain a combination of these things. I have had a number of dreams where I am shown various string instruments that I have never seen before, and as far as I know, do not yet exist in physical reality (like the dream of a spring-string instrument I had this morning, before writing this paragraph). Alternately, some 'music' dreams come more in what seems to be a guidance perspective, encouraging me to work with certain musicians, or work on a certain song, or make certain actions related to musical outreach. This is also true for other artists, including some described in this book.

Intriguing Music Dream Personal Examples

Here is a personal example of a music 'guidance' dream:

> *Two women are speaking with me and encouraging me to get my song out there more. I express my appreciation for their enthusiasm, then ask which song they are referring to, since I have a number of completed and partially written ones. They do not respond before I awaken, yet I somehow know that their names are Polly and Muriel.*

Association via similar or identical-sounding words (homonyms) is a dream interpretation principle whereby dream symbols and especially dream character names link the dream with waking events.

Soon after waking, I laughed, realizing a strong connection between their combined names and my playful environmental song-in-progress at that time titled *Polymers*.

Thanks to the dream, I then polished and recorded that song largely as a result of the dream, and have had the good fortune to have it shared a number of times on radio and elsewhere. Hopefully, the song offers a playful nudge about the vital need to address the serious problem of all the artificially-created materials and chemicals in our lives that challenge our health and environmental ecosystems.

I don't want to give the impression that all guidance dreams are easy to follow. A day or two after beginning a lovely vacation retreat in Hawaii, I had a rather clear dream that encouraged me to go back to Canada very soon (in the middle of winter), and that it was going to be important for sharing music. I contemplated the dream and choice all day, and realized that another dream before I left on the trip had encouraged me to do the same thing. There was no logical reason that I knew of to return, but I eventually convinced myself that my commitment to try my best to follow inner guidance was stronger than my wish to enjoy another couple of weeks of my (already-paid-for) tropical vacation. I followed the dream, and as things turned out, I met someone the next week who I would not have met otherwise, and it led to a few years of regular performances that seem to have inspired many people. The dream's wisdom seems easier to understand in retrospect than at the time it came. To go against logic, it required a trust I have learned over many years of happily having followed (and also of painfully having not followed) dreams and intuitive guidance, and some dreams were harder to follow than the one shared above.

Dreamy Audio Effects

An intriguing example of what I call an audio effect dream came one day when I awoke to a fascinating sound of what I thought must be a large truck starting up, or a piece of heavy machinery being operated outside, since it had an odd rhythmic motor-like rumbling sound. I soon grew very perplexed, quietly arose, and walked to the window to see what was going on. It was tough to localize the odd sound, but I eventually realized that what I was hearing was actually an echoed version of my nearby sleeping friend who was snoring loudly! It was as though I had a 5-second reverb/echo effect inserted into my regular hearing! I was not frightened, yet I was surprised and very intrigued so I experimented with light tapping sounds to discover that they exhibited the same odd echo. The fascinating effect lasted for a minute or two until the peculiar experience slowly dissolved back to regular hearing. Many years later I learned that French singer-songwriter Melody Prochet had a similar echo experience in a dream.

In a related and equally intriguing experience I had on the border between sleeping and waking, I listened for about half a minute to two soft, low-frequency piano notes playing alternately. As I gently transitioned into wakefulness, I realized that the alternating notes corresponded to my inhalation and exhalation.

The audio aspect of a dream can also sometimes stimulate lucidity, which is to say, it can help me recognize *during* a dream that I am dreaming. I had the good fortune to be part of the Stanford University team that helped bring lucid dreaming into the mainstream, and we did so because the experience can be life-changing and can also powerfully enhance the various benefits dreams offer.

One example of a sound-triggered lucid dream was an interesting scene where I became aware during the dream that the voices of the other characters were lagging a few moments after their lips moved, much like a poorly-edited film. This oddity encouraged me to look at my hands to check whether I was dreaming. Much to my surprise, my 'hands' looked fuzzy and wavy (as they usually do in dreams) and I realized that I was indeed dreaming, and that these were dream hands (i.e. not physical hands). I had not considered any such possibility up until that moment because the scene was otherwise very believable and seemed like so many waking life moments.

I have had the good fortune to experience well over a thousand lucid dreams, many of which have offered powerful revelations and changed me forever. While being lucid (conscious) during a dream is often exhilarating, it can also be helpful for dreaming creatively, as demonstrated by one of my lucid dreams:

A lively instrumental musical phrase is playing repeatedly. I become lucid and listen closely to memorize the tune so I can record it when I awaken. One or two instruments suddenly go quiet so that I hear the pizzicato strings much more distinctly. Then about 5 white horizontal lines appear in what looks like a musical staff yet each line also seems to correspond with an instrumental track since some lines disappear in the middle for the tracks that are 'switched off'. I mentally 'choose' just to hear piano—then only the piano track is playing. I am intrigued and do the same with the drums, which then play alone, continuing the lively beat. I like that I can focus on individual tracks, just like with my music software in waking life. I am unsure about remembering all the details when I awaken, but I am enjoying the process, and it seems like a great 'dream skill' to develop.

In lucid dreams, I know that I am dreaming. However, the distinction of being awake or dreaming is not always so clear, and sometimes the subjective experience of sound is also unclear as to its source, i.e. whether it is coming from inner hearing or outer physical hearing. Sounds and songs (such as a radio playing while one sleeps) can be incorporated into dreams, and sounds and melodies from dreams can seem very much as though they are coming from the outer world. On one occasion, I heard my name clearly called from what sounded like my friend sleeping in an adjacent room.

I called over to him, "What?"

He responded, "What do you mean 'what'?"

"Didn't you just call me?"

"No," he replied.

"Sure sounded like you did."

"I assure you," he answered back, "I did not."

We were both confused but found the episode very intriguing when we discussed it later that day, since I was sure that he had spoken to me, and he was certain that he had not, at least not in waking state. Although it is difficult to tell what actually happened or why, perhaps my own subconscious (i.e. not my physical friend in the adjacent room but an inner 'friend' at a deeper level) was trying to get my attention, since a similar sounding voice spoke in my dream that night, and it surprised me so much that I quickly awoke.

Inner Music as Intuition

I mention the possibility of inner music being akin to, or an aspect of, intuition, since I have many times noticed that the title of the song and especially the exact line of lyrics that I remember from a dream (or notice playing in the background of my thoughts during daytime hours) offers a clear, helpful insight for a question I have been contemplating or a challenge I am facing in my life. From such moments and similar experiences of my students, it seems as though intuitive insights can arrive via music from the inner muse, and they usually come particularly clearly this way.

Some music-related dreams seem to be able to tune into events I could not otherwise consciously know about. Here is a performance-related dream example:

> *R. gives me his guitar to play on. I'm impressed since he seems to have made it himself with a central 'neck' pole that has strings attached to its top but spread around a 180-degree semi-circle rather than being strung in a flat plane like a regular guitar. I'm amazed how low the bass string is, sounding like a true bass guitar, but then I see how loose it is (curly and dangling) and I say I will have to tighten it for now to make it more playable. He seems fine with that.*

Knowing that my dreams often reveal things that I am not consciously aware of, I emailed the dream to my friend R., since he had agreed to lend me his guitar for a performance a couple of weeks later.

He replied, "I've been reading how the first string instruments that many Delta [blues] guitar players had as kids were single string 'guitars' though made with a broom handle [just like the central 'neck' from my dream]. Also, I got the guitar I'm lending you partially because of the bass sound—it just vibrated in a way I liked. And I do often tune it down, increasing that effect." When I met him and heard the guitar, I found that it was indeed tuned much too low (symbolized by loose strings in my dream that sounded like a bass guitar), and I had to tune it higher so the strings didn't buzz against the neck.

This is one instance among many of how it is quite possible for dreams to 'tune in' to situations that we have no normal way of knowing about. I share it as an example of abilities I have developed and my students all develop and enhance, and therefore I hope it encourages you to keep an open mind regarding the surprising revelations your own dreams can offer.

Chapter 4

Seeing Music, Hearing Images

"A painter paints pictures on canvas...musicians paint their pictures on silence." –**Leopold Stokowski**[59]

Sight and Sound on the *Innernet*

Since light is a universal symbol for consciousness, 'seeing' generally represents knowing and understanding and therefore also relates with the reasoning mind. This is why figurative expressions like 'shedding light on the situation' or 'seeing things more clearly' or 'I see what you mean' are common. In a similar manner, hearing can symbolically represent intuition. Since recalled dreams are a strong aspect of intuition and since music has a powerful connection with and effect on feelings, then dreaming and dream-inspired music may well be contributing significantly to the profound global shift mentioned in the introduction. A core aspect of this vital shift is that intuition, emotions, and empathy are not only gaining importance, but also functioning more and more harmoniously with intellect and reasoning—a welcome change that seems to be slowly happening throughout our beloved, yet in many ways quite challenged, world.

"As [the] pure organ of Feeling, [music] speaks out the very thing which Word-speech in itself cannot speak out—...that which, looked at from the standpoint of our human intellect, is the Unspeakable." –**Richard Wagner**[60]

Regarding music in dreams, I wonder if all dreams may actually have an associated 'soundtrack' that most of the time we simply don't tune in to or remember. I mention this not only due to the surprising amount of success that my students had incubating musical dreams the first time they tried (as detailed in the Techniques chapter), but also because I sometimes awaken from a dream with music that I remember too vaguely to record, and at other times, I spontaneously find a new melody going through my mind shortly after waking or later that day.

On a similar note, a dream of mine offers an even more interesting possibility:

> *As I watch, these yellow plastic curled petals morph into curly red and gold Christmas ribbon tassels. I become aware of this pretty musical phrase playing that I seem to know I have created at some other time. As I very slowly begin to awaken, rather than the music being a soundtrack separate from the dream imagery, it seems as though the lovely notes actually <u>are</u> the pretty-colored ribbon, yet simply perceived in a different way.*

So perhaps the 'inner light' that composes dream images and the 'inner sounds' that form dream music are both perceptual translations of a single underlying energy. By this I mean that some source energy, whatever it is, can be perceived as visual dream images and symbols from one perspective and dream music or sounds from another just like the flip sides of a coin, although appearing different, are simply impressions of, and both composed from, the coin's metal.

"What makes us feel drawn to music is that our whole being is music: our mind and body, the nature in which we live, the nature which has made us, all that is beneath and around us, it is all music." –**Hazrat Inayat Khan** (Sufi master)[61]

The subjective experience of blending or interchanging different sensory faculties is called synesthesia. One possible basis for such experiences may be hinted at by my dream above where the same source energy is perceived through different sensory channels. In an uncommon form[62] of this phenomenon, I sometimes have the subtle yet intriguing and occasionally quite exquisite experience of 'hearing' touch sensations. While completing this book, I also had a dream during which I genuinely 'felt' (in my dream body) music and sound that someone near me was playing in the dream. The sensation was so exquisite that I just kept standing there as music poured across and through my arms and torso. Needless to say I awoke quite full of joy, yet also very intrigued by this fascinating experience.

"Within your system, colors may be perceived as sound. Their connection with human moods is only too apparent [63] *...Sound can be felt as well as heard.*[64]*"* –**Seth**

Quite a number of musical artists have auditory-visual synesthesia, a somewhat dream-like experience of "seeing" sound or music as colors. Dream-inspired artists Billy Joel,[65] Billie Eilish[66] and her brother Finneas O'Connell,[67] Lady Gaga,[68] Lorde,[69] Jimi Hendrix,[70] Tori Amos,[71] and composers Beethoven,[72] Richard Wagner,[73] and György Ligeti[74] all report having this experience, as well as Beyoncé and composer Shirish Korde who both appear here below. A few among many others include Stevie Wonder,[75] ColdPlay's front man Chris Martin,[76] Eddie Van Halen,[77] Kanye West,[78] classical composer Franz Liszt,[79] and John Mayer who describes his experience of how "melody is color".[80] Dream-inspired artist Pharrell Williams also sees sounds as colors. "There are seven basic colors: red, orange, yellow, green, blue, indigo, and violet," Pharrell said, adding his viewpoint that the 7 colors correspond with the 7 musical notes in the octave.[81] Not only has dream artist extraordinaire Sting reported seeing imagery while composing or listening to certain types of music, the visual cortex of his brain was also shown to be activated while composing,[82] perhaps in a musical visualization experience related to the composing process of Mozart.

Mozart

The great 18th-century Austrian classical composer **Wolfgang Amadeus Mozart** was also accomplished on keyboard instruments and violin. Mozart was incredibly prolific during his short 35-year life, producing over 600 musical works, and is reported to have heard a number of melodies in dreams which he transcribed upon awakening.[83]

In a letter to his cousin, Mozart described his remarkable and quite dream-like composition process:

> *[It] kindles heat in my soul—that is if I am not disturbed—and it gets bigger and bigger, and I spread*

it out and make it wider and brighter; and the whole thing is almost finished in my head, even if it is a long piece, so that afterwards I can see in my mind at a single glance, as if it were a beautiful picture or an attractive person, and similarly, when I rehearse it over in my imagination, I do this not just in sequence, as it will have to be produced later, but I hear it all together in the same moment. What a feast! The whole process of finding and making music takes place in me as if it were a lovely and vivid dream; but the best part of it is hearing everything all together like that.[84]

Beyoncé

A modern artist who, like Mozart, seems to experience dreamlike musical-visual synesthesia (i.e. a blending or transposing of sensory impressions) is megastar **Beyoncé Knowles**, who has won 35 Grammy awards, the most of any artist ever.[85] The American singer-songwriter posted a video on her Facebook page to explain the inspiration for *The Visual Album*: "I see music. It's more than just what I hear. When I'm connected to something, I immediately see a visual or a series of images that are tied to a feeling or emotion, a memory from my childhood, thoughts about life, my dreams or my fantasies. And they're all connected to the music."[86]

The concept for her touring and performance band to be only made up of women came to Beyoncé in dreamland. "What a great dream!" she recalled. "We were all just rocking it and we felt connected." She shared the dream the following day with her then all-male band who were doubtful that she'd find talented enough female musicians, but she did indeed and her new tour band **Suga Mama** was born.[87]

Beyoncé also reported that dreams inspired *all* the songs on her 2006 *B'day* album,[88] which she completed in a couple of weeks, and which was nominated for seven Grammys (over two years) and won the Grammy for Best Contemporary R&B Album.

Musical "Gestures" and "Colors in Music"

Modern world-music composer **Shirish Korde** harvests both musical and visual elements of his dreams for inspiration. He had a dream containing "fragments of music" and birds flying at varying speeds—a "musical gesture" which he incorporated as note positions and rhythms into his composition for solo flute, *Tenderness of Cranes*. "I wrote it as quickly as anything I ever wrote," explained Korde, adding that he finished the piece in a single weekend. The composition garnered the National Flute Association[iv] Award for new music as well as the Suzanne and Lee Ettleson Composer's award.

Rasa is another composition where Korde dreamt a blend of music and visuals to inspire the piece. In a dream, the image-sound of "colors in music" and "notes in color" apparently emerged from nowhere. It is interesting to note, as pointed out by author Deirdre Barrett, that Bharati Mukherjee's novel *Jasmine*, upon which Korde's musical-theatre piece *Rasa* is based, also incorporated a dream sequence by Mukherjee that inspired the book's ending.[89]

Visual Cello Music Rapture

[iv] The National Flute Association is the world's biggest flute organization with ~5,000 members from over 50 countries

Amateur ballerina, former computer administrator, and epilepsy sufferer **Charlotte Rohrer** made what she called a "particularly foolish" decision to stop her epilepsy medication for serious seizures. She experienced a powerful near-death experience that sounds, subjectively-speaking, like various lucid dream experiences I have had and that students, clients and others have communicated with me. One evening, after a day of deeply mourning the death of a good friend, she watched the sun set and then suddenly slipped into empty blackness. She felt a slight wind on her face and mugginess in the air, and became aware that the only things present were her dog Otis, occasional colors, and loud rock music. She realized she might be dying and decided to surrender to the situation, at which point "beautiful cello music" began playing. Rohrer explained that she "saw" the music—not just written like musical notes on a staff—she actually visually became enraptured in the sound as a male voice from behind her left shoulder told her, "You made this. This is your reward. Enjoy it."[90]

Dream Winds Align into Composing Skill Revelation

Miami University Associate Music Professor **Roger Davis** started dreaming of music in his teens and often uses dreams for inspiration in his compositions. At about age 21,[v] he had a powerful dream that he felt showed him how to effectively compose what is known as a musical climax.

Davis' dream involved trees blowing back and forth in the wind. Not only did he see the swaying motion, he also heard the movement musically. All the leaves and branches and

---

[v] A common age for life-calling dreams due to the 7-year cycle principle described elsewhere in this book (21 = 3 x 7).

corresponding musical notes were initially going in different directions, but then they began to align and their individual forces combined and grew in tension towards a powerful emotional and musical peak. Davis awoke with the realization that the dream had experientially shown him how to compose a musical climax. The dream seems to have also revealed to Davis his career calling since he began his formal musical training only after the dream. Like many 'calling' dreams, the revelation Davis received took a number of years to properly embody. Davis seems to have done so successfully with his doctoral degree composition *The Dancing Difference*, completed at age 38, which was one of only four compositions chosen worldwide that year to be recorded for the Vienna Modern Masters' 'Music from Six Continents' series.[91]

Chapter 5

Music, Premonition Dreams, and Life in the Balance

"They tease me now, telling me it was only a dream. But does it matter whether it was a dream or reality, if the dream made known to me the truth?" **–Fyodor Dostoevsky**[92]

Research shows that two out of three people report at some point having experienced a premonition dream that they feel later came true.[93] I share this not to prove that such experiences are possible, since it is clear to me from my own almost daily precognitive dreams and from similar experiences of my students and many others that it is indeed possible. I mention it to show that such experiences are more common than most people think. So if precognition seems hard to believe, I suggest at least keeping an open mind about it being a possibility. I have presented on the science and experience of precognitive dreaming, and spoken to many people whose first experience after seeing a prescient dream come true in their life is fear that precognition could even be possible. Or else, like Patti Smith did, some people feel guilt about not having prevented the situation their dream warned about, even when lack of details or clarity make reasonable actions impossible. After working with thousands of dreamers worldwide and hearing many premonition dreams, I would like to offer my perspective that although such dreams can warn us about unfortunate probable future events, they do not come to bring fear or guilt. If we miss an opportunity to follow a dream's foretelling guidance, then hopefully the situation catches our attention enough so that we consider such dreams more carefully the next time they come calling. Ideally, we also get the hint about our underdeveloped inner abilities that can, if honed, protect or guide us and others in the future. Furthermore, the same inner skill can also bring us glimpses[vi] of very bright possible futures along with valuable guidance about how to get there, as exemplified clearly by Charlie Wilson's experience (detailed later in this chapter). In my view, this last point is true for most of the experiences shared in this book which show how artists who acted on their dreams thereby creatively brought bright possible futures into reality, boosting their careers as well as entertaining and inspiring many people.

"Dreams are that of which the subconscious is made, for any condition ever becoming reality is first dreamed."
                                                    –Edgar Cayce[94]

Nightmare Saves Husband

Canadian folk composer and CBC radio host **Clary Croft** was inspired for his song *Black Sails* by the tale of a shocking warning dream that saved a man from death by shipwreck.[95] The Annie M.

[vi] while such dreams are sometimes called visions, the feeling in the dream is very important.

Pride, a wooden schooner built in 1889 in Halifax, Nova Scotia, Canada, was to set sail for her maiden voyage one fateful day five years later from Mabou, Nova Scotia to deliver fish and lumber. The first mate's wife awoke in tears and horror from a haunting vision of the ship with an ominous gray hull and all sails set, yet the sails were black instead of their usual white. She pleaded with her husband not to go on the expedition that day, and he finally agreed and went to inform the ship's captain of his decision and the dream that changed his mind. Captain James Pride, who then needed another crew member, unfortunately took no heed of the warning and headed out with his 12-year-old son instead. In a blinding snow storm on November 6th, 1894, the ship containing its load of lumber and 800 quintals of fish ran aground about 400km away in Bear Cove, Nova Scotia. The vessel ended up as a wreckage and Captain Pride, his son, and three other sailors sadly perished.[96]

I had the pleasure to meet Clary and learn the heartbreaking story behind the song. I also learned another fascinating fact. During his youth, and still to this day, Croft has a half-model of a ship (i.e. cut down the middle along the length of the ship) on the wall of his room. After a bit of investigation, he learned that before a ship is built, the shipwrights often first create a scaled-down half-model to make sure everything is properly measured and works correctly. Eerily, the half-model on Croft's wall, labeled the 'Annie M. Pride', turns out to be the original 1/11th-sized half-model of the wrecked ship! Clary also learned not only that the ship was named after the wife of Captain James Pride, Annie Burns Pride, who was left widowed and without a son by the horrible wreck, but also that she was his maternal relative![97]

John Lennon's Creative Dreams & Death Premonitions

"The best songs are the ones that come to you in the middle of the night, out of a creative space, and you have to get up and write them down." –**John Lennon**[98]

According to his biographer Frederic Seaman, **John Lennon** was no stranger to the practice of harvesting dreams for creative inspiration.[84] One example of Lennon tapping dreams for songwriting is *#9 Dream*, for which the chorus was directly inspired by an odd multilingual sentence he heard in a dream. He awoke and wrote the words along with the melody.[99] On December 6th, 1980, in his last recorded interview two days before his death, Lennon told BBC radio host Andy Peebles, "I just sat down and wrote it, with no real inspiration, based on a dream I had. I wrote it around the string arrangement I'd written for the Harry Nilsson album I'd produced of Many Rivers to Cross, the Jimmy Cliff number…And it was such a nice melody on the strings. I thought, this is a tune! So I just wrote words to the string arrangement. That was *#9 Dream*. Kind of psychedelic dreamy kind of thing."[100] It is interesting to note that the number nine is symbolically linked with dreaming,[vii] and especially that the song's top position on the charts came when it reached none

---

[vii] For those interested in synchronicities and other numerical connections between dreaming and the number 9, 9/9/9 is a numerological date sequence occurring only every 9 years. This book was first officially published on 9/9/2016 (note that 2+0+1+6=9), and the formal second edition on 9/9/2025 (2+0+2+5=9). On 9/9/2007 (2+0+0+7=9), I was at the start of a high profile world tour of invited presentations about dreams and was taken to visit the house of Sigmund Freud. Additionally, the number 3 symbolically aligns with creativity, and so is closely linked with dreams and with 9 (e.g. 3x3=9, 3^3=9+9+9). I just so happened to first meet dream-inspired director James Cameron on 2010-3-3, which numerologically becomes 3/3/3 since 2+0+1+0=3.

other than #9 on the Billboard Hot 100 on February 22nd, 1975.

Dream #9 and **The Beatles** song Revolution 9 hint at Lennon's deeper connection with the number 9. His birth was on the 9th of October as was his son Sean's, and his first address was at 9 Newcastle, Wavertree, Liverpool (note: three 9-letter names of 3 syllables each = 9 syllables). He passed in 1980, a year that is linked with 9 numerologically (which only happens every 9 years) since it is divisible by 9 so the sum of its digits reduce to a 9 (1+9+8+0 => 18, then 1+8 = 9). Although some sources question the claim, Lennon shared in 1971 (another '9' year) that he derived the Beatles' less-known track *Sun King* from a dream.[101]

An event as important as murder will often show up beforehand in dreams of either the victim or their loved ones. In late December 1979, before his tragic shooting, **John Lennon** dreamt about eating at a restaurant with his wife when a chubby stranger wearing spectacles came to their table. When Lennon asked the man to confirm that he was not a nutcase, the stranger became anxious and the police appeared and informed Lennon that the man had entered the restaurant with a loaded revolver. Awakening, Lennon was upset not to recall any further details from the foreboding dream.[102] Warning dreams about very important potential events usually come more than once, though not always. Although the first dream by itself strongly foreshadowed the events that were to come, Lennon also had two more dreams to start the year and new decade. In the first, he was inside a mirror, smiling at his own reflection. He then walked through the glass, and became clear and fully awake. The star was sure the dream was psychic. In the second, a horrifying nightmare, Lennon was reading his own obituary. He learned that he had been charged with his own murder that occurred at The Dakota where he lived with Yoko Ono and their son Sean, and he frantically tried to convince anyone who would listen that he was not guilty.[103] In what retrospectively seems a tragic combination of the first and last dreams, on December 8th, 1980, a deranged, chubby fan wearing glasses shot Lennon with a revolver in front of The Dakota.

Years earlier, Lennon's friend Wayne Barrett lost his mother. In order to console him, Lennon commented, "Death is just a dream."[104] With the hope that his comment hints at some aspect of a larger truth, perhaps Lennon's dream shared above about smiling at his own reflection also came true, suggesting that in some invisible manner, the deceased Beatle's spirit walked freely out of the mirror of life and death, both clear and truly awake.

Lynyrd Skynyrd

Ed King was **Lynyrd Skynyrd**'s rhythm guitarist in late summer of 1973 when the band recorded their US top 10 hit *Sweet Home Alabama*. He heard band mate Gary Rossington play an interesting riff during practice one day and decided that evening to write a new song. That night, King dreamt of the main D-C^9-G chord progression and both guitar solos "absolutely note for note—all the transition points, the fingering, the chord voicings." King added, "I woke up out of the dream and it was done."[105] Rossington's riff also made it into the recording, offering a counterpoint melody in the verses to the dream's chord progression played by King, who also played one of the two dreamt guitar solos.[106] Interestingly, the song's lyrics, written by the band's founding lead singer Ronnie Van Zant, included at least four lines in response to another dream-inspired artist—Neil Young.

Sadly, Van Zant died in a plane crash on October 20, 1977 along with 2 other members of the band, their assistant tour manager, and the plane's two pilots. Twenty others were injured during the crash, including 6 band members,[107] managers, road crew, a cameraman, and others connected with the band. The deaths and injuries may well have been averted had they heeded a clear warning dream foretelling the crash that came to band backup singer JoJo Billingsley the night before the disaster occurred. The band did four shows that year without all three of the regular backup singers that they had affectionately dubbed the "honkettes". But in the fall of 1977, Van Zant phoned Billingsley and asked her to come back and join them immediately in Greenville, South Carolina. However, during the call, she heard an inner voice clearly say one word: *"WAIT."* Therefore, she agreed to meet them only a few days later for their next show in Little Rock, Arkansas. That night, she had an ominous foretelling dream.

"It was like the most vivid dream I ever had. It was like in Technicolor," recalled Billingsley. "I saw the plane, and saw it smack the ground."[108] She was staying at her mother's house and awoke from the nightmare screaming and crying and shared the dream. Her mother told her (what I generally consider to be unwise advice), "It's just a dream, go back to sleep." However, the next day, Billingsley was still so upset that she called the band, told them the dream, and beseeched them not to get back on the plane. Eerily, one of the plane's engines had exhibited some abnormal operation the day before.[109] The band discussed her dream and urgent warning and took a vote about whether to take the flight. Band guitarist Allan Collins and backup singer Cassie Gaines had even made alternate travel plans. The vote outcome, which is now very unfortunate history, was that the band's flight that day from Greenville to Baton Rouge, Louisiana would be their last trip on that plane but that they would take it anyway.[110]

Jojo Billingsley had originally asked Cassie Gaines and Leslie Hawkins to join the band, and later Cassie helped get her brother Steve in as guitarist after Ed King left the group. Cassie, Leslie, and Steve were all active and traveling along with the group when Billingsley had her shocking nightmare, perhaps offering one connection as to why the premonition dream that she warned the band about might have come to her.

A particularly strange yet perhaps very fortuitous event for the survivors was that the emergency medical team who arrived at the crash site had run a drill just 6 weeks earlier practising how to get 25 passengers off none other than a Convair 240—the very same plane that the band was on! The band's plane crashed about a mile from where the drill had taken place with 26 passengers instead of the 25 that the rescue team's recent practice had been for. Two additional amazing synchronicities may also have helped many of the passengers survive. The first is that the Red Cross had just finished a local blood drive and had not yet sent the blood to state headquarters, so the large amount of blood needed to keep the surviving passengers alive was immediately available. The second serendipitous situation is the timing of the crash, since the victims arrived at the small local hospital right during shift change and were therefore fortunate enough to have a double shift of 31 doctors, nurses, and medical professionals present.[111]

A clear, and especially a repeated warning dream not fully considered is rather risky business.

Dream Warning for Sparklehorse

In a hauntingly similar vein to the Lynyrd Skynyrd tragedy, the grandmother of American singer, songwriter, and musician **Mark Linkous** best known as the leader of **Sparklehorse,** woke up crying each night for a week from a terrifying dream without really remembering why. She soon gained more insight and called Mark's father to quite strongly warn him, "something is wrong with one of the boys." Mark's father replied that Mark's stepbrother broke an elbow playing football, but that everything was all right. Hearing that was a great relief for her. However, the same nightmare returned that night, then the next, until the bad news arrived that her grandson, a brilliant musician yet former drug addict, had been found unconscious yet breathing in a hotel bathroom where he had been slumped for 14 hours, cutting off the circulation in his legs. His heart stopped when the medics moved him, and he was clinically dead for 2 minutes before he was revived and taken to St. Mary's Hospital in London.

On a more upbeat note, the title for Sparklehorse's first album, *Vivadixisubmarinetransmissionplot,* was inspired by one of Linkous' dreams in which he heard music playing inside a submarine as he swam towards it. The music was distorted by the water, and he knew that Robert E. Lee, a confederate army general from the American civil war, had built the submarine.[112]

Diana Ross & The Supremes

As **The Supremes** rose to stardom and their packed schedule became more and more stressful, Motown iconic singer **Diana Ross** started having horrific dreams.

"I dreamed of a cat leaping on me, digging his claws into me," revealed Ross to her band mates in the back of a limo on the way to their next performance in Boston, giving an example of increasingly regular nightmares about "frightening things like that because we're always being harried."

About half-way through the third night of their Boston engagement, Ross suddenly backed away from the microphone, put her hands over both ears, and then started moaning and swaying as she had the experience of "getting smaller and smaller." The show was cancelled, as was the rest of the Boston engagement, and Ross was taken back to Detroit and hospitalized for exhaustion.[113] Ross recovered, but the episode offers another important, practical, health-related example about the value of warning dreams.

Ross also had a dream where she was playing Dorothy in what later became *The Wiz*, an adaptation of the *The Wizard of Oz*. At 5 a.m., she called her producer, Motown Records founder Berry Gordy, and told him she just had the dream and wanted to play Dorothy. He had never thought of it before and told her to go back to sleep. However, he later pitched the idea, and the 33-year-old Ross did indeed end up as Dorothy, a 24-year-old kindergarten school teacher, in the 1978 film alongside Richard Pryor as the wizard and none other than Michael Jackson as the scarecrow, in Jackson's film debut.[114]

Patti Smith

"I often write songs out of a dream." –**Patti Smith**[115]

In 1964, at age 18, American singer-songwriter and Rock and Roll Hall of Fame inductee **Patti Smith**, found a spot near the front of a peaceful auditorium before a Rolling Stones concert but was crushed into the stage as throngs of screaming female fans surged forward when the band emerged. She remembers grabbing hold of Rolling Stones founder Brian Jones' ankle just as something to hold onto, and that their gaze locked for a short moment while they smiled at each other.[116]

Smith says she later had a premonition or a dream vision where the roles had reversed and Jones was in danger, hurt, and about to sink beneath the surface. In her dream vision, Jones' hand reached for something to grab onto, just like her hand had done in reality. When she learned on July 4th, 1969 that Jones had drowned in a swimming pool the previous evening at a party while friends apparently looked on, she felt guilty that perhaps somehow she could have helped avoid the tragedy.[117]

She decided to express her feelings about the tragedy creatively, which was wise artistically, since the poetry that she crafted about Brian Jones[118] in the form of a requiem set to a rock and roll rhythm developed into an important, unique characteristic of her artistic style. Her choice was also wise psychologically since as I mentioned at the start of this chapter, premonition dreams do not come to bring us guilt. Smith was wise enough to consider such dreams more closely when they happened again because soon thereafter, she started having ominous dreams about her father's health. Given how her precognitive dream about Brian Jones had played out, she decided to act on the new series of dreams and return home from Paris. She arrived just days after her father Grant Smith was hospitalized by a surprise heart attack, right as doctors announced he would survive.[119]

Smith revealed that although her dreams are now more filled with deceased loved ones, she harvested dream inspirations for many of her early songs and poetry, such as her song *Blakean Year*[120] and poem *Skunk Dog* which was "a complete dream." Another example is her song *Break It Up*, co-written with Tom Verlaine, which is directly inspired by her dream of deceased maverick rocker Jim Morrison from The Doors, "half-encased in marble— literally trapped by being turned into an icon."[121] Smith elaborated elsewhere that in the dream, Morrison was lying naked on a marble slab with stone wings, and she was dreaming from the point of view of a young boy yelling, "Break it up!" until the wings broke and Morrison rose freely up and away.[122] That Jim Morrison appeared in her dream is interesting, since Smith also revealed that dreaming about The Doors' song *Soul Kitchen* is what motivated her to make her own cover version of the song.[123]

Smith's song *Constantine's Dream* refers to a dream by Roman emperor Constantine on October 27th, 312 CE, the night before an important army battle against his brother-in-law Maxentius. Reports vary, but early Christian author Lactantius stated that in the dream, Christ told Constantine to employ an insignia, most likely the Chi-Rho symbol (χ) or something close to it, to win the battle.[124] The Chi-Rho is a combination of the Greek chi (X) and rho (P) symbols that start the Greek word for 'Christ'. Whether Constantine's forces used the symbol on their shields the next day in the battle of the Milvian Bridge is uncertain, however Constantine did win and became the new emperor in Rome. Record keeper and Roman Bishop Eusebius also wrote about Constantine's dream, yet reporting that it occurred further in advance of the Milvian Bridge battle. In a strange twist of fate, Eusebius' son, also named Eusebius yet better known as St-Jerome, was given the important task of translating The Bible into Latin about a half century later. The Hebrew term 'anan', meaning witchcraft or soothsaying, appeared in the pre-translated Hebrew scriptures ten times. Unfortunately, St. Jerome at least twice[125] translated the phrase as 'observing dreams' ('*observo somnia*' in Latin) in places where it cast a very unfavorable light upon dreams and even forbade working with them altogether. By the end of the 4th century, practising dream interpretation had been prohibited—an edict that endured for about fifteen centuries until modern times when the mistranslation was corrected.

Why is the above history important? It reveals a key reason why interest in dreams and practices involving them, such as dream interpretation and using dreams for artistic inspiration, has been somewhat limited in Western culture until the 20th century.

Charlie Wilson –
Dream Predicts Grammy-Nominated #1 Hit

Not all precognitive dreams are ominous, some are positive
visions calling us to bright future possibilities. The result of not
acting on them is not necessarily disastrous, but can result in
missing great opportunities, as may have been true for composer
Hector Berlioz. American R&B and gospel singer-songwriter and
former lead singer for **The Gap Band**, **Charlie Wilson**, revealed
that his wife Mahin had a dream that motivated him to compose
his Grammy-nominated hit *If I Believe*. Wilson recounted that she
awoke, "grabbed a pen and paper and began to write the lyrics".[126]
She then told him, "We need to make this record. God showed it
to me, and it's gonna be nominated for a Grammy." Wilson
finished and recorded the song for his album *Love, Charlie*. Not
only was the song nominated for the 2014 Best Gospel Song
Grammy, the album also hit #1 on Billboard's R&B albums chart
and #4 on their Top 200 Albums list. "I'm so glad her vision was
right," added a very grateful Wilson.[127]

Craig Sim Webb

Chapter 6

Dream-Sparked Musical Collaborations

It seems as though an entire unexpected level of communication and support transpires between various artists invisibly, on deeper levels, which aligns with the *innernet* concept I described early in this book. In addition to intriguing cases described in the chapter on dream visits from the deceased where living musicians are helped by deceased colleagues, dreams have also sparked collaborations between living artists.

Roy Orbison

In a vivid 1963 dream, music legend **Roy Orbison** heard a radio disc jockey say, "Here's a new song from Elvis Presley." Orbison remembered the song in perfect detail upon waking, and realized the song was not Elvis' at all but his own.[128] Within 20 minutes of waking,[129] he had completed his hit which became the title track for his album *In Dreams*.

In Dreams is not the only dream-inspired song Orbison recorded. Having originated in dreams, perhaps the song *In Dreams* has its own inspirational effect on or "in" others' dreams, as you will discover in the following fascinating account by Bono.

Bono/U2

Irish band **U2**'s lead singer **Bono** was stressed before a performance at Wembley Arena with his band in the mid to late 1980s and lay half awake "all night" with the soundtrack of David Lynch's *Blue Velvet* film playing on repeat, which includes and weaves together dreamy visuals for Roy Orbison's hit song *In Dreams*. "It kept stopping appropriately on *In Dreams*," said Bono. "I couldn't sleep and this song was going through my head. When I woke up the next day, I had a song in my head which I presumed was another Roy Orbison song that was on the soundtrack. And I looked for it but I couldn't find it. Where's this tune? Maybe I've just written it."

Bono took the song to the sound check that day to see if the band liked it, mentioning that it had a Roy Orbison feel to it—'Mystery Girl, she's a mystery to me.' The band really liked it, and after the concert, in their dressing room, Bono continued working on the song since it really stuck with him and he wanted to finish it. Suddenly there was a knock at the door. It was the band's security guard John who said, "Roy Orbison and his wife Barbara are outside. Can I bring them in? They'd really like to meet you."

"The band looked at me," explained Bono, "and thought I'd either been winding them up or there was some voodoo in me. I told them I had no idea he was here. 'I swear to ya.'" Orbison came in, said he really liked the show, and then strangely, out of nowhere, asked if they had a song for him. "Everyone was falling around and no one could believe their ears. I played him right there and then this song '*she's a mystery to me*', which he loved." The rest is history.[130] The song became Orbison's new album's title track, and Bono and band mate The Edge ended up producing it. The album was Orbison's last, released after his death, and reached #5 on the US Billboard 200, and #2 on the UK Albums Chart,[131] and became central to Marvel's first Aquaman film soundtrack where Aquaman meets the film's leading lady.

*"I wake up with a melody in my head in the morning and I have to write it down. I don't have to write it down because we need another song for the record. I write it down because I'm excited by the idea of making music." –***Bono**[132]

Orbison wasn't the only iconic colleague that Bono's dreams led him to collaborate with. One night in the late 1980s while staying in Beverly Hills during their Joshua Tree tour, Bono dreamt of **Bob Dylan** singing a song and awoke with the tune playing in his head.[133] He quickly jotted down the words and went back to sleep. Come morning, the U2 front-man was not sure if the lyrics were his or Dylan's. Dylan had been a hero of Bono's for many years, so Bono called him. Dylan spontaneously invited Bono to come to his place in nearby Malibu and play him the song.[134] Together the two worked on *Love Rescue Me* all afternoon and a new country ballad was born thanks to Bono's dream muse. Dylan originally sang the lead vocal but decided not to use it due to his involvement at the time with The Traveling Wilburys all-star band.[135] He does however sing the backing vocals on the U2 recording, and both stars have performed the song live.

Veteran TV host David Letterman interviewed U2 in Dublin for the 2023 Disney+ rockumentary *A Sort of Homecoming*.

"It's literally the middle of the night. I wake up with an idea. So I have to get out of bed, find the phone, find the guitar," explained U2's guitarist, **The Edge** who has a huge collection of "6000 voice notes" on his phone that contain creative inspirations.

Amazed by U2's surprising talents for tapping dreams for

songwriting, Letterman exclaimed, "Honestly, you guys are like a magic act!"

"Well we have some magic for you," replied Bono. "We want to write a tune for you called *Forty Foot Man*." The night before that interview was scheduled to be filmed, **The Edge** had a musical dream at 3am, and he and Bono had already fleshed out a song with rough lyrics by the time of the interview. They knew the song was "for" Letterman since the latter had been anxiously considering yet avoiding doing a cold plunge in the Irish Sea on the south east side of Dublin known as 'the 40 foot' swim.

By the end of the filming, perhaps thanks to the dream-inspired musical gift and nudge from The Edge's subconscious, Letterman finally mustered the courage to plunge in for an invigorating swim in the frigid waters.[136] The dream-inspired song plays during the film's closing credits, and according to Letterman, "Makes the first 35 years of being in television well worth the effort."[137]

As lead singer of the band with the most ever Grammy wins (twenty-two),[138] Bono revealed his belief that artists can do their "great work" in dreams while they are "…Yes. Unconscious."[139]

Jimmy Webb

American singer-songwriter **Jimmy Webb** stands alone as the only artist to have won Grammy Awards for music, lyrics, and orchestration.[140]

One night in London, a terrifying chase nightmare[viii] besieged him. He woke covered in sweat, but fortunately for him and for music lovers, there was a piano in his suite. He went directly to it and crafted the dream into the lyrics of the first verse of his song

---

[viii] Statistics show that being pursued is a common nightmare theme reported by about 4 out of 5 people.

The Highwayman. Since the idea of reincarnation really intrigued Webb, he combined that with the dream as a powerful motif for the next three verses of the song.[141]

The dream crystallized as the song's title, and Webb recorded it on his 1977 album *El Mirage*. Glen Campbell decided to record a cover version of the song the following year, and wanted to release it as a single, but his label, Capitol Records, refused. The song's dream-sparked alchemy seems to have come into play, since the disagreement marked the beginning of Campbell's break with Capitol's main studios[142] where he had exclusively recorded and released 30 albums over a period of 15 years. Campbell then released his version of the song on his 1979 album *Highwayman*.

The invisible power of Webb's dream creation sprang up yet again in 1985, inspiring the name of a super group called **The Highwaymen** that included Willie Nelson, Kris Kristofferson, Waylon Jennings, and dream-inspired artist Johnny Cash. The Highwaymen recorded Webb's nightmare-inspired creation as the title song and lead single of their first album *Highwayman*, which hit #1 on Billboard's Top Country Albums and achieved platinum-selling status. Their rendition of *The Highwayman* song reached the top spot on Billboard's Hot Country Songs, remaining on the chart for 20 weeks and earning Webb the 1986 Grammy for Best Country Song.[143]

Webb also wrote a tribute song about dream-inspired songwriter P. F. Sloan.

Johnny Cash

Genre-spanning singer-songwriter **Johnny Cash** has the very rare honor of being inducted into not only the Country Music Hall of Fame, but also both the Rock and Roll and Gospel Music Halls of

Fame. His hit *Ring of Fire* was written by June Carter and country singer-songwriter Merle Kilgore who joined Cash on tour in 1962. Carter would later become Cash's wife after accepting his on-stage marriage proposal in front of 7000 people in London, Ontario on Feb. 22nd, 1968.[144] But in 1962, she was upset about Cash being such a wild man, yet also painfully aware that she couldn't resist him.[145] One night, she and Kilgore were trying to compose a song inspired by an underlined phrase in a poetry book of her uncle's which obviously resonated with her—'Love is like a burning ring of fire'. Later that night, her sister Anita Carter called from the recording studio needing another song for a session she was doing there. Amidst the sudden pressure and her tumultuous feelings for Cash, the song was born like a phoenix from the fire and Anita recorded it. After listening to Anita's rendition, Cash dreamt that he heard the tune arranged with a mariachi-style horn section.[146] One account states that in Cash's fateful dream, he found himself singing the song along with "Mexican bullfighting trumpets" added in, and that the dream came the night before he planned to record the song himself.[147] However, the liner notes for Anita's album *Ring of Fire* report that Cash dreamt he heard the Mexican horn section playing as he listened to the record in his dream, and that he later told Anita, "I'll give you about five or six more months, and if you don't hit with it, I'm gonna record it the way I feel it."[148] Indeed about five or six months later, in spring 1963, Cash recorded the tune with the two Carter sisters and their mother Maybelle singing harmony vocals. Regardless of exactly when the dream came, it definitely brought unexpected information since trumpets were a rather unusual arrangement for a country song. However, Cash and his producer Jack Clement really liked the inspired arrangement suggested by Cash's dreaming muse. So they went ahead and incorporated what are now the song's signature Mexican horn phrases that helped turn *Ring of Fire* into not just a #1 hit and a recipient of the 1998 Grammy Hall of Fame Award, but also

Cash's overall best-selling song.

"The Truth moves through us even when we sleep."
    –**Singer-songwriter Roseanne Cash** (Johnny's daughter)[149]

Johnny Cash was a very prolific songwriter. On his 87th album, released not long before his death, is the tune *The Man Comes Around*. Cash explained that the idea for that song came to him in a dream after reading a book called ***Dreaming of the Queen*** which talked about the great number of The English who dream that they are with Queen Elizabeth II. In Cash's dream, he entered Buckingham Palace to find Queen Elizabeth II knitting or sewing with a basket of fabrics and lace nearby, and a woman beside her with whom she was talking and laughing. As Cash approached, the Queen looked up at him and exclaimed, "Johnny Cash, you're like a thorn tree in a whirlwind!"[150] Of the dream, Cash said, "It kept haunting me…I kept thinking about it, how vivid it was, and then I thought, maybe it's biblical." Cash researched the queen's thorn tree reference, found it in the bible's book of Jobs. Seven years later he finished composing the song which also draws elements from the bible's Book of Revelation as well as other biblical sources.[151] The song inspired the title for his 67th album, and Cash revealed that he spent more time on that song than any he ever wrote.[152]

The inspiration for Cash's entire 1964 album *Bitter Tears* came during a dream he had with Willie Nelson circa 1962, though he had not seen Nelson in three years. In Cash's dream, he and Nelson were in a dressing room swapping songs. Cash shared a song called *The Ballad of Ira Hayes*, and Nelson told him, "You should do an album of Indian songs." Still dreaming, Cash replied that he'd never thought of doing a whole Indian music album.

Nelson answered, "You will…Let me sing you one, John. I thought of you when I wrote it: *They're All the Same*." Cash reported that the dream ended as Nelson finished playing the song. In the morning, Cash had his secretary look up a phone number for Nelson, who he had not seen (in waking life) in three years. Cash called him, told him the dream, and asked if he had a song titled, *They're All the Same*. An incredulous Nelson replied that he did, and agreed when Cash requested him to send a copy of it to listen to so that Cash could record a cover version.

Although Cash received the tape, he later lost it and never recorded what might have been for him another dream-inspired hit.[153] However, he and Nelson did later come together to form the country super group **The Highwaymen** based on the nightmare-inspired song *The Highwayman* by Jimmy Webb.

Cash's backup singer, rockabilly guitarist **Luther Perkins**, a member of **The Tennessee Three**, bought his first guitar at age 9 thanks to a dream. In his dream, Perkins journeyed to the rainbow's end and found a pot of gold. The dream was vivid enough for Perkins to recognize the actual waking world location where he had found the pot of gold in the dream, so he and his brother went there and began digging. Though they did not find gold, they did unearth an old house. Perkins gathered the bricks and sold them to a local construction company for $9, which in 1937 was enough to buy his first guitar.[154]

Scott Mathews, John Hiatt, B.B. King & Eric Clapton

American music producer, composer and multi-instrumentalist **Scott Mathews**, sometimes dubbed the fifth member of The Beach Boys, has collaborated with and written or produced songs for many musical dreamers including Roy Orbison, Johnny Cash,

The Beach Boys, Todd Rundgren, Dr. John, Pat Monahan (of Train), Elvis Costello, Tom Waits, Keith Richards, Van Morrison, David Bowie, Neil Young, David Crosby, Taj Mahal, Lady Gaga, and Taylor Swift.

It is not surprising then that Mathews has musical dreams, including "whole chunks of songs in their finished version." Once, when producing musical dreamer Todd Rundgren, the latter kindly offered Mathews a few tips about how to dream music.

"Sometimes I'd dream musical pieces where I'd hear a record, wake up and rush to an instrument and play what I'd heard," recalled Mathews. "There was a period of time when I kept a cassette machine at my bedside waiting for melodies or lyrics that might be worth catching. Hey, making a living in your sleep…what's wrong with that picture? Truth be told, some of the best songs come that way. It almost makes me feel like it's not right that only my name appears as writer when I was just the receiver…but let's not take things too far! I may be sleeping but it's still me! Some interesting pieces were followed up on but the return was about 50/50. There were some glorious things I heard in dreams that turned out to be duff." [155]

One song inspired by Mathews' dreams that became a winner was American rock guitarist, pianist, singer, and songwriter John Hiatt's *Riding With The King*, which also became the title track for one of Hiatt's albums.

In 1983, Hiatt was living at Mathews' house in San Francisco and Mathews was producing songs for what would later become Hiatt's new album. One day over breakfast, Mathews shared the previous night's dream where he was flying in an old plane with Elvis Presley, but could not see Presley's face. "All The King's men were huddled around him," Mathews explained, referring to Elvis' entourage (since Elvis is also often dubbed 'The King'). Mathews did however see reflections from The King's rhinestones and gold rings, and added that, "The only real glimpses I had of Elvis were flashes of light from his fine jewelry. He could have been wearing a crown for all I knew—those jewels were plentiful and the diamonds shined brightly!

"One detail [not included in the song lyrics] is that Elvis and his crew were up in front in their own section. I was sitting behind along with all the other regular riders. In other words, I wasn't on the plane as a musician or having anything to do with him…it was The King and commoners headed for the Promised Land.

"This particular dream was by no means atypical compared to most of my dreams," Mathews explained, "but for some reason I opened up about it in great detail and John (being the consummate writer he is) jotted it down. That was that and I never gave it another thought until I saw the cover of the record—*Riding with the King*—a phrase I had used when describing the dream.

"I was definitely taken aback but I just rolled with it, and I liked the title so I decided to take it as a compliment. But when I heard my words describing my dream put to some blues changes on the song…it was kinda startling. John was a dear friend and I suppose you could say I took the high road when I didn't put a stop to the fact my name did not appear with his as songwriter and that my publishing company didn't own half the song. I took a 'win some, lose some' attitude, since life is short and relationships like we had don't grow on trees. Years later when we were writing together in Nashville for a band project he and I were planning to do along with Big Al Anderson, he told me he always felt he should have done the right thing and given me the co-write. I deeply regret that I made a crucial mistake and did not take him up on clearing the whole thing up right then and there, because in 2000, Eric Clapton and B.B. King chose it as a signature song for their new album!"

B.B. King and Eric Clapton's cover version of *Riding With The*

King also became the title track for their album and not only hit #1 on Billboard's top blues albums, but also won the 2001 Grammy Award for Best Traditional Blues Album.

"So it became a déjà-vu," explained Mathews, "except this time the album sold millions instantly upon release. John bought a big ranch outside of Nashville, which he richly deserves, but sadly, my attempts to even discuss the situation with him were blocked." Although Mathews regrets not asking Hiatt to credit him as co-writer, he decided that friendships are more important than money, yet adds, "Hey, it's never too late!" Warner Brothers were aware of the situation, and in a kind gesture, sent Mathews an RIAA award when Clapton and King's cover version of the song went double-platinum.

In retrospect, with Hiatt receiving all the song royalties and moving into a big ranch in Elvis' home state of Tennessee (a cross-country flight away from where Mathews had the dream), the dream's depiction of Elvis with sparkling jewelry near the front of the plane in a section separated from Mathews may well contain precognitive elements.[156]

Arcade Fire

Neil Young was asked to perform the song, *A Band with My Friends*, that came in a nightmare to **Win Butler**, singer-songwriter and multi-instrumentalist for Montreal rock sensation and 2011 Album of the Year Grammy Award winners **Arcade Fire**.

Butler revealed during a live performance, "I had a dream…we were sound-checking and there were huge bright lights in my face and it was empty and people started leaving…I woke up and remembered everything. I was half asleep and I started playing it and wrote down the lyrics and listened back to my tape recorder and it was basically a Neil Young song."

The band contacted Young, who loved Arcade Fire and the song and joined them to perform it as part of an annual benefit concert Young organizes to assist children with severe physical impairments and complex communication needs. Butler introduced the song live as "*I Dreamed a Neil Young Song*", adding that, "This song is by Neil Young, in my head." The dream melody's reminiscent, flowing feel combined with Young's harmonica does indeed give it a strong Neil Young feel.

In an interesting example of dreams-come-true, thanks to Win Butler acting on the dream even beyond crafting it into a song, Neil Young actually appeared on stage in a band with his new fellow-Canadian friends Arcade Fire singing Butler's dreamt lyrics 'since I was young…I had a dream about playing in a band with my friends'.[157]

Barry Manilow & Bette Midler

American singer-songwriter and producer **Barry Manilow** has sold over 85 million albums, and won many prestigious awards including a Grammy, 2 Emmys, and 3 American Music Awards, among others. Manilow claims that his optimistic tune *One Voice* arrived from dreamland already complete. "The thing woke me up, I ran to the piano, croaked One Voice into the cassette machine—lyrics and music, and that was the song."[158] Manilow also had a dream that inspired an entire album by Bette Midler.

With three Grammy Awards, two Academy Awards, four Golden Globes, three Emmy Awards, and a special Tony Award, **Bette Midler** has been successful as both a singer and an actor.

Midler's 2003 album *Bette Midler Sings the Rosemary Clooney Songbook*, a tribute album to Rosemary Clooney who died in 2002, was conceived in a dream earlier that year by Manilow, who interestingly has the same initials as Midler.

In Manilow's dream, set in the 1950s, he saw Midler (a respected female singer/actor) singing songs by respected American cabaret singer/actor Rosemary Clooney, the aunt of well-known actor George Clooney. Manilow explained, "Bette and I hadn't spoken in years, but I picked up the phone and told her I had an idea for a tribute album. I knew there was absolutely no one else who could do this." Midler adored the concept since she respected Rosemary Clooney and loved her "magical" songs. She also missed Barry, so the album was completed within months.[159]

Cole Porter & a Life-Long Dream-Inspired Partnership

Esteemed songwriter and composer of the early 1900s, **Cole Porter**, ran into trouble developing his 1934 comedy musical later named, *Anything Goes!* It was originally about a shipwreck, but a few weeks before the show was to open, the U.S.S. Morro Castle cruise ship had a terrible fire just off the New Jersey shore and over 130 lives were lost, so a comedy about a shipwreck was no longer acceptable. The original story writers were busy with other projects. However, Howard Lindsay, who was engaged to direct the show, agreed to write a new libretto on the condition that they find a co-author. Porter's producer Vinton Freedley searched for a suitable writer all weekend without luck.

Meanwhile, Porter attended a party hosted by his friend Neysa McMein where Porter mentioned that his team needed a librettist. In the morning, McMein, who believed in the importance of dreams, called and told Porter that she had dreamt about Russell

Crouse, who had also been at the party.[160] According to Porter, McMein's dreams were taken seriously around town,[161] so he contacted Freedley who tried in vain to reach Crouse all day. However, in the evening Porter happened to look out his office window and see Crouse in a window across the street. Crouse accepted the job and within an hour started crafting the new story with Lindsay, allowing the production to open on schedule five weeks later.[162]

In retrospect, Porter's decision to follow McMein's dream-inspired librettist suggestion had a powerful, lasting impact over many years. Not only did *Anything Goes!* become the 4th longest-running musical in all of the 1930s, winning countless awards up to the present day as well as a Grammy nomination, it also brought about a lifelong writing partnership between Lindsay and librettist Crouse. The pair's work together included 15 plays and musicals, almost all of which were critically and financially successful.[163]

Chapter 7

Little-Known Musical Dreams that Rocked the Modern World

"There are some people who live in a dream world, and there are some who face reality; and then there are those who turn one into the other." –**Douglas Everett**[164]

Paul McCartney

'Scrambled eggs, oh my baby how I love your legs' were the initial lyrics for a melody **Paul McCartney** received in a dream one night in 1964 while sleeping at the home of his girlfriend Jane Asher.[165] He woke up, got out of bed, and played the tune in his head on a nearby piano to avoid forgetting it. McCartney at first wondered if he had copied someone else's work. Explained Sir Paul, "For about a month,[166] I went 'round to people in the music business and asked them whether they had ever heard it before. Eventually it became like handing something in to the police. I thought if no one claimed it, after a few weeks then I could have it."[167] McCartney recalls further, "I checked this melody out, and people said to me, 'No, it's lovely, and I'm sure it's all yours.' It took me a little while to allow myself to claim it, but then like a prospector I finally staked my claim; stuck a little sign on it and said, 'Okay, it's mine!' It had no words. I used to call it 'Scrambled Eggs'." About the song, Beatle John Lennon later recalled, "We made up our minds that only a one-word title would suit, we just couldn't find the right one. Then one morning Paul woke up and the song and the title were both there, completed."[168] However, The Beatles' manager George Martin claims he first heard the song at the George V hotel in Paris in January 1964. Martin shared, "Paul said he wanted a one-word title and was considering *Yesterday*, except that he thought it was perhaps too corny. I persuaded him that it was all right."[169]

Having claimed the tune, McCartney began writing the lyrics. A little more than a year later, in late May 1965, McCartney finished the lyrics in the back seat of a car during a five-hour drive from Lisbon airport to the holiday house in Albufeira, Portugal of guitarist Bruce Welch from the musical group The Shadows.[170] *Yesterday* seems to be amongst the top few most covered songs of all time.[171] In 2016, Rolling Stone Magazine ranked the song at #13 in their 500 Greatest Songs of All Time[172], though it is currently #72 as off this writing.

Yesterday is not the only dream-inspired mega-hit by Sir Paul, who claims that the idea for *Let It Be* also came in autumn 1968 during a difficult period before the Beatles parted ways. Sir Paul's late mother Mary, who died from an embolism after surgical treatment of her breast cancer when young Paul was just 14, came to visit 12 years later in a dream "somewhere between deep sleep and insomnia". McCartney attributes that dream as the inspiration for the 'Mother Mary' lyric.[173,174] Sir Paul is quoted as later saying, "It was great to visit with her again. I felt very blessed to have that dream. It got me writing *Let It Be*."[175] He elaborated in a separate interview that his mother, in the dream, did indeed speak the now-famous words of wisdom.[176] "There was her face, completely clear, particularly her eyes, and she said to me very gently, very reassuringly, 'Let it be.' It was lovely." McCartney woke feeling as if he'd been touched by an angel. "When something happens like that, as if by magic," added McCartney, "I think it has a resonance that other people notice too." Soon after the dream, he met his wife-to-be Linda Eastman. McCartney shared his belief that "it was as if my mum had sent her."[177] The song won the 1973 Grammy Award for Best Original Score Written for a Motion Picture or Television Special, and is ranked at #20 in Rolling Stone Magazine's 500 Greatest Songs of All Time.[178]

McCartney also described the dream that inspired the **Paul McCartney and Wings** song *No Values*: "I was with the Rolling Stones. They were all there, Mick, Bill, Charlie and Keith. Mick was up front." He awoke thinking how much he liked that song that the Stones do, but quickly realized that the Stones have no song titled *No Values* nor any like the song in his dream, and knew therefore that he had just created it.[179]

In the mid-1980s, McCartney's songs shifted somewhat suddenly from softer ballads back to a harder, psychedelic rock sound with the release of his 1986 album *Press To Play*. The former Beatle explained that a dream by his album co-producer Hugh Padgham triggered the abrupt style shift. In the early stages of creating the record, McCartney said Padgham recounted a dream in which "he woke up one morning and had made this really bad, syrupy album with me, an album he hated, and that it had blown his whole career." McCartney added, "We took that as a little warning."[180]

McCartney continues to harvest his own dreams for creative insights and explained that the robot 'Newman', with whom he dances in his 2014 *Appreciate* music video, was conceived in a dream. McCartney elaborated, "I woke up one morning with an image in my head of me standing with a large robot."[181]

Although artists' dreams often inspire their music, sometimes they can suggest valuable career directions and choices. As a youngster, McCartney had a recurring dream of digging in the garden with his hands and finding a tin can. Yet when he met and started jamming with his future band mate and songwriting partner John Lennon, the dream's ending changed for the better: "In this dream, I found a gold coin. I kept digging and I found another, and another." What is perhaps most intriguing is that John Lennon shared with him that he'd dreamt the same dream. Shared (sleeping) dreams are somewhat rare, and often come to catch the dreamers' attention and offer important insights. In retrospect, McCartney feels the dream was a premonition about what he and Lennon could accomplish writing songs together and performing with the Beatles. "I suppose you could say it came true," commented McCartney,[182] whose net worth is over a billion dollars.

Billy Joel

Billy Joel admits the Beatles inspired him to start writing hit songs[183] and told Sir McCartney when he first met him that some of that motivation came after the Beatles broke up and stopped putting out songs. Like McCartney, Joel's music is inspired directly by dreams. "I dream music all the time," revealed Joel.[184] The American singer-songwriter added that he doesn't always remember his dreams, but affirmed that, "All the music I write, I've dreamt."[185] Joel elaborated that he is not always able to reel in the music that comes to him during sleep: "I've lost songs because I don't remember the dream...I put a tape recorder next to the bed and a notebook."[186]

"When I'm asleep…I go back to the primeval artist who is at the core of me. There's no restraints, there's no editors—they close up shop, they go home," explained Joel. "I say to people, 'if you only could have heard what I dreamt, if you only could have been there.' When you hear a new piece of music, it makes you feel an emotion that's very difficult to explain. So to try to explain a dream or to try to translate a dream is a similar kind of difficulty, and it takes a great deal of effort to do it, but that's my job." Joel summarized the challenge, common to many dream-inspired musicians, "What I'm fleshing out, what I'm recording…isn't as good as what I've heard in my dreams."[187]

Joel explained that rather than dreaming scenes, he generally dreams of "abstractions—shapes, colors, sounds, symphonies."[188] "Normally I don't come up with a lyric idea in the dream, the dream is usually musical. I don't usually dream scenarios or words. I dream sounds and I dream arrangements, I dream solos, I dream even the production of a recording, but not lyrics. But this time I did wake up saying 'I go walking in my sleep in the middle of the night.'"[189] That dream became the inspiration for his *River of Dreams* album's title song. The album's cover is a painting by his former wife, supermodel Christie Brinkley, depicting compelling images from some of the dreams that inspired Joel's music. "I tried not to write that song," said Joel. "It was another one of those dreams. I am not going to write that. I am not that guy. It was like gospel. Who the hell am I to try to pull that off? I'll take a shower and wash this song away." Joel adds that the song kept coming more and more in the shower, and he realized he had to write it.[190]

During a 1993 Discovery Channel documentary in which I also had the good fortune to appear, Joel explained that he has created many compositions from dreamt music that is "classical in scope." Regarding his song *Lullabye* from the *River of Dreams* album, Joel revealed that he composed it from a longer piece of music which he dreamt was performed by "a classical chorus, a Vienna boys' choir…or an operatic kind of choir…there was no lyric, it was just piano and a chorus, an angelic chorus." Joel decided not to arrange the song exactly as he dreamt it.[191]

About his song *Just the Way You Are*, Joel explained, "It happened pretty fast. I dreamt the melody and chord progression and wrote the lyrics over a few days after the dream re-occurred to me."[192] Joel later elaborated that at first he "dreamt the melody, not the words," and awoke "in the middle of the night and going, 'This is a great idea for a song.'" Joel continued, "A couple of weeks later, I'm in a business meeting, and the dream reoccurs to me right at that moment because my mind had drifted off from hearing numbers and legal jargon. And I said, 'I have to go!' I got home and I ended up writing it all in one sitting, pretty much. It took me maybe two or three hours to write the lyrics."[193]

The song won the Grammy for Song of the Year, and was included on Joel's album *The Stranger* which won the Grammy for Record of the Year. *The Stranger*'s album cover depicts dream-like objects—boxing gloves hanging on the wall of a bedroom behind Joel in suit and tie leaning back on an unmade bed and staring at a polished mask on the pillow beside him. As one might guess, the imagery also came to Joel in a dream.[194] *Just The Way You Are* made the top 10 in at least 6 countries, including the #1 position on Billboard's Easy Listening list in the US, and #3 on Billboard's Hot 100.

Joel revealed that the musical artist whose creative process most resonates with his own is dream-inspired artist Sting,[195] who says that he consciously employs the "shamanic art of rhyming…to re-enter that realm…halfway between sleep and waking",[196] who sometimes gives concerts alongside Joel, and who I just so happened to have guiding me in a dream this morning—the day that I am updating these pages for this book's new edition.

Sting

"Any artist who ignores their dreams is ignoring half of their creative potential." –**Sting**[197]

"Some songs take months," explained seventeen-time Grammy-winning artist[198] **Sting** about songwriting. "The best come quickly and are very simple. They are given to you."

One such song "given" during sleep to Sting was *Every Breath You Take.* "I woke up in the middle of the night with that line in my head, sat down at the piano and wrote it in half an hour," elaborated Sting,[199] who was lead singer and bass player for **The Police** at the time. *Every Breath You Take* became a monster hit, winning two of the three Grammy Awards it was nominated for in 1983, including Best Song of the Year and Best Pop Performance by a Duo or Group with Vocals. It remained at #1 on Billboard's Top 100 Singles for 8 weeks and their Top Tracks chart for 9 weeks, as well as atop the UK Singles Chart for 4 weeks. It also ranked #28 on Billboard's Hot 100 All Time Top Songs.[200]

The song appeared on The Police's *Synchronicity* album, for which the title track and album were inspired by famed psychiatrist and dream analyst Carl Jung's concept of meaningful coincidence.[201] *Synchronicity* was also The Police's last album, capping their seven-year journey as a band[ix] at the height of their major international success.

Sting's first solo album, *The Dream of the Blue Turtles,* also had its title inspired by a dream[202] in January 1985, the night Sting arrived in Barbados. "I dreamed I was sitting in[203] the walled

---

[ix] An example of how the 7-year cycle principle applies to partnerships and groups, not just individuals.

garden behind my house in Hampstead, under a lilac tree on a well-manicured lawn, surrounded by beautiful rosebushes."[204] The beautifully maintained garden, Sting elsewhere explained is "very English, very disciplined, with a flower bed, a square lawn and a lilac tree." Recalling the rest of the dream, Sting says, "Suddenly, a big hole appears in the garden wall and out of it come four massive, prehistoric blue turtles with long, scaly necks. They are very macho and athletic and drunk on their own virility. They start doing back flips and somersaults, and in the process they destroy this garden, just wreck it.[205] "They were not only the size of a man, they were also blue and had an air of being immensely cool, like hepcats, insouciant and fearless… digging up the lawn with their claws, chomping at the rosebushes, bulldozing the lilac tree. Total mayhem."[206] Sting says that he awoke to the sound of his new band mate Branford on the floor above him "riffing wildly on his tenor saxophone" and then laughing.[207] The former **Police** front man, who has done Jungian analysis, links the four turtles with the four musicians from his band, noting that blue is a good color for jazz musicians. He says the dream confirmed for him that it was okay to destroy the "safe back yard" formula he used when making **Police** records, and to instead "churn up the land like a farmer does when he wants it to be fruitful a year hence." He adds how the dream, in this case, brought him the emotional realization that although upheavals can be "frightening and dramatic, ultimately you'll be rewarded."[208]

Sting records his dreams in a bedside journal. One of them is a recurring "classic anxiety dream" where he is aboard a plummeting jet that's narrowly missing people, bridges and buildings. "The meaning is fairly clear to me," said Sting. "The plane is a symbol of my rather extraordinary life and a subconscious fear that it is out of my control."[209]

His bedside journal also holds notes scribbled late at night that led to **The Police**'s hit, *Walking on The Moon*. Sting reported being unable to fall asleep with a "boom ba boom bass line" and rhythm running through his mind, so he arose from bed and penned down[210] what shortly developed into the band's second #1 hit in the UK. The song also hit #1 in Ireland.

Another example of Sting's nightly adventures that have sparked songs is *The Wild Wild Sea*. The former lead singer of **The Police** wrote in his book *Lyrics*, that the song began as "disjointed fragments recalled from a night of fitful sleep." He added that he crafted the dream vignettes into song, using among other tools, "the shamanic art" of rhyming, about which he elucidated that "to follow its winding path is to re-enter that realm that is halfway between sleep and waking, where the mysterious imperative of the subconscious can reveal itself on the page."[211]

In the liner notes for his *Nothing Like the Sun* album, **Sting** writes, "*Lazarus Heart* was a vivid nightmare that I wrote down and then fashioned into a song. A learned friend of mine informs me that it is the archetypical dream of the fisher king."[212]

"If I'm ever asked if I'm religious, I always reply, 'Yes, I'm a devout musician.' Music puts me in touch with something beyond intellect, something otherworldly, something sacred."

–Sting[213]

In the 1980s, Sting also lived in New York City in the same building as Paul Simon, and the two stars ended up touring internationally together in 2014-2015.[214]

Paul Simon

"Sometimes stuff'll come in the middle of the night in a dream."[215]

–**Paul Simon**, sixteen-time Grammy-winner

Master singer-songwriter **Paul Simon** for years suffered from performance-related nightmares about the microphone being too high for him to reach, or placed such that he was facing away from the audience and yet was not able to budge it, or that nobody could hear him since he was singing in a glass booth.[216] His upsetting recurring dreams offer an interesting perspective on the title of **Simon & Garfunkel**'s megahit ballad *Sounds of Silence*.

On January 15th, 2019, Simon had a dream that told him to work on a new piece called *Seven Psalms*. The dream "was strong enough that I woke up and wrote it down in the middle of the night. I didn't even know what the word 'psalm' meant," recounts Simon. A little over a year passed, then Simon started to dream words that he would wake up and write down, "I would wake up between 3 and 5 a.m. with words...If I used my experience as a songwriter, it didn't work. I just went back into a passive state...it was just flowing though me...at a pace that was comfortable. This is really fun. I'm really not working at all, it is just like kind of a gift." While working on the album during covid, Simon was surpised that his hearing started to disappear in his left ear. Gradually at first, then more rapidly, which he initially found annoying though strangely it didn't interfere with his work on Seven Psalms. By the time he had finished the piece, he had mostly lost hearing in his left ear.[217]

"All of these guitar pieces came out of dreams...and I thought, 'this is so easy and this is so much fun, and now this [hearing problem] is a real interuption', and I'm angry. Then I started to think, 'maybe this is a wrong idea...it's possible that this is a piece of information that will be of value to this creation.'" That new perspective helped him shift his interpretation and feelings around the hearing loss: "It's a disability, but it's not a problem."[218] Simon's 15th solo album Seven Psalms was nominated for a Grammy. Interestingly, the album includes a line from the dream-inspired Battle Hymn of the Republic.[219] Simon was quite surprised by the process of the album's music flowing so easily in his dreams. Quite intriguing is that his dream download experiences started in early 2020 which aligns very closely with Feb 11, 2020, the date when shamanic dreaming artist and LadySmith Black Mambazo founder and lead singer Joseph Shabalala passed on.

Thanks to his 1986 *Graceland* album and ensuing tour, Simon was responsible for bringing African artist and master-dreamer Joseph Shabalala and his group Ladysmith Black Mambazo into the international spotlight. The album was Simon's most successful and won the 1987 Grammy Award for Album of The Year, and sold over 18 million copies.[220]

Joseph Shabalala & Ladysmith Black Mambazo

Modern artists who tap dreams for enhancing their art and performances are much like creative public shamans in this big world tribe that we call our society.

Zulu songwriter and master dreamer **Joseph Shabalala** is a good example since his father actually was a traditional African shaman who used plant medicine. Shabalala shared how people would tell him that his "father healed them with his medicine and I healed them with my music." "Oh yes," Shabalala would reply, "but my father's medicine is bitter…my music is sweet."[221]

The group that Shabalala formed, **Ladysmith Black Mambazo**, has won many awards including five Grammys, sold many millions of albums worldwide, and worked with numerous high-profile performers including dream-inspired artists Paul Simon, Stevie Wonder, Michael Jackson, as well as Sarah McLachlan and many others. A documentary film about the group, *On Tip Toe: Gentle Steps to Freedom*, was also nominated for an Academy Award.

They sing in the African Zulu a cappella style called 'isicathamiya' which also incorporates traditional Zulu dance and related choreography. Although Shabalala founded the group in 1960, it took a few years to hone their sound. Neither Shabalala nor the group could read music, so he taught them to sing harmonies by ear.[222] "I like this music very much, but I knew that it wasn't quite right yet. I was thinking about it [a lot]."[223] Then in 1964, Shabalala received inspiration and training about how to arrange and sing powerful harmonies from a "marvelous" dream.

"A dream came to me to show how to bring the people together to take their mind back to their roots, to their tradition—African soul," recalled the Zulu songwriter.[224] "I saw children…not white, not black…floating in between the sky and the stage. They are singing very perfect harmony. And then I learned to produce that harmony and I learned to teach [it]. And I learned many things—even action [for choreography]—I learned from those children."[225] Elsewhere Shabalala elaborated, "It was a marvelous dream. My ears were filled of just merriment, and listening [to] that harmony. I learned from them how to sing the bass, how to sing the tenor, how to sing the alto. I called them the choir from heaven." "The dream" continued as a recurring theme for Shabalala over a period of about 6 months,[226] during which time he claims to have dreamt *every night* of music taught to him by the otherworldly choir of children.[227]

In 1972, the group received an invitation from jive saxophonist and producer West Nkosi to come with him to Johannesburg to record an album. At first, Shabalala had concerns about businessmen from Johannesburg, but then the group reminded him about a dream he had shared with them not long before in which he saw "a car from heaven come down with a crane." The crane then placed the car on the ground and disappeared.[228] They suggested that maybe this new offer was the car and they should accept it. Shabalala agreed and apologized to Nkosi for his initial mistrust, and the group members squeezed into Nkosi's minibus and headed to Johannesburg. The album of traditional Zulu music that they recorded, *Amabutho,* became a huge success across the country and was the first album by black musicians from South Africa to achieve gold disc status.[229] Likely only because the group followed Shabalala's "car from heaven" dream and recorded the successful album with Nkosi, did they become well enough known to attract what happened next.

In 1984, Shabalala and the group met Paul Simon and rose to international stardom thanks to the collaboration with Simon on his 1986 *Graceland* Grammy-winning album and tour. Ladysmith Black Mambazo wrote and performed with Simon the songs *Homeless*, *Diamonds on the Soles of Her Shoes*, and *You Can Call Me Al.*

For years, Shabalala honed the music and sometimes adjusted the arrangement or lyrics that he dreamt. However, for the group's 1988 album *Journey of Dreams*, the composer decided to record the music "exactly as my dreams would tell me."[230]

His subconscious source of musical inspiration, arrangement, and harmony training seems to hold an element of invisible truth or at least wide appeal, since the group has received seventeen Grammy nominations (beginning in 1987), and has won the coveted award five times for: *Shaka Zulu* (Best Traditional Folk Recording, 1987, produced by Paul Simon, as well as for *Shaka Zulu Revisited* in 2018), *Raise Your Spirit Higher* (Best Traditional World Music Album, 2004), *Ilembe* (Best Traditional World Music Album, 2008), and *Live: Singing For Peace Around The World* (Best World Music Album, 2013).[231]

Accentuating the process that brought him so much success, Shabalala affirmed:

"You must learn the way to follow the dream."

–Joseph Shabalala[232]

Billie Eilish

Pop sensation **Billie Eilish** is the youngest female to reach #1 on the UK Albums chart for her debut effort *When We All Fall Asleep, Where Do We Go?* which also rose to the top of the charts in 15 countries, achieved best-selling album of the year status in Canada, and had its track *Bad Guy* become 2019's biggest digital single[233] that also hit #1 on Billboard's *Hot 100*.

Collaborating with her older brother Finneas, Eilish and he masterfully crafted archetypal nighttime experiences into art that seem to resonate with many, many millions of people worldwide given that their songs have surpassed 50 billion streams.[234]

"The album is basically what happens when you fall asleep," Eilish shared with Zane Lowe of Apple Music, explaining that the songs are inspired by night terrors, nightmares, lucid dreams, and sleep paralysis.[235]

The singer admitted that she has terrifying dreams, and that they deeply influenced her multi-platinum song *Bury A Friend*, adding

"I probably wouldn't have made that song the way it is if I hadn't had sleep paralysis and nightmares."[236]

Everything I Wanted is another track from the album that divulges her dreams. In a nightmare, Eilish leapt off the Golden Gate Bridge thinking she could fly but then fell to her death. She noticed that friends, colleagues and fans didn't cry or pay attention to her tragic end, and then awoke with a sense that although she attained 'everything [she] wanted', some people around her still see her as disposable.[237]

Many of Eilish music videos and performances incorporate elements from her nightmares, sleep paralysis, dreams, synesthesia experiences, and surreal daydreams. In her live performances, she has even flown around midair singing from a floating bed.[238]

Michael Jackson

Motown records founder Berry Gordy dubbed superstar singer-songwriter and multi-talented artist **Michael Jackson** as "the greatest entertainer that ever lived."[239] Jackson had thirteen #1 singles in the United States, and his album *Thriller* became the best-selling album of all time. He won 13 Grammy Awards, the Grammy Legend Award and Grammy Lifetime Achievement Award, and many other awards including 26 American Music Awards[240] (more than any artist except dream-inspired Taylor Swift).

Given all the dream-inspired successes collected in these pages, it is perhaps not surprising that Jackson credited dreams as the source of "many" of his artistic and musical ideas,[241] including his top 10 duet with Paul McCartney *The Girl is Mine*.[242] "I wake up from dreams and go 'Wow, put this down on paper,' the whole thing is strange. You hear the words, everything is right there in front of your face. I feel that somewhere, someplace it's been done and I'm just a courier bringing it into the world."[243]

While alive, Jackson often experienced the common worldwide dream theme of flying.[244]

Michael's late father, talent manager **Joe Jackson**, revealed that he dreamt of his deceased son smiling and singing in such a way that his voice echoed out the door. The dream became lucid as Joe Jackson realized he was dreaming, followed by an experience that is called a false awakening (i.e. he dreamt that he 'awoke' within the dream). He went to the room's doorway, following Michael's voice and then (actually) woke up.[245] Experiencing lucid dreams, and thereby realizing that who we are exists beyond the physical body (like Gennadius did), is an important spiritual development that can bring more peace about death. Just thirteen months after the dream, Joe Jackson tragically suffered a stroke and three heart attacks.[246]

The Rolling Stones

On May 7, 1965 in Clearwater, Florida, only a few weeks before McCartney finished the lyrics for *Yesterday*, **Rolling Stones**' guitarist **Keith Richards** awoke in the middle of the night with a short melody. He played the dream-delivered riff on acoustic guitar into his tape recorder along with the mumbled lyrics "I can't get no satisfaction" and then fell back to sleep. "When I woke up in the morning, the tape had run out," Richards recalled years later. "I put it back on, and there's maybe 30 seconds of *Satisfaction* in a very drowsy sort of rendition. And then suddenly the guitar goes 'CLANG!', and then there's like 45 minutes of snoring." Richards thought the melody was sort of a joke, but the

Stones liked it. Mick Jagger wrote the lyrics "in 10 minutes" by the pool the next day, and much later commented that Richard's subconscious may have also gained inspiration from Chuck Berry's *30 Days* which contained the line 'I don't get no satisfaction from the judge', since they played those records a lot back then.[247] Nonetheless, three days after the song was finished, they brought it into Chicago's Chess studios on May 10th, 1965, and then completed it on May 12th after a flight to Los Angeles and an 18-hour recording session at RCA Studios. In L.A., Richards played the riff on his guitar using a Gibson fuzz box effect, even though he had initially envisioned the melody being played by horns. The rest is history. In June 1965, *Satisfaction* launched the Stones to superstar status as their first #1 single in America, and was later included on the American version of that year's *Out of Our Heads* album.

In 2005,[248] when *Rolling Stone* magazine ranked the song #2 on its 500 Greatest Songs of All Time, it added that Richards' dream "spark in the night…was the crossroads: the point at which the rickety jump and puppy love of early rock and roll became rock."[249]

Keith Richards claimed that he also composed *Robbed Blind* within 15 minutes right after he woke up. The song appears on his 2015 solo album *Under The Influence*.[250]

Taylor Swift

Pop megastar and singer-songwriter **Taylor Swift** says that, in a few cases, dreams have inspired her lyrics. As an example, a single piercing word she screeched during a dream became the seed for her song *All You Had to Do Was Stay* from her best-selling album *1989*. Swift candidly recounted her dreamland experience about an ex-boyfriend arriving at her door,[251] which appears to contain a slight variation of the common dream theme where the dreamer cannot speak or make any sound:

> *"In the dream I was trying to talk to somebody and all that would come out of my voice was that sound, and I was embarrassed. It was like a social humiliation dream, and I was so embarrassed that I woke up and I was haunted by this sound. I was like, 'why? that's the weirdest sound!' But it was the word 'stay', screeching, high-pitched, and so the next day I went into the studio and wrote a song and incorporated that into the chorus."*[252]

Another arrangement addition came in the middle of the night. While writting and recording her song *I Did Something Bad*, Swift awoke on October 18th, 2018 with the staccato vocalisation "ra ri di di di di di di di di tya" and had it mixed in that day to the latter part of the song's chorus.[253]

The superstar also divulged that she has recurring nightmares about waking up and her tour is not planned, which she says motivates her to organize her tours well ahead of time. Swift further confided that she has another recurring nightmare of "being arrested for something I didn't do,"[254] and more specifically about "being framed for murder"—sometimes so well that she doesn't even know in the dream whether she committed the crime or not. The stress of being a high-profile artist seems to often affect Swift's dreams since she has yet another recurring anxiety dream about her room being bugged, and she has to smile because paparazzi are in her room taking photos of her as she is sleeping.[255]

Ed Sheeran

For a colloboration with Taylor Swift on her song *End Game,* master pop singer-songwriter **Ed Sheeran** shared that he wrote a verse at 8 o'clock in the morning in bed in a New York City hotel, thanks to a dream that he'd just had: "I woke up 'cuz for some reason, I'd, like, dreamed it in my head what I was gonna do."[256]

Lady Gaga

Pop artist **Lady Gaga** is no stranger to turning nightmares and dreams into art and confided that, "My biggest fear is I'll die before I get all my ideas out—I have nightmares about it."[257]

She also had a huge childhood fear of an angler fish which she spun into her *Monster Ball* stage show.[258] Her performances have also drawn inspiration from a recurring dream "where there's a phantom in my home...he takes me into a room and there's a blond girl with ropes tied to all four of her limbs, and she's got my shoes on from the Grammys...and the ropes are pulling her apart." Gaga added that she witnesses the girl whimpering but never being dismembered as the phantom tells Gaga that if she cuts her own wrist, he will stop torturing the girl and Gaga's family will be okay. He provides a special wrist-cutting tool and a Tupperware containing honey that looks like New York MSG-infused sweet-and-sour sauce that he wants Gaga to pour in the wound and cover with cream and gauze.[259]

"I wonder if the way I process trauma is these semi-fantastical nightmares...spinning them into something beautiful," Gaga pondered, explaining that her 2025 *Mayhem* album draws inspiration from many dreams about her past[260] including dark "gothic dreams...symbols of life and metaphors that I then turned into pop songs."[261]

Gaga has another nightmare where the devil tries to take her, and admits that she has often asked author Deepak Chopra for help with her nightmares.[262]

Sexxx Dreams is a Gaga song that incorporates her "really bizarre" erotic dreams and night visions that contain "sexy sculptures",[263] and she also credited the sexual dreams her private chef Nate would tell her at breakfast during her 2012-13 *Born This Way* tour.[264]

Gaga's Joanne album was named after a young woman she saw in a recurring dream. "In the dream," shared Gaga, "I'm playing at an amphitheater outdoors, and beyond the seats, there's a field in back — it's the cheap tickets." She goes on to describe the girl as seated, wearing a Hanes sweatshirt, her mom's rolled-up jeans, a lot of fake jewelry alongside one real heirloom piece, holding a cigarette and a glass of Pinot Grigio, and has two of her three babies running around her. "This girl is singing every word," explained Gaga, "and she thinks, 'How is it possible that Lady Gaga understands how I feel?'". Gaga concluded insightfully, "That girl — it's me."[265]

Teddy Swims

Mainstream artist **Teddy Swims** also experiences disturbing dreams so regularly that he is anxious about going to sleep and even avoids sleeping when possible. He admits to "having nightmares all the time" and occasionally has bouts where he wakes up from upsetting dreams every half hour. As an artist, he decided to openly express his previously private challenging experiences as musical art with his hit *Bad Dreams* and frame it as a love song linked to his current partner who helps him deal with his tough overnight episodes. The song describes his ongoing nightmares, and shows how sleep brings him "nothing but stress" as hinted at by his reference at the end of the first verse to grinding his teeth, although he adds that he does experience a specific recurring dream about his teeth crumbling and falling out (that is actually a fairly common dream theme worldwide). The chorus describes another of Swims' nightmare motifs that is also experienced by many people — trying to scream and having no sound come out.[266] *Bad Dreams* reached #1 on iTunes' US chart and landed in the top 40 in UK and several other countries.

Shawn Mendes

Pop star Shawn Mendes revealed that his song *Lost in Japan* was sparked by an intriguing dream, "I was lost in this country and I woke up the next day and we had this cool piano part and the song was birthed."[267]

The song was featured on his self-titled third studio album which was nominated for the Best Pop Vocal Album Grammy, and Mendes was also invited to the American Music Awards where he performed a remix of the song on October 9, 2018.

Jimi Hendrix

"We want our sound to go into the soul of the audience, and see if it can awaken some little thing in their minds...'Cause there are so many sleeping people." –**Jimi Hendrix**[268]

In what seems it may have been a precognitive dream, sixties superstar **Jimi Hendrix** revealed, "I used to dream in Technicolor that 1966 was the year that something would happen to me."[269] Indeed, that year Hendrix was catapulted from being virtually unknown into mega stardom.

"I dreamt a lot and I put a lot of my dreams down as songs," explained Hendrix. "I wrote one called *First Around the Corner* and another called *The Purple Haze*, which was all about a dream I had that I was walking under the sea."[270] Hendrix elsewhere commented that the dream was linked to a story in a science fiction magazine about a purple death ray.[271]

"In the dream," recounted Hendrix's lover Monika Dannemann, "he looked down on earth and saw an unborn fetus waiting for its birth as if it were pointing at the time for it to be born. At the same time, he saw spirits of the dead leaving earth. Later in the dream he went on a journey through the dimensions, and was walking under the sea." The song's original working title was *Purple Haze - Jesus Saves.*[272] Dannemann also reported that Hendrix told her that his faith in Jesus saved him when he became engulfed by and lost in a purple haze near the end of the dream as it became a nightmare.[273] Hendrix's official cause of death was asphyxiation, with the autopsy confirming that he had ingested alcohol—which included wine, according to Dannemann,[274] and specifically red wine, according to Hendrix's friend Meic Stevens who was with him the night before he died.[275] During asphyxiation, blood cells are deprived of oxygen creating a condition called cyanosis where the skin turns blue or purple.[276] The *Purple Haze* lyrics crafted from Hendrix' dream include "Oh, no, no, help me, help me" and originally also included "down on the ceiling, looking up at the bed…See my body painted blue and red"[277]—perhaps containing an eerie premonitory hint about his unfortunate death. In 2008-9, *Rolling Stone* magazine ranked *Purple Haze* at #17 in their 500 Greatest Songs of All Time[278] and as #2 in their 100 Greatest Guitar Songs of all time.[279]

Dannemann also reported that Hendrix told her his song *Machine Gun* was inspired by an astral travel dream experience he had one night during which he found himself "next to a dying and groaning soldier."[280]

Hendrix's song *Angel* was also inspired by a dream from his childhood: "My mother was being carried away on this camel, and it was a big caravan," recalled Hendrix. "She's saying, 'Well, I'm gonna see you now,' and she's going under these trees, you could see the shade, you know, the leaf patterns across her face when she was going under [were green and yellow shadows]…She's saying, 'Well, I won't be seeing you too much anymore, you know, so I'll see ya.'…And I said, 'Yeah, but where are you going?' I remember that. I will always remember that. I never did forget. There are some dreams you never forget." About two years after the dream, Hendrix's mother died.[281] Although he started working on the song in October 1967, Hendrix finished recording *Angel* on July 23, 1970, just weeks before he himself headed to spirit realms on September 18. The song was released in March of the following year as the lead single on his posthumous album *The Cry of Love*.[282]

"Don't be dismayed at good-byes. A farewell is necessary before you can meet again. And meeting again, after moments or lifetimes, is certain for those who are friends."

–Richard Bach[283]

Peter Gabriel

Peter Gabriel is another superstar artist who has been visited by the dream muse. His song *Here Comes the Flood* was inspired by "an apocalyptic dream in which the psychic barriers which normally prevent us from seeing into each others' thoughts had been completely eroded, producing a mental flood. Those that had been used to having their innermost thoughts exposed would handle this torrent and those inclined to concealment would drown in it."[284]

Gabriel's hit *Red Rain* also originated from a dream, a recurring scene where he would find himself swimming in a sea of red water.[285] Released in 1986, the song reached #3 on Billboard's Mainstream Rock chart.

Bobby Braddock

As a member of the Country Music Hall of Fame and Nashville Songwriters Hall of Fame, American country artist, songwriter, and record producer **Bobby Braddock** has created numerous hit songs. Among his thirteen #1 hit singles, one was voted by the BBC as the best country music song. Braddock claims that he has intentionally "slept on" lyric and melody ideas for pretty much every song he wrote, "waking up with it all there, worked out overnight" by his subconscious. He adds that one of his songs recorded for Mercury Records on his *Gloria the Magnificent* album, was completely formed in a dream, down to background vocals and instrumentation.[286]

Carl Perkins

Carl Perkins says the lyrics for his rockabilly hit *Blue Suede Shoes* came to him overnight after performing for a dance at the Roadside Inn on December 4th, 1955.

"I heard this boy tell the girl he was dancing with 'Watch out, don't step on mah suedes' and I looked down at his feet, and he had on this pair of blue suede shoes," recalls Perkins. The incident stayed on his mind all night and then his subconscious and dreams went to work. In the early morning hours he got up and quickly penned the song's lyrics on the only nearby writing surface he could find—an old brown paper potato sack. He then started finding the chords on his Les Paul guitar, beginning with an A chord. The song was recorded in a single take less than 2 weeks later on December 17, 1955, and released on New Year's Day, 1956.[287] On March 17 that year, Perkins became the first country artist to reach the #3 spot on the rhythm & blues charts.[288] By mid-April, the song reached gold status with over a million records sold,[289],[290] and was the first million-selling country song to cross over to both rhythm and blues and pop charts.[291]

Elvis Presley performed the song three times on national television in 1956, and released his own up-tempo cover version as the first song on his groundbreaking RCA Records album entitled *Elvis Presley*. Elvis' version rose even higher on the charts than Perkins' original.[292] Numerous artists besides Elvis also later covered the song including The Beatles, Buddy Holly, Bill Haley and His Comets, Jimi Hendrix, Jerry Lee Lewis, and many others.[293]

David Crosby of Crosby, Stills & Nash

Music legend **David Crosby** of **Crosby, Stills and Nash** got the spark for the band's song *Shadow Captain* from a dream that occurred close to 3am while he was, appropriately, sleeping on his boat. He had never conceived of anything at all like it before, but happily recorded the complete song lyrics word for word, then went back to sleep.[294]

The former **Byrds** singer and guitarist noticed similar experiences starting to happen more and more around the late 1980s, especially as he started to nod off. Just before he slipped fully into slumber, Crosby would sometimes awaken with a clear inspiration, scramble for a light, and pour out pages of lyrics.[295] His song *Thousand Roads* is one example among many, and he added that he has also received music in the same twilight mental state[296] that is known to science as hypnagogic dreaming.

Neil Young

Neil Young's film *Journey Through the Past* included his music as the soundtrack, as well as a scene which is a recreation of one of his recurring dreams where twelve men wearing black hoods and riding black horses in a cavalry charge towards a man in a pickup truck.[297]

According to radio host Sherman Baldwin (who has interviewed both Neil Young and me), the veteran rocker dreamt up at least three of his songs "including I think *Like a Hurricane* and two others," said Baldwin.[298] Young's song *After the Gold Rush* speaks of a powerful dream where he saw many things including a future where space travel might help humanity survive environmental destruction.[299]

Mamas and the Papas

In 1964, John Phillips woke his wife Michelle from a deep sleep in the middle of a "very cold" New York winter night. Not long before, he had awoken from a dream with the phrase *California Dreamin'* and had started crafting a melancholy song around it that he wanted her to help him write. She didn't want to get out of the cozy bed and said she'd help him work on it "tomorrow," but at his insistence she admitted, "I made myself get up—thank God—and we wrote the song."

Hundreds of people have told Michelle Phillips in the years since the song was released that after hearing it, they packed their bags and headed to California. Surely many others that Phillips never spoke to acted similarly, so the dream-sparked song ended up having quite a transformational effect on the lives of many.[300]

California Dreamin' entered the Grammy Hall of Fame in 2001 and is ranked as #89 in Rolling Stone Magazine's 500 Greatest Songs of All Time. The song has been in numerous film and TV soundtracks and has been recorded by many artists including, among others, The Four Tops, America, R.E.M., The Carpenters, as well as The Beach Boys, whose version hit #57 on Billboard's Hot 100.

The Beach Boys

The Beach Boys were inducted into the Rock and Roll Hall of Fame in 1988. Band leader and co-founder, Grammy-winner **Brian Wilson**, was inducted into the Songwriters Hall of Fame in 2000 by dream-inspired colleague **Sir Paul McCartney**,[301] as well as into the UK Music Hall of Fame in 2006.

Wilson shared that while recording their *Pet Sounds* album, and especially the song *God Only Knows*, he and his band mate and younger brother Carl would "pray to the Lord for guidance and maximum love vibes for this single." Brian Wilson revealed a dream that came to him during that time about "a halo over my head, but people couldn't see it,"[302] and added, "God was right there with me. I could see—I could find that feeling in my head, in my brain."[303] Brian Wilson shared his understanding that the dream "might have meant that the angels were watching over *Pet Sounds*."[304]

The album was named the greatest album of all time by The Times (of London),[305] NME,[306] and Mojo[307] magazine, and in 2003, Rolling Stone Magazine ranked the album second on their 500 Greatest Albums of All Time, the position it still holds today,[308] and the song God Only Knows as #11 in their best songs of all time.[309]

Fleetwood Mac & Stevie Nicks

In early 1970, when he was experimenting with LSD, British guitarist and songwriter **Peter Green**, the founder of **Fleetwood Mac**, had a terrifying nightmare in which he was taking care of a green[x] stray dog that barked at him, and yet he somehow knew that the dog had been dead for a long time.[310] In an experience hinting at what science calls sleep paralysis, Green reported that in the dream, he found himself dead and unable to move, though he eventually managed to struggle back into his body and wake up. In the darkened room, he wrote out *The Green Manalishi*, and soon recorded a rough version of all the parts on his home Revox.[311] Green associated the dog with money and decided he wanted to give all of the band's income to charity, but the other band members disagreed. Fleetwood Mac released the song on Friday, May 15. Five days later, Green left the band over the money dispute.

Fleetwoord Mac member **Christine McVie** explained that the tune *Songbird* arose from a nocturnal "spiritual experience". McVie elucidated further, saying "I woke up in the middle of the

---

[x] An interesting color, considering Green's family name.

night, and the song just came into my head. I got out of bed, played it on the little piano I have in my room, and sang it with no tape recorder...from beginning to end: everything. It was as if I'd been visited – it was a very spiritual thing." She felt anxious to replay *Songbird* on the chance she'd already forgotten it. So, in the morning, she rang her producer with urgency saying, "I've got to put this song down right now." In the studio that day, she played it nervously but managed to recall the whole song. "Everyone just sat there and stared at me." added McVie, "I've never had that happen to me since."[312] The final *Songbird* version for the band's album *Rumours* was recorded in California's Zellberbach auditorium with a spotlight on a bouquet of red roses on the piano being played by McVie around 3 a.m. — very close to the time that the song came to McVie.[313]

McVie's band mate **Stevie Nicks** also harvested a dream to write her song *Show Them The Way*. In 2008, after a long day in studio working on a concert tour documentary, she returned home and watched the USA's democratic primary elections as well as civil rights movement documentaries. That night, reported Nicks, "I had a dream that was so real...a cinematic story; it had a beginning, middle and end...every detail, every colour, every smile was there."[314] Upon waking, Nicks had unusually clear recall[315] and recorded "every little bit" of the dream in which she was invited to perform at a benefit party full of influential political figures including John F. Kennedy, Bobby Kennedy, John Lewis, and others.[316] "I saw myself walking with Martin Luther King from the back, like I was standing on the other side of myself," explained Nicks. "I walked down the hallway with him into that room with the Kennedys, and all the people surrounding the piano said, 'Play for us.'" Nicks soon crafted the experience into a poem, and later evolved it into an anthemic single. Although she really liked the tune, it was only released in 2020 before the USA's presidential election, with dream-inspired artist Dave Grohl playing drums.[317]

Dream-Sparked Career for Dave Grohl
(Nirvana/Foo Fighters)

Singer-songwriter, producer, actor, drummer, and guitar player **Dave Grohl** has had a rockin' career, including as drummer for the grunge band **Nirvana**, founder and front man for the **Foo Fighters**, session drummer for Paul McCartney, David Bowie, Tom Petty and the Heartbreakers, Stevie Nicks, among other well-known artists, and has been involved in various film and TV projects, including as director of the movie *Sound City*.

Grohl divulged that his first heart throb was in grade 8, a beautiful girl named Sandy Moran who was "the best-looking girl in the school." The couple were together for "all of two weeks" after which, the rocker confided, "She dropped me like a hot potato." That night, Grohl dreamt he was rocking out on guitar on stage in a massive arena. "The audience was going nuts and she was in the front row crying," he said, recalling the dream, and explained that it was his initial motivation to become a mega rock star.[318]

The Foo Fighters' music video *Everlong,* nominated for Best Rock Video at the 1998 MTV Video Music Awards, portrays multiple dream scenarios. In the video, Grohl's hand twice grows significantly in size, and each time he positively transforms what are portrayed as intertwined dream scenarios. This is interesting since it demonstrates both how to become lucid (conscious) in a dream, as well as what can happen as a result of becoming lucid. The practise of verifying hands to test whether one is awake or dreaming is a lucid dream induction technique called '**reality checking**'. It was originally proposed by 19th century Russian mystic, philosopher, and composer, George Gurdjieff, and about seven decades later by author Carlos Castenada in his book *Journey to Ixtlan*. I have triggered lucid dreams this way many times, checking my 'hands' and watching in surprise as they grow extra fingers or otherwise appear unusual, at which point I realize that they are 'dream hands' and that I am experiencing a dream, even though the scene often seems quite 'real'. Once lucid, I can then consciously guide the dream to differing extents, for fascinating adventures and insights. This key plot element of the *Everlong* video was chosen on purpose, inspired by the dreams of the video's director Michel Gondry[xi] who in childhood would often have dreams of his hands growing larger.[319]

An idea for the music video of the Foo Fighters' song *Monkey Wrench* came from a dream of Dave Grohl's where he traversed a hotel lobby with a bag of food and greeted the receptionist.[320]

Grohl also opened up about another dream: "My entire life, I've had the same recurring dream about a house I've never been to." In the same interview in US Weekly, Grohl also revealed that he left high school at age 17, before graduating, to tour with a band. He added that he has toured "almost every year since," which suggests he spends a great deal of time away from home and therefore may offer insight about his recurring dream.[321]

Pharrell Williams

As previously mentioned, American singer-songwriter, rapper, and music producer **Pharrell Williams** experiences visual-auditory synesthesia, often "seeing color" when he listens to music,[322] hence the title *Seeing Sounds* for the third album by his rock, funk, and hip hop band **N.E.R.D.**

His song *Gust of Wind* was also downloaded from dreamland. "It's from a dream, would you believe? It's the only time that's happened. I woke up, and immediately texted my wife." Williams

---

[xi] Gondry also directed the lucid-dream-like movie *Eternal Sunshine of The Spotless Mind*.

says the song is his favorite from his very successful *G I R L* album, which was nominated for multiple awards including the American Music Award for Favorite Soul/R&B Album and the 2015 Grammy for Best Album of the Year, and won Billboard's Top R&B Album award and the 2015 Grammy for Best Urban Contemporary Album.[323]

Pharrell is no stranger to dream-like states however, explaining that while recording in the studio, he sometimes likes to sit quietly with the lights off and a recording of rain playing in the background as he intentionally enters sensory deprivation and starts having the "craziest visions"—a process that sounds a bit like Salvador Dali's edge-of-sleep technique (described at the end of the Techniques chapter). The eleven-time Grammy-winner elaborated, "When you meditate, you let go of the senses and allow your inner essence to just flourish and bring to you images of whatever it's going to."[324]

Black Eyed Peas

Black Eyed Peas' singer/songwriter *will.i.am* (born Will Adams), says that a lot of songs come to him while he is dreaming,[325] including the tune for their chart-topping hit *I Gotta Feelin'*. "I've written songs right from a sleep," will.i.am told BBC's Newsbeat.[326] "Have you ever had a dream where there's a melody in your dream? I'll wake up out of my sleep and record that! *I Gotta Feelin'* was one of those songs. From a random mumble, listening to talking in the back and making sense of melodies."[327] The song reached #1 on the US charts and 20 other charts worldwide, won the Grammy for Best Pop Performance By A Duo Or Group With Vocals,[328] was 4th on Billboard's Hot 100 Songs of the Decade,[329] and is, as of this writing, iTunes most actively downloaded song of all time (as of 2012)[330], and has sold about 20 million downloads worldwide.[331]

Fergie

American solo artist and **Black Eyed Peas**' singer **Fergie** revealed that she named her son Axl Jack because of a musical dream in which she was at an outdoor concert where Jim Morrison came on stage singing, followed by Bob Marley, then Axl Rose. "I was in heaven in this dream," recalled Fergie. "And I'm dancing and just getting into the music, and then all of a sudden, boom boom! And I wake up, and it's the first time my son kicked me in the stomach. It was like he was feeling the music with me. It was amazing!"[332]

A little-known fact of particular interest, since it demonstrates consciousness principles[xii] and also seems to shed light on her dream, is that Fergie remembers how she used to want to "be with" Axl Rose and then later longed to actually "be" him. She would practise singing and performing in the mirror pretending she had Axl's then band-mate **Slash** playing guitar behind her. "So it's a dream for me to actually have the real thing now…to actually be in that role and have him play with me,"[333] explained Fergie, referring to singing on stage with Slash. How did the collaboration come about? Slash heard Fergie singing a cover of **Heart**'s 1970s hit *Barracuda*,[334] which led to the two performing *Barracuda* at a few concerts including Slash's birthday bash, followed by **Guns N' Roses**' biggest hit *Sweet Child O' Mine*.[335] The latter song is interesting in relation to Fergie's child-naming dream not only due to its title, which grew from the song's chorus written by Axl Rose, but also due to the fact that Rose wrote the lyrics about his then-girlfriend, Erin Everly, daughter of Don

---

[xii] such as what is commonly known as 'the law of attraction'.

Everly from the Rock and Roll and Country Music Hall of Famers **The Everly Brothers**. The Everly Brothers biggest hit is arguably *All I Have to Do Is Dream*,[336] a phrase which accurately describes all that Fergie had to do to come up with the name for that sweet child of hers. By dreamily imagining herself in Axl's role beside Slash, *All I have to Do Is Dream* may well also describe a key thing Fergie did to almost magically later end up singing on stage alongside Slash. Considering the performers in Fergie's baby-naming dream, it will be interesting to see if young Axl Jack follows in the footsteps of musical mavericks like Morrison, Marley, or Rose.

Train

Music group **Train**'s lead singer **Pat Monahan** says his #1 hit *Drops of Jupiter* that won two 2001 Grammy awards (Best Rock Song and Best Instrumental Arrangement With Accompanying Vocalist) was directly inspired by a dream in 1998, shortly after his mother's death from cancer. While on a trip to his hometown in Pennsylvania, and under intense pressure from his record label to produce a hit, he awoke with the opening lyrics clear in mind: "back in the atmosphere". Recalled Monahan, "Loss of the most important person in my life was heavy on my mind, and the thought of 'what if no one ever really leaves? What if she's here but different?'"[337]

"I fell asleep briefly—it felt like five seconds—and woke up with the lyric 'she's back in the atmosphere,'...I'd dreamed she'd gone through this incredible journey and came back to tell me about it."[338] When Train accepted the Grammy that *Drops of Jupiter* earned for Best Rock Song, Monahan thanked his mother.

Monahan values dreams to the degree that, like Fergie, he named his son Rock Richard because of them. His sister-in-law Summer reported dreams before the birth of her new nephew in which the baby visited and insisted on the name "Rock". Initially, father-to-be Pat was not keen on the name since it seemed too connected with his music. The dreams continued however, including one where baby-to-be apparently grabbed Summer's face and insisted for her to tell his parents to start listening to the dreams since his name needed to be Rock, and another in which young Rock was playing baseball and wearing a [Colorado] Rockies' uniform, and drew his future aunt's gaze to his jersey, "Look, my name's on."[339] Sure enough, like his father and older brother Patrick, young Rock is indeed publicly performing music.[340]

Lorde

New Zealand musical artist and two-time Grammy-winner **Lorde** posted on her Facebook page on December 3, 2013 that the video for her hit song *Team* was

> *"borne from a dream i had a few months ago about teenagers in their own world, a world with hierarchies and initiations, where the boy who was second in command had acne on his face, and so did the girl who was queen. i dreamt about this world being so different to anything anyone had ever seen, a dark world full of tropical plants and ruins and sweat. and of this world, i dreamt about tests that didn't need to be passed in order to be allowed in: sometimes the person who loses is stronger."*[341]

LL Cool J

Rapper and two-time Grammy winner **LL Cool J** shared that Michael Jackson was one of his childhood idols and a great source of inspiration. Cool J reported the lyrics for his *Billie Jean* remix came to him in a dream after he learned of Jackson's tragic death.[342]

Drake

Canadian superstar rapper **Drake** revealed the reoccurring dream behind his song *Fireworks* in which he finds himself in a field near where his uncle often golfed and also beside his grandfather's burial. "I kept having this dream that I was standing in the middle of that field and watching these fireworks go off." Drake contemplated the dream for quite a while and concluded that it shows how the high level of success he has reached offers him the opportunity to "make a lot of things happen for not only myself but a lot of people around me."[343]

Katy Perry

About her hit, *I Kissed a Girl,* American pop singer **Katy Perry** commented, "The chorus actually popped into my head when I woke up. It was one of those moments where you hear artists talking about songs they get in dreams or in the middle of the night."[344] Singer-songwriter Jill Sobule remarked that the song's title is the same as one she wrote and released in 1995, claiming that Perry signed a music deal with the same person that signed her back in 1995.[345]

Perry said that she found the song idea interesting, but that it sat on the back-burner for about a year and a half until two days before she was to finish recording her *One of the Boys* album. She and producer **Dr. Luke** found they had the chorus stuck in their heads, so they decided to flesh it out and record it.[346] The song was released as the lead single for the record and became a huge hit, holding the #1 spot on Billboard's Hot 100 chart for 7 weeks in a row, hitting the top spot on similar charts in nearly twenty countries, and winning the 2009 People's Choice Award for Best Pop song.

The *I Kissed a Girl* music video depicts Perry waking at the end as if the scene that the song describes were a dream.[347]

Meghan Trainor

American pop artist Meghan Trainor explained that her song *Like I'm Gonna Lose You* was directly inspired by nightmares in which a loved one has died and she wakes up in tears and covered in sweat. Trainor continued, "Then you have to go check on them to make sure they're still alive and they are and you're like, 'Oh my God—thank God'. It's like I'm going to love you like I'm going to lose you because I know what it feels like from that dream and I'm not going to let it happen."[348] The song appears on her album *Title* which debuted at #1 on Billboard's Top 200 and was nominated in 2014 for the Record of the Year Grammy Award.

Miley Cyrus

Pop singer **Miley Cyrus** credits dreams she had the night a friend's cat died as the inspiration for her original tune, *The*

Twinkle Song. "I write about death a lot," shared Cyrus. "My friend, she lost her cat and I had these crazy dreams. I feel her cat kind of told me what I was supposed to say to get her through it…It was more therapy to me than anything."[349] The song's lyrics do indeed seem to speak about multiple dreams.

Madonna

Pop star and singer **Madonna** attributes a lot of importance to her dreams, and not only records them in journals, but also shares them with friends. In 1988, she dreamt that she and actress Sandra Bernhard had survived a catastrophe and were the only two people left on the planet. Bernhard was a casual acquaintance she had met a few years earlier. However, about 2 weeks later, she discovered that the dream was either precognitive or telepathic, since she attended an off-Broadway play that Bernhard was in and was amazed to hear the actress share a fantasy where she and Madonna survived WWIII and were the last two people alive. It is interesting to note that Madonna's biography containing this dream was published about two weeks after September 11th, 2001.[350]

Dolly Parton

"Sometimes I wake up in the middle of the night and write something down of something I've dreamed."[351] –**Dolly Parton**

On her 77th birthday, Jan. 19th 2023, country music superstar **Dolly Parton** released her new song *Don't Make Me Have To Come Down There* and posted on Instagram: "It's a song that kind of came to me in a dream…it's special to me."

I had a dream about God standing on a mountain looking down on us, saying don't make me have to come down there. Then it woke me up. I got up and I started writing this song, and over a period of weeks and months, I finished it...and I just felt like I should drop it on my birthday."[352]

Blake Shelton

In May 2015, during his divorce from Miranda Lambert, country music superstar **Blake Shelton** dreamt a meandering gospel melody and 4 lines of lyrics. It wasn't the first time Shelton had dreamt music, but it was the first time he remembered such a dream, so the former coach from The Voice awoke and recorded every detail he could remember as a smartphone voice memo. The dream carried not just a creative inspiration but also a special healing alchemy, because initially Shelton interpreted the the dream to mean, "I'm so sad and pitiful that even God feels sorry for me and [is] crying for me." But he started to soon realize "No, it's just that [God is] on this journey with me and [is] walking with me."[353]

He invited songwriters Jessi Alexander and Jon Randall to help him finish the song. Randall worked on it and sent back the completed version of *Saviors Shadow*. Whether it was the lyrics, the music, the dream-choreographed-process timing, or perhaps all three, Shelton played the song three time and divulged, "I cried as if someone I loved just died in front of me."[354]

R.E.M.

R.E.M. lead singer **Michael Stipe** explains that dreams are a creative tool for his songwriting: "The words come from everywhere. I'm extremely aware of everything around me, whether I am in a sleeping state, awake, dream-state or just in day-to-day life."[355] Regarding R.E.M.'s song *It's The End Of The World As We Know It*, Stipe revealed, "A weird part of that song is that I had had a dream about a party very similar to the one for Pylon [held around 1970 by Lester Bang in New York City] and everyone at the party had names that started with the initials L.B. except for me. It was Lester Bangs, Lenny Bruce, Leonard Bernstein." Stipe added that the dream is what inspired the song's verse that starts with "Cheesecake…".[356]

Stipe also received the song *Pretty Persuasion* as a visual dream download of "an unknown Rolling Stones' single." In Stipe's dream, each side of the 45 rpm mini-record showed a picture of Rolling Stones' founder Brian Jones who appeared "very beautiful, sitting on the end of a pier." Stipe elaborated, "and as I watched the single rotate in space, on one side was written 'Pretty', and on the other—'Persuasion'."[357]

Electron Blue, the third single released from the band's album *Around The Sun,* came from Stipe's recurring dream concerning a drug made of light. Stipe also claims that the song *Feeling Gravity's Pull* was inspired by his dream world.[358]

Bruce Springsteen

American singer-songwriter **Bruce Springsteen** revealed that he often experiences dreams in which he is writing new music that sounds great within the dream, yet does not always inspire his waking mind. He was, however, happily surprised to receive from a dream his song *Surprise Surprise*, which is included on his appropriately-titled album *Working on a Dream.*[359]

The Fray

"I dreamt I ran into God on a street corner. He looked like Bruce Springsteen and was smoking a cigarette," revealed **Isaac Slade**, lead singer of four-time Grammy-nominated rock band **The Fray**. "I had it out with him and asked, 'Where were you when all this bad stuff was happening to these very undeserving, good people?'" While some sources describe that Slade "dreamt" the meeting with God,[360] others say he imagined it.[361] Slade had been going through a period of tough times, and both his parents were missionaries,[362] which added impetus for the strong discussion with God. Whether a sleeping dream or daydream, the experience nonetheless inspired Slade's lyrics of the band's big hit *You Found Me,* which became the promo song for ABC's 2009 season of the successful TV series *Lost,* won the 2010 APRA award for International Work of the Year, and was nominated for the Teen Choice Awards' Rock Track.

Slade claims he wrote the lyrics in early 2006,[363] so his dream occurred before then. Offering an interesting perspective on the dream, 'The Boss' (i.e. Springsteen) spontaneously showed up with his daughter Jessica Rae at one of The Fray's New York concerts in 2009. Springsteen's presence was a pleasant surprise for the band, so they invited him and his daughter backstage. At Slade's request, Springsteen shared some thoughts on marriage that Slade found very valuable.[364]

Queen

Guitarist and singer-songwriter **Brian May** from the British rock group **Queen** had a feverish dream[365] about people having done something wrong and experiencing a retribution. "It was something like a flood...the whole thing had to start again," recalled May. "People were walking on the streets, trying to touch each other's hands, desperate to try to make some sign that they were caring about other people."[366]

"The words really came from a dream that I had…I woke up with all this strange stuff in my head about a prophet who said various things, and it was very vivid…I could hear some of the melody in there as well…Very often you get little snippits… some words and a tune at the same time. So 'ohh, people of the earth' was going around, obsessing in my head."[367]

"In the song is this guy who also appeared in the dream. I don't really know whether he was a prophet or an impostor, but anyway, he's standing up there and saying, 'Look, you've got to mend your ways.'"[368]

Released in November 1975, *The Prophet's Song* appeared on Queen's album *A Night at the Opera* which debuted atop the UK albums chart and ranked in the #1 spot on four non-consecutive weeks. It was a breakthrough album for Queen in America, peaking at #4 on The Billboard 200 top albums chart, becoming Queen's first entry into the top 10 albums, and reaching triple-platinum status.

Sir Bryan May also received from dreamland the inspiration for Queen's renowned hit *We Will Rock You*, released in 1977 on their *News of the World* album.[369]

The Kinks

On a cold February morning in 1967, **Ray Davies,** lead singer and songwriter for the British rock band **The Kinks**, awoke from a dream with a new song "all there". Davies' 'dreamchild' started out being about Liverpool, but he soon switched the focus to

London. Davies explained, "I knew London better than I knew Liverpool…Waterloo was a pivotal place in my life."[370] *Waterloo Sunset* reached #2 on British charts, and became one of the band's best-known hits as well as an anthem for London. Rolling Stone magazine ranks it as #14 on their 500 Greatest Songs of All Time.[371]

Ray's brother Dave, The Kinks' lead guitarist and vocalist, also reeled in from dreams the title track for his 2014 solo album *Rippin' Up Time*, which is about bridging past, present, and future moments in his life. 'There is madness here! There is madness here!' was a lyric he awoke with that seeded *Rippin' Up Time*, "and the other songs grew out of that."[372]

David Bowie

Superstar **David Bowie**'s album *The Rise and Fall of Ziggy Stardust and the Spiders from Mars* opens with an announcement that the world will end in 5 years, followed by his song *Five Years*. Bowie told TV host Dinah Shore[373] that the song was the direct result of a dream he had in 1971, where his late father told him that he had only five years left to live and that he must never fly again.[374] Fortunately, the dream was not literally true, since Bowie lived another 45 years, but it did nonetheless serve as a powerful creative spark.

Bowie admitted that he "frequently" got creative ideas from his dreams and therefore kept a tape recorder near his bed.[375]

Donovan

Scottish singer-songwriter **Donovan** claims that the inspiration for his song *Hurdy Gurdy Man* came from a dream in 1968 where he saw a hurdy-gurdy man rising above the waves on a Hawaiian beach. Apparently, Donovan had originally hoped Jimi Hendrix would play on the song, but Hendrix was unavailable.[376] Donovan played a tanpura on the track, which was a gift to him from George Harrison during time they spent together in India. At Donovan's invitation, Harrison wrote an additional verse for the song, which was not included in the single due to song duration limits for singles at the time, but which speaks about the 'Hurdy Gurdy Man' who sings songs of love. According to Donovan, the Hurdy Gurdy Man is the one who re-awakens transcendental consciousness.[377]

Van Morrison

A native of Ireland, **Van Morrison** crafted his song *These Dreams of You* from a dream he had in which there was an assassination attempt on the life of Ray Charles. Morrison explained that the song from his *Moondance* album is "the result of a dream I had about Ray Charles being shot down. That started off the whole song." The singer-songwriter from Belfast added that, "The song is basically about dreams."[378] The album lifted Van Morrison to stardom in 1970 peaking at #29 on Billboard's pop album charts. In 1999, it was also inducted into the Grammy Hall of Fame, and in 2003 was ranked #65 in Rolling Stone Magazine's Top 500 albums of all time.

The language of dreams mostly uses **the principle of association** rather than linear logic or direct literal representation to link dreams with corresponding waking events—and the association is often through a feeling common to the two.

The principle is clearly demonstrated by a soon-to-be-shared dream of Phish's Mike Gordon, but the connection can happen through a dream character's identical or similar-sounding name (as shown previously) or identical initials. The connection can also occur according to the time when a certain dream symbol, character, or setting appeared in the dreamer's life, or other such associative links. When dream symbols and their related waking counterparts are similar though not exactly the same, the reasons for any differences can be important. For example, dream characters are sometimes similar to the waking people they are connected with yet have altered traits such as a different face.

I highlight the above principle so that you can explore it yourself to help understand your dreams, and also to offer an interesting potential connection to Morrison's dream. Martin Luther King was assassinated less than two years before Morrison released the album, though likely even closer than that to the time that the singer composed *These Dreams of You*, and possibly closer still to when he had the dream. Intriguing then that King is a prominent Black figure shot in an assassination (like Ray Charles was in Morrison's dream) right around the time Morrison had the dream. Another possible link is that King's most famous words (and the title for his best-known speech) are, "*I have a dream*", and that the word "dreams" also appears in and is central to Morrison's song title and chorus. Ray Charles was also a strong supporter of the civil rights movement and of Martin Luther King, though the fact that both Morrison and Ray Charles are musicians (who sing lyrics) rather than orators like King (who speak words) may explain why Morrison's assassination dream starred Ray Charles.

A couple of additional possible connections: following the dream principle of name association, the last name of the man convicted for shooting King was "Ray",[379] and Ray Charles cited Nat '*King*' Cole as his biggest influence and also as who he closely imitated during the early part of his career.[380] It is also interesting that Van Morrison's fellow Irish rockers, U2, who are also dream-inspired songwriters, released 14 years later (i.e. two seven-year cycles[xiii] after Morrison's *These Dreams of You*) their hit *Pride (In the Name of Love)*, which in the third verse specifically references King's assassination in Memphis on April 4, 1968. Following the principle of feeling association, King's assassination was strongly linked to racial tensions, and both Van Morrison and U2 grew up near ongoing ethnic-political tensions and conflicts in Northern Ireland.

Although there seem to be a number of intriguing connections described above, I would like to offer an important guideline here to keep in mind (and heart) when contemplating other people's dreams: while dream principles and techniques can often help draw associations that may offer fresh insights, it is wise and respectful to let the dreamer, in this case Van Morrison, be the one to finally decide what their dream means for them.

Rush

Alex Lifeson, guitarist for Canadian rock trio **Rush**, crafted some

---

[xiii] Seven-year cycles are important generally. Elsewhere in the book, I show how this cycle was important for composer Hector Berlioz. The 7-year duration is also linked with what is commonly called the 'seven-year itch' in relationships. To investigate this 7-year principle yourself, ask a few people if major, important event(s) happened in their life around age 28 (i.e. 4 x 7, which can be an even more significant cycle than the 7-year one). I believe that you will find that the majority of people, at that age began or changed their main career, or moved, or got married, or had a child, or experienced a powerful catharsis such as a spiritual awakening, a serious accident, or the death of a loved one.

of his upsetting dreams into the song *La Villa Strangiato* on the band's *Hemispheres* album. Lifeson admitted that the rather unusual 12-part instrumental is a "musical recreation of some of my nightmares!" Rush's late virtuoso drummer **Neil Peart** added that "Alex has some of the most bizarre bad dreams, especially when we're away touring on the road…he'll wake up either Geddy [Lee] or me…and start telling us about these terrible dreams…"[381]

Peart got dysentery while staying at the Happy Hotel in Cameroon in 1988, and reported having a "crazy dream" one night in which he heard a ballad titled *The Larger Bowl* "about loneliness and the misfortunes in life." He had never heard the song before and liked its name, which he used as the title of the 5th chapter in his book *The Masked Rider: Cycling in West Africa*. Peart wrote, "I only remembered the title, but I knew I had to write that song. Make a dream come true, as it were."[382] *The Larger Bowl* became the title of the 4th track on the band's *Snakes and Arrows* album[383] and its 3rd single, climbing into the top 30 on the Mainstream Rock and Media Base Mainstream charts.

Radiohead

Radiohead singer-songwriter **Thom Yorke**, says part of the inspiration for his song *How to Disappear Completely* came from a nightmare. "We did this show in Dublin which was by far the biggest show we'd ever done, and we were headlining in front of about 33,000 people. It was sheer blind terror. My most distinctive memory of the whole year was the dream I had that night," Yorke revealed. "I was running down the Liffey [River], stark bullock naked, being pursued by a huge tidal wave."[384] Perhaps not too surprisingly, the dream's universal themes (tidal wave, being naked) strongly suggest the nightmare was about performance anxiety.

On December 19, 1999, while the song was being recorded, Yorke posted on the Radiohead website message board a fuller message suggesting that the song may also incorporate another of his dreams, "I dreamt I was floating down the Liffey and there was nothing I could do. I was flying around Dublin and I really was in the dream. The whole song is my experiences of really floating."[385] It sounds like the blog post's second half is a different dream from the tidal wave nightmare, and may have been a lucid dream, since aside from flying which is a common lucid dream experience, the song's lyrics also include the experience of walking through walls which is quite possible in lucid dreams, in my own experiences and those of my students.

Deep Purple

On December 4, 1971, heavy metal rockers **Deep Purple** were settled at their hotel in Montreux, Switzerland a day before they were to begin recording their new album *Machine Head* at the Montreux Casino where **Frank Zappa and the Mothers of Invention** were performing that night. During the Zappa concert, a fan fired a flare gun at the ceiling, setting the casino ablaze. As the members of Deep Purple watched from their vantage point on the edge of Lake Geneva, they could see smoke from the fire spreading across the water in the down draft from the nearby Alps. Bassist **Roger Glover** credits a dream he awoke from a day or two later for their megahit song's title *Smoke On the Water*.[386] In that half awake state between dreams and waking he actually spoke the song title that summarized the experience. Glover elaborated, "I woke up then and asked myself if I actually did say out loud [the four words before waking], and I came to the conclusion that I did. I pondered upon it and realized that it was a potential song title."[387]

Not only did *Smoke On The Water* immediately become a huge international hit that peaked at #4 on the US Billboard Hot 100 and rocketed the band to stardom, it has since been covered by various artists, and continues to appear in mainstream media and pop culture as an iconic anthem of heavy metal rock.

The Cure

Robert Smith, co-founder, lead vocalist, and primary songwriter for **The Cure**, has harvested dreams for lyrical inspiration over the years, and dream themes appear in a number of their songs such as on *The Walk* (B-side), *The Dream*, and their 2008 record *4:13 Dream*.

"I'm blessed, or cursed, with the ability to remember what I've dreamed. When I was 11 or 12, I used to write them down as soon as I woke up, and after doing that for two years, I found that I didn't have to...my dreams are very flamboyant."[388]

Smith experienced a recurring nightmare in his teens of being slowly eaten by a giant spider and he wove it into The Cure's *Lullaby*. Dreams as a motif recur throughout the band's songbook, from The Walk B-side, The Dream to the 2008 album 4:13 Dream.[389]

Iron Maiden

Heavy metal rock band **Iron Maiden**'s vocalist **Bruce Dickinson** revealed that the band's title track for their 1982 *Number of the Beast* album was inspired by a nightmare about Satan who warned that many of the group's messages have been misinterpreted.[390] The album was a break-through for the band, being their first to reach #1 on the UK albums chart and go platinum in the USA. 'The Beast' has even become an occasional nickname for the band, including in their compilation album title *Best of the Beast*.[391]

Black Sabbath

Among many other awards and honors in the heavy metal music genre, **Black Sabbath** has won two Grammys for Best Metal Performance and were inducted into the UK Music Hall of Fame in 2005 and the Rock and Roll Hall of Fame in 2006. Lyricist/bassist **Geezer Butler** was inspired by a dream for the lyrics and song title for the band's *Behind the Wall of Sleep*.[392] Another dream by Butler about mythologies and the creation of the universe is reported as the source for the band's song *Symptoms of the Universe*.[393]

Chapter 8

Music Inspired by Dream Visits from the Deceased

Dreaming of the deceased is one of the most common dream themes across cultures. A number of artists inspired by dreams of the deceased are mentioned elsewhere in this book, such as rock icons Paul McCartney, Jimi Hendrix, David Bowie, and Pat Monahan from Train, as well as classical composers Gustav Mahler, Robert Schumann, and Anton Bruckner for whom at least three compositions seem to involve musical gifts from the departed. I grouped other such experiences together here to highlight a very important principle:

dream visitations from the deceased often bring valuable, practical insights for the dreamer.

Stevie Wonder

Lula Mae Hardaway, the mother of 22-time Grammy-winning superstar **Stevie Wonder**, passed away on May 31st, 2006. Stevie and his mother were very close and she even co-wrote some of his hits including *Signed, Sealed, Delivered I'm Yours*,[394] so her transition was particularly difficult for Stevie. He told his agent and the president of his company that he was going to take a year off from performing to grieve his mother's death. However, shortly after he put his mother to rest, Stevie explained that she arrived in a dream and said, "you can't let everything that God blessed you with stop for a year when there's so much for you to do and say, and you should really go and continue everything you were going to do and spread your message of love." So during what he calls his time of deepest pain, Wonder continued making music, thereby also "serving [his] greater purpose".[395] On August 2, 2007, he also announced his first concert tour in more than a decade: *A Wonder Summer's Night*, with 13 performances across the United States, and later added dates in Europe and Japan. By June 2008, Wonder also began work on a gospel tribute album *A Gospel Inspired By Lula* to keep a promise he made to his mother before her death.[396]

A dream also bestowed Wonder with the title for his album *Songs in the Key of Life*. "That title came to me in a dream," Wonder revealed, "and I worried maybe that it doesn't make sense because we can never, never write all the songs in the key of life. No one can."[397] Whether or not the phrase made sense, the dream-titled album spent 13 consecutive weeks atop the U.S. Billboard charts, garnered two 1977 Grammys including for Best Album of the Year, and was certified as Diamond status by the RIAA.

Marc Anthony & Jennifer Lopez

After working for three years with his wife on her first Spanish-language album, **Marc Anthony** received a dream visit from famous Spanish singer **Rocío Dúrcal** just two weeks after she lost a long battle with cancer. In the dream, Dúrcal was in Anthony's home and asked him to listen to a song that she emphasized was "exclusively for Jennifer." Anthony awoke and shared the dream gift with his then wife, **Jennifer Lopez**. He didn't want to forget the tune, so Lopez promptly called their voice-mail in order for her half-awake husband to sing the dream song into her phone and record it for safe-keeping.[398] Within a few weeks, Anthony and collaborators crafted the dreamt melody into the Latin rock song *Qué Hiciste*, which became not just the album's first single and a commercially successful hit internationally, but also Lopez's first Spanish-language song to enter Billboard's Hot 100. Lopez admitted that singing in her parents' tongue was "a dream come true."[399]

Stevie Ray Vaughan

Influential electric guitar virtuoso **Stevie Ray Vaughan** was no stranger to his dreams, and married his girlfriend Lenora 'Lenny' Darlene Bailey on December 23, 1979 after he dreamt of Lenny sitting on the knee of one of his idols, blues singer Howlin' Wolf.[400]

According to Lenny, Stevie even played guitar in his sleep, perhaps honing his skills during dreams. She explained to Austin Chronicle columnist Michael Ventura that she was once awakened in the middle of the night to find her husband apparently performing in his sleep "with his fret hand and pickin' hand moving hard and fast, and his face scrunched up the way it was on stage."

Offering an 'inside' perspective of what may have even been the same night, Vaughan himself also revealed to Ventura how he dreamt about Jimi Hendrix showing him "secret chord changes", although when awake, he couldn't always recall his dreamland guitar lessons from the deceased electric guitar master.[401]

On August 26th, 1990, Vaughan shared with his band mates an ominous nightmare where he was present at his own funeral feeling "terrified yet almost peaceful" amidst thousands of mourners.[402] Sadly, the dream came true the following evening after Vaughan played a show alongside special guests including his older brother Jimmie, Buddy Guy, Robert Cray, and Eric Clapton. Could the dream have served Vaughan as a warning if he had paid more attention to it? Possibly. After the show, one of four helicopters for the band and crew was reserved for Stevie, his brother Jimmie, and Jimmie's wife Connie to fly them home to Chicago. When the trio arrived at the helicopter, their seats had been taken by Eric Clapton's agent, bodyguard, and assistant tour manager. There was one remaining seat, so Stevie asked Jimmie and Connie if they minded him occupying it since he really wanted to return to Chicago that night. The couple agreed. In an unfortunate twist of fate, the helicopter crashed into a nearby hillside not long after take off, most likely due to heavy fog.

The Allman Brothers

Apparently the late Hendrix is active in other guitarists' dreams as well. **Duane Allman** from **The Allman Brothers** wrote only one song without the help of the other band members, however it seems he may have had a collaborator from 'the other side'. The song was *Little Martha*, recorded in October 1971, interestingly only weeks before Allman died in a motorcycle accident. He explained that the song's melody came to him in a dream where Jimi Hendrix played it for him in a Holiday Inn motel bathroom, using the room's sink faucet as a guitar fretboard.[403] Only guitarist Dicky Betts plays with Allman in the final version of the song on their 1972 *Eat A Peach* album, although bassist Berry Oakley's part was mixed back in for the Allman Brothers 1989 box set entitled *Dreams*. The tombstone of Martha Ellis, a twelve-year-old girl buried at the Rose Hill Cemetery is the inspiration for the song's title since the Allman Brothers Band would pass her grave on frequent trips to that cemetery in their home town of Macon, Georgia. Eerily, it is also where Duane Allman and Berry Oakley were both buried less than a year after the song's first release.[404] Another strange synchronicity is that Jimi Hendrix was the one who played the melody in Allman's dream and that *Little Martha* was about the deceased, because musical dreamer Hendrix was also buried shortly after releasing his dream song *Angel* about his mother who visited him in dreams and hinted that she would soon pass from this world.

Ziggy Marley

Reggae artist **Ziggy Marley**, son of the late Bob Marley, believes dreaming is very important and disclosed that he continues to connect with his father through his dreams, even though his father is no longer physically alive. "Our culture is one that believes in dreams as a way to see things, to understand and communicate with the past. Many of our ancient prophets communicated through dreams." The seven-time Grammy winner not only trusts and uses dreams for communicating with his father, he also harvests them creatively, and composed the song *Keep on Dreamin'* about his dream experiences in order to share with others what is possible.[405] The song is featured on his second solo album *Love Is My Religion,* which garnered the 2006 Grammy for Best Reggae Album.

Rachmaninoff Coaches Pianist Olga Kern As She Sleeps

Olga Kern's most memorable early influence is of having seen dream-inspired performer Vladimir Horowitz play piano in Moscow.[406] Many years before, renowned Russian pianist **Rachmaninoff** played piano to accompany Kern's great grandmother as vocalist one night[407] when her regular accompanist got sick and Rachmaninoff just happened to be in the same city.[408]

When she was just 17 years old, Kern (née Pushechnikova) was the youngest pianist in Moscow's first-ever Rachmaninoff International Piano Competition.

"Playing Rachmaninoff demands an enormous psychological input," commented Victor Merzhanov, chairman of the competition's jury of judges. "Despite her young age, Pushechnikova was able to demonstrate perfect control over the music. Not only is she technically very gifted, but she can convey Russian spirituality, which is so quintessential about Rachmaninoff's work."[409]

Strangely enough, given Merzhanov's comment, Rachmaninoff appeared to young Olga in a dream just before the semi-final round of the competition. Kern recalled that in the dream he was "sitting in a big concert hall playing piano, and he said, 'Olga, you're late to have a lesson together.'" She played for the legendary piano master the piece of his music that she had been practising called *The Barcarolle*. He complimented her rendition, yet proceeded to show her how he felt the piece should be interpreted. Kern reported that her famous dream guide played his own composition "really great" though faster "and a little bit dry."[xiv] She awoke very inspired and told her parents about the dream.[410] Boosted by her excitement and the unique advantage of being coached by the competition's namesake in her dream, she "stunned" the judges and blew past 65 other international

---

[xiv] in regards to piano, this usually means playing with little or no sustain pedals.

experienced pianists to win the contest.[411] When Rachmaninoff's remastered recordings were released on CD two years later, Kern purchased a copy right away and listened in shock to the master's recorded rendition of the Barcarolle. "It was the same that I heard in my dream. He came to me somehow." Kern added that since the dream, she "always wanted to play more Rachmaninoff."[412]

Kern's dream-mentored win, talent, and discipline has led to incredible success. She has toured extensively internationally, often performing Rachmaninoff, and is a laureate of numerous piano competitions. She was the first woman in 30 years to win the gold medal at the prestigious Van Cliburn International Piano Competition in Texas, which leads to more intriguing connections. American pianist Van Cliburn rose to international fame when he won the first International Tchaikovsky Piano Competition in 1958, an interesting parallel to Kern winning the first ever International Rachmaninoff Piano Competition. Both events were held in Moscow, where Kern is from. Not only was Tchaikovsky one of Rachmaninoff's early influences, he was also a "very good friend" of Kern's great-great grandmother,[413] who also played piano, as do both of Kern's parents.

There are also other interesting connections between these great pianists. The recording of Van Cliburn's competition-winning performance became the first ever gold record of classical music,[414] so the event likely contributed significantly to the creation of the competition bearing his name that Kern won years later to lift her career to a new level of success. When Kern revealed to Van Cliburn the story about her dreamland lesson by Rachmaninoff, he confided to her, "I always felt Rachmaninoff behind my shoulder when I played his music."[415] More intriguing still is that in winning the Moscow competition in 1958, during the height of the cold war between America and Russia, Van Cliburn powerfully inspired another master dream-inspired artist—Billy Joel, who was only 9 at the time. Kern discovered that fact when she met Joel in New York and he invited her to one of his monthly performances at Madison Square Gardens in early 2015.[416] Before coming on stage, Kern recounted that Van Cliburn's competition-winning rendition of Tchaikovsky began playing along with a video where Joel explained that when Van Cliburn won the Tchaikovsky competition, [Joel's] 'dream' became to go to Russia and perform there.[417] She was blown away, and intrigued to learn that Joel was composing classical pieces and looking for pianists to perform them.

Reminiscent of the initial dream-inspired piano competition win that sparked her tremendous success as a pianist, Kern now has a new way to recognize other great pianists since she is Artistic Director and President of the Jury for The Olga Kern International Piano Competition in Albuquerque, New Mexico. Among many other accolades, she also shares the rare title, as does piano man Billy Joel, of being an official Steinway Artist.[418] She is, however, not the only pianist being visited in dreams by past great piano masters, as you will see just below.

Musical Prodigy Downloads Dream Gift from Mozart

Reminiscent of Mozart, modern day musical prodigy **Alma Deutscher** by age 4 was already talented on the piano and playing Händel sonatas on her violin. By age 6, she had composed a complete sonata, by 9, a complete concerto for violin and orchestra that she premiered herself as solo violinist,[419] and by 10, a full length opera.[420] The young artist wisely places a tape recorder by her bed to capture music that comes at night. At age 7, she wrote an opera *The Sweeper of Dreams* that arrived in a dream. "Mozart composed this piece in my dream," revealed the young Deutscher, "and when I got up, I sat down and played it and my father recorded it." The work barely missed placing in a

2012 national English opera competition for adult composers and was highly commended by the English National Opera.[421]

The Grateful Dead

Giving a fascinating depth of meaning to their band name, Grammy Lifetime Achievement winners **The Grateful Dead** seem to continue their avant-garde musical explorations by collaborating on songs through the veil between life and death.

Speaking of his deceased band mate and friend **Gerry Garcia**, Grateful Dead co-founder **Bob Weir** confided that "the guy comes to me in my dreams every now and then and we get some laughs in."

Weir revealed that Garcia came to him in a dream and introduced to him a jazz ballad that the two were going to "work on together" and "do a duet on."

Weir elaborated that in the dream, "The song itself was a living critter, not unlike a great big ethereal sheep dog. It came up and sniffed me and I batted it around a little bit, and it sort of nipped back at me, and we got to be friends, and we got to like each other. And that sort of confirmed a notion that I've been harboring for a long time that a song is an actual living entity of some sort. It just comes and visits us through the artist who acts as a portal for it."[422]

Sammy Hagar & Eddie Van Halen

As lead singer for a dozen years with the Grammy-winning rock group **Van Halen**, **Sammy Hagar** developed a profound friendship with band co-founder Eddie Van Halen that seems to endure beyond death. The latter passed in 2020 and Hagar wanted to create a tribute song for his friend as a "final bow to that part of my life." About a year after he passed,[423] Eddie appeared in Hagar's dream in a room with a bunch of people. "It was not like he was passed, but he had just been out of my life and we hadn't seen each other for a while," Hagar said, describing the dream and adding that Eddie exclaimed, 'Man, let's write some music!' Hagar heartily agreed. "He had a guitar around his neck," Hagar continued, "he just started playing this riff, and I started singing."[424] Van Halen then showed Hagar a guitar lick that he had played for him many years before during the band's 2004 reunion tour. "He did this harmonic thing and he slid it up to a chord, like a slide guitar," remembered Hagar, who then awoke inspired and fleshed out a song he initially titled 'Thank You.'[425] Three years later, with help of his band mates, Hagar released the song as *Encore. Thank You. Good Night.*, highlighting his musical inspiration dream with Van Halen as "100% a communication from the beyond."[426]

Sinéad O'Connor

Motivation and help with decisions sometimes comes in dreams also. In September 2001, Grammy-winning, outspoken Irish singer-songwriter **Sinéad O'Connor** was unsure about recording her album *Sean-Nos Nua* until her late manager, Steve Fargnoli, who had died just days earlier, visited her in a dream and told her: "Look, I understand now what this record means to you. That's what you have to do. Go and make this record."

Fargnoli's dream-delivered message contrasted with the view he had expressed to O'Connor before his death where he had taken the alternate position of wanting to sell a lot of albums, even though O'Connor felt that this more niche album meant a lot to her personally. Also present in the dream was an image of a recording industry acquaintance she had met over a decade before. O'Connor recognized the man as John Dunford, managing director of Irish roots label Hummingbird Records, so she called him shortly after waking, and Hummingbird Records ended up releasing the album.[427]

"Make sure you're good, but don't worry about being popular."
–Mike Posner[428]

The Barenaked Ladies

Ed Robertson of **The Barenaked Ladies** is reported to have written the song *Leave* about a strange dream he experienced where he saw his deceased brother who was killed in a motorcycle accident.[429]

Lyrics from the band's other tunes such as *When You Dream* also discuss dreams, hinting at other inspirations that arrived thanks to the dreaming muse. As an interesting synchronicity, while I write this paragraph, their song *Pinch Me* just started playing on the radio! Maybe life is indeed like a dream, as the song's lyrics suggest. Pinching myself to see if I'm awake may not work as the best 'reality check' though, since I have tried pinching myself in lucid dreams before and the dream continued, plus I actually even felt a bit of something akin to pain! So to check if I'm dreaming right now, I just looked at my hands which did not become wavy or odd (as they almost always do in dreams), so I guess if you are reading these words, we can assume I was awake while writing this paragraph.

Rodney Crowell

Country singer-songwriter and six-time nominee and two-time Grammy Award winner **Rodney Crowell** revealed that his departed parents came to him in a dream and helped him finish his album *The Houston Kid*. For a while, he felt he was missing something to complete the record, but he wasn't sure what. "Then I dreamed my parents came and showed me around their new house," he explained. "They said they liked the record, but they didn't think I was telling the whole story."

He awoke with a flash of insight and the clarity he had been looking for. "What was missing was forgiveness," Crowell revealed. "I lived through this, I'm a better man for it, and toward the end, my relationship with both parents was really good." Inspired by the dream, Crowell wrote the healing song *I Know Love Is All I Need*, which naturally found its place at the end of the album.[430]

The album also includes *I Walk The Line Revisited,* which features Crowell's former father-in-law, dream-inspired singer-songwriter Johnny Cash.

Florence Welch (Florence & the Machine)

It is more common than one might guess for grandparents to appear in powerful dreams. British singer **Florence Welch** from the Grammy-nominated group **Florence and the Machine** revealed that her song *Only if for a Night*, was inspired by a very emotional dream from which she awoke in tears.[431] While touring in Germany, Welch's deceased grandmother paid her a dream visit, shining in gold and pink, and offered her the advice, "Concentrate on your perfect career." Welch was quite surprised, commenting, "Can you imagine? It's like, 'You've left your laundry out and it's going to rain.' 'Ok Grandma, thanks!' I thought it would be something, y'know, more cryptic."[432] The song's album, *Ceremonials*, debuted at #1 on the UK charts and #6 in the United States.[433]

The Killers

Brandon Flowers, lead singer and keyboardist for the American alternative rock band **The Killers**, said he sometimes experiences musical dreams, though admitted he almost never recalls them. Fortunately, he remembered just one and it delivered the melody for the band's song *Enterlude* on their 2006 album *Sam's Town* which reached #2 on the US Billboard and #1 on the UK top albums charts.[434] "It sounds ridiculous," recalled Flowers, "but it was Kurt Cobain on a ship in the clouds! He was singing this melody and I remember thinking he sounded like Bob Dylan, so that made it even weirder!"[435]

Dr. John

New Orleans blues, pop and jazz musician and late singer-songwriter **Dr. John** (born Malcolm John 'Mac' Rebennack) was a professional musician for an impressive six decades. In 2014, he recorded thirteen songs by the dream-inspired late jazz music icon Louis 'Satch' Armstrong because, John says, Armstrong appeared in a dream and instructed him to do so. "He told me to do his music; his music, my way," claimed Dr. John, who then recruited top jazz trumpet players and other musicians such as Bonnie Raitt and The Blind Boys for his 2014 album *Ske-Dat-De-Dat...The Spirit of Satch.*[436]

Rory Block

"Don't ask yourself what the world needs. Ask yourself what makes you come alive, and then go and do that. Because what the world needs is people that have come alive."

–Rev. Dr. Howard Thurman[437]

About her songwriting process, traditional blues guitarist, singer, and composer **Rory Block** admits, "It wasn't until I dropped all attempts at commercial format and just told the story from the heart that I suddenly had commercial success." Block adds that an important element of her creative shift included harvesting her dreams for inspiration,[438] and reveals a powerful musical dream that played a key role in shaping the sound and feel of her album *Confessions of a Blues Singer*:

> *"One night I had a dream and woke with the slide riff from Charlie Patton's Bo Weavil Blues soaring through my brain with great clarity and volume. This was extremely odd as I had never focused on that particular song nor had I heard it for 30 years. I couldn't even remember the title and had to listen to the entire CD collection to find it. I realized I was meant to record it, and that focused this album. I decided I was going to go for 'feel' over 'perfection.' I wanted to move in the spirit of the early recordings where spontaneity and musical freedom were at the core of everything, all soul and raw power and no technological advantages save the on/off button on the tape recorder."[439]*

No less than four of Block's dreams acted as creative updrafts for the lyrics of her song *Silver Wings* on her album *Ain't I A Woman*. All of the dreams were recurring themes, which Block noted were "strangely intensified" in Holland where she wrote the song. The lyrics weave together her almost nightly themes of flying, visiting with her deceased friend Wendy who was an "endless source of wisdom", being back in a former much-loved house that she had to leave under duress, and having a new baby.[440] The dream-inspired lyrics and Block's soulful voice and rhythmic guitar mastery create a powerful song.

Block has won five Blues Awards[441] (Traditional Blues Female Artist in 1997 and 1998, as well as Acoustic Blues Album of the Year in 1996, 1999, and 2007), and two NAIRD awards for Best Adult Contemporary Album of the Year in 1994 and 1997 for her albums *Angel of Mercy* and *Tornado* respectively.

Alfred Hayes & Earl Robinson

Screenwriter, novelist and poet **Alfred Hayes**' best known poem is *I Dreamed I Saw Joe Hill Last Night*, written circa 1930, thanks to the fact that it gained enduring renown as the folk song classic *Joe Hill*.[442] Hayes handed the poem to singer-songwriter **Earl Robinson** in 1936 while the two were working as staff at a summer camp and needed a campfire song, and Robinson set it to music in about 40 minutes.[443] Hayes' poem was inspired by an experience he had one night which seems to be a visitation dream of the late workman hero Joe Hill who appeared near his bed and spoke with him. Often performed by folk singers Pete Seeger and Paul Robeson, the song was also performed and recorded by various other artists including Bruce Springsteen and the E Street Band, The Dubliners, Scott Walker, Billy Bragg, and perhaps the best known performance and recording was by Joan Baez at Woodstock in 1969 which was included in the corresponding 1970 Woodstock documentary and soundtrack album. Bob Dylan's hit *I Dreamed I Saw St. Augustine* offers a slight variation on the song title and opening phrase, and hints at other similarities such as recounting a dream, suggesting the song may have been inspired by Hayes and Robinson's folk classic.

Elsiane

Canadian eclectic artist **Elsieanne Caplette**, singer-songwriter for the band **Elsiane** that has toured internationally and performed for Cirque du Soleil and other high profile hosts, explains that when she is going through tough situations, she actually hears the soundtrack for the events that are occurring, like in a movie. In 2002, she received the inspiration from the dream realm for the band's breakthrough song, *Mend*. Near 4 or 5 a.m., in the borderland between dreaming and waking, she heard the main melody of the chorus that unfolded into the rest of the song. She started working on the melody a day after the dream and admitted, "the creative flow was incredible. Composing that song went so well. It came so naturally." *Mend* became a key that really started opening doors for the band, catching the attention of a producer and then a label. "People still really love that song the most it seems," shared Caplette. "In call-in interviews, they sometimes ask 'Is there going to be a song like *Mend* on the new record?'" She explains that she is a different person now and that there has been an evolution in her songwriting. However, she does continue to receive powerful dream insights from the muse.

Another unfinished piece was conceived in a dream where she heard a beautiful song playing. Waking, she sang the melody into a voice recorder right away. "In the dream, I had tears in my eyes because it was so beautiful," she remembers. "I wanted to find out what it was, so I walked into the room where the song was coming from and saw a sound engineer in a room mixing the song and then suddenly realized it was mine!" Caplette added, "it feels like the time to complete that song hasn't been right yet."

However the band's single *The Motive* is derived from a similar rich-feeling dream that she experienced while the band toured in Russia in the fall of 2013. Again, a remarkably beautiful song played in her dream and she awoke in the early morning hours from a visitation dream from a deceased grandparent and immediately recorded what she'd just heard. "In that dream, I saw my grandmother, who was really like a mother to me. I was crying and it was very intense…so powerful, a profound feeling of hope and light and beauty. I thought I was dying because she took my hand and said, 'it's time to leave'. I knew I had to go with her. Life brought some difficult times since then, and I felt her presence following me everywhere. On a tour in Peru, I decided to visit her tomb." Caplette began writing the song in November 2013, however it is intriguing that she just finished recording it the day before I interviewed her.

Tegan and Sara

Canadian singer-songwriter **Sara Quinn** of the **Tegan and Sara** sibling duo revealed the upsetting dream that inspired her song *Knife Going In*: "After my grandma passed away, I had this really upsetting dream where I was in her bedroom and she wasn't in the bedroom, and there were intruders and they came in and they stabbed me. It was super intense and I didn't die."[444]

Megadeth

Although it was dream-inspired, **Megadeth**'s song *A Tout Le Monde* has sometimes been misinterpreted to be about suicide, since the lyrics can be heard as a suicide note. On September 13, 2006, Kimveer Gill went on a shooting rampage at Dawson

College in Montreal, eventually shooting himself. He was a fan of Megadeth and mentioned the song on his blog, encouraging others to listen to it. As fate would have it, Megadeth had a performance in Montreal two weeks later. Songwriter and lead singer **Dave Mustaine**, who wrote the song, was furious to learn that Gill mentioned it in his tragic plans for Dawson College.

"I was so angry that this guy would use my song, and that he would try and turn that beautiful song into something ugly and nasty," said Mustaine, adding that he composed the song about his mother who died when he was a child. "I had a dream that she came back to me, and said 'I love you.' That's the whole song." He continued to explain how the song is in memory of the living, "It's for those who lost their lives, and it's a gift to those who are in the process of healing."[445]

Dreams also delivered to Mustaine the melody for the band's song *Public Enemy No. 1,*[446] and apparently the song title for *Have Cool, Will Travel* which came from a dream in which those words were spoken by drummer Nick Menza as he left the band.[447]

Timbaland: Dream Visit from the Late Aaliyah

Producer/rapper **Timbaland**, whose producing credits include Justin Timberlake, Rihanna, Drake, Jay-Z, Ludacris, Madonna and many others, said that the late singer **Aaliyah**, whom he had produced, came to him in a dream and told him, "Tink is the one." Timbaland felt she was giving a thumbs up from beyond the veil to have the up-and-coming singer **Tink** perform a tribute with him for Aaliyah at SXSW 2015 by singing Aaliyah's hit *One in A Million*, and so it happened that way.[448]

Chapter 9

Dream-Inspired Baroque, Classical, Romantic, and Modern Composers

Richard Wagner

German composer and conductor **Richard Wagner** deserves a special spot in the roster of dream-inspired musical artists. Like other artists described here, he often had dreams containing music and incorporated such dreams into his compositions. However, Wagner also publicly proposed theories about dreams, and even portrayed how to use dreams in the songwriting process, as well as the importance of doing so, with his opera *Meistersinger von Nürnberg* (*The Mastersingers of Nuremberg*). The music from the dream-based opera was later recorded by esteemed conductor Sir Georg Solti and post-homously brought him his final Grammy win in 1998 for Best Opera Recording.[449]

Wagner often shared his dreams with his wife Cosima, who kept a diary containing many specific details. According to psychiatrist and frequent musical dreamer Heinz Prokop, who sifted through Cosima's extensive diary, at least 24 of Wagner's dreams recorded there directly refer to or contain music, and another 16 relate to musical performance. Cosima also shares at least one musical dream of her own where she heard her first husband, Hans von Bülow, playing piano.[450]

For about 5 years, Wagner did a great deal of contemplation and musical sketching, yet was unable to find a way to begin what would eventually become his gigantic 26-year, four opera cycle *Der Ring des Nibelungen* (*The Ring of the Nibelung*).[451] Then a powerful nightmare bestowed the solution upon him in September 1853, according to his autobiography *Mein Leben* (*My Life*). After a feverish, sleepless night followed by a long day hike through a pine woods in hill country, Wagner recounted that he dozed off on a hard couch in his room in a hotel in La Spezia, Italy, and then in a dream, sank into a rushing stream of water. "The rushing sound formed itself in my brain into a musical sound, the chord of E-flat major, which continually re-echoed in broken forms," he wrote. "These broken chords seemed to be melodic passages of increasing motion, yet the pure triad of E-flat never changed, but seemed by its continuance to impart infinite significance to the element in which I was sinking.

"I awoke in sudden terror from my doze, feeling as though the waves were rushing high above my head. I at once recognized that as the orchestral overture to *Das Rheingold* (*The Rhinegold,* the first opera cycle of The Ring of Nibelung), which must long have lain latent within me. Though it had been unable to find definite form, [it] had at last been revealed to me. I then quickly realized my own nature; the stream of life was not to flow to me from without, but from within."[452]

Accordingly, *Das Rheingold* is set at the bottom of the Rhine River, and Wagner opens the opera with an E-flat drone that slowly builds into E-flat triads spinning out into a busy expanse of notes, building the world into existence. Wagner does not change from the dream's E-flat major chord until the opera's 137th bar which is about five minutes into the piece (depending on the tempo).

The late orchestral and operatic conductor Sir Georg Solti won 31 Grammys,[453] the second highest amount of any artist ever after dream-inspired megastar Beyoncé who has won 35. From over 250 recordings that Solti made, likely the most famous is his recording of Wagner's dream-inspired The Ring of Nibelung which has at least twice been honored as the greatest recording ever made,[454] and won him the 1966 Grammy for Best Opera Recording.[455]

Wagner also publicly proposed concepts relating to dreams such as the unconscious, condensation, and secondary revision that predated by half a century their investigation by renown neurologist Sigmund Freud who is generally recognized as the father of psychoanalysis.[456] Before Freud was born, Wagner had also publicly analyzed the Oedipus myth in terms of its psychological significance.[457] Other key elements of Freud's dream theory also strongly resemble Wagner's ideas, and author Cora L. Díaz de Chumaceiro shows how the latter were almost certainly considered by Freud in formulating his own interpretation of dreams.[458] Physician George Groddeck even considers Wagner's *Ring of the Nibelungen* cycle as "the first manual of psychoanalysis."[459] Wagner had his own influences, acknowledging that the writing and philosophy of Arthur Schopenhauer strongly affected him including, among other ideas, Schopenhauer's concepts of a "dream-organ" that can perceive events at a distance and/or across time, as exemplified in the chapter on precognitive and warning dreams.[460]

"Talent hits a target no one else can hit; genius hits a target no one else can see." –**Arthur Schopenhauer**[461]

Another of Wagner's works inspired by his dreams was *Tristan & Isolde*. About the opera, the composer wrote to a friend, "For once you are going to hear a dream. I dreamed all this. Never could my poor head have invented such a thing purposely." [462] In the opera, Tristan denounces the realm of daylight which he claims is false, unreal, and keeps the two lovers apart. Wagner claims that it is only during night—likely his metaphor for dreams—that they can truly be together, and that only in the "long night of death" can they be eternally united (*"O sink' hernieder, Nacht der Liebe"*).

As mentioned above, Wagner creatively expressed his concept and experience of the dream-inspired artistic process in his opera *Mastersingers*. The opera's hero Walther von Stolzing awakens from a "wonderfully beautiful" morning dream[463] which has moved and inspired him, yet he fears he might forget the dream or experience rejection if he expresses it. Under the guidance of instructor Hans Sachs, Walther finds courage to craft the dream into a 'master song', creating and singing two stanzas of the new song with the hope to win over the heart of the woman he is interested in. Sachs stresses to his student the close relationship between dreams and the process of crafting verse and music, hinting at the opera's main theme:

> *"My friend, it is the poet's work;*
> *to find in dreams what meanings lurk.*
> *Believe me, our deepest wisdom here,*
> *is oft in dreams to us made clear.*
> *All songs[464] and poems the world has known*
> *are nought but truths our dreams have shown."[465]*

Sachs then encourages Walther to continue writing the song. After a little while, he finishes the third stanza and Sachs christens the song as "the blissful morning-dream-interpretation-melody". By the word 'interpretation', it seems clear that Wagner is referring to the connotation of 'interpretation' as an artistic rendering of the dream rather than an intellectual explanation of its meaning.[466] This new 'mastersong' transports all the opera's characters into a moment of enraptured bliss. All five characters sing phrases from the song, and Wagner has each of them ask, "Is it only a morning dream?"[467]

In the first version of the song, Walther describes a dream meeting with a beautiful woman in paradisiacal garments, which contained a "glorious tree" with "juicy", "golden fruit".[468] He also imagines the woman offering him "the fruit so precious of The Tree of Life"[469] and later sees a "host of stars" taking the place of the laurel tree fruit.

The storyline is notably similar to novelist and poet **James Joyce**'s 1916 book *A Portrait of the Artist as a Young Man.* The book's hero, Stephen Dedalus, awakens hearing "sweet music" and is filled with ecstasy and poetic inspiration from a dream or vision he has had during the night.[470] This inspires Stephen to compose six stanzas of a villanelle poem. Later in his book *Ulysses*, Joyce also writes of a "heaventree" full of stars and fruit much like Wagner's, but instead describing the fruit as "humid" and "night blue". The parallels are very likely more than chance since Joyce is quoted as having said about his *Sirens* episode in Ulysses that a "quintet occurs in it too, just like *Mastersingers*, my favorite Wagner opera."[471]

Wagner's Mastersingers, performed by the Chicago Symphony Orchestra and conducted by Hungarian maestro Sir Georg Solti, won the 1997 Grammy for Best Opera Recording.[472]

George Frideric Händel

"Music is a dream…Music is God."

> –**Alice Herz-Sommer**, 109-year-old pianist, holocaust survivor, and star of the Oscar-winning documentary *The Lady in Number Six: Music Saved My Life.*[473]

Beginning on the 22nd of August, 1741, German-British baroque composer **George Frideric Händel** retreated for 24 days into his small London house on Brook Street. Although a fine meal was delivered each evening, Händel left the bowls and platters mostly untouched as he worked tirelessly on what may well be his greatest work, *Messiah*. One evening as the waiter made Händel's evening food delivery, the startled composer, tears streaming down his face, cried out, "I did think I did see all Heaven before me, and the great God Himself."[474] He had just finished writing the hallelujah chorus, the closing movement of the second part of his now famous oratorio. While Händel does not seem to have specifically mentioned the word 'dream' regarding his creative process, he did later describe his dream-like composition experience by quoting St. Paul, "Whether I was in the body or out of my body when I wrote it I know not."[475] In response to a resounding ovation for his final performance in 1759, Händel also cried out, "Not from me…but from Heaven… comes all."[476]

Ludwig van Beethoven

"Music is indeed the mediator between the life of the senses and the life of the spirit." –**Beethoven**[477]

Among the four dreams reported by famed German pianist and

classical-romantic composer **Ludwig van Beethoven** is the following account written in a letter to the Archduke Rudolph: "Last night I dreamt of [Your Imperial Highness]. Although no music was performed, it was a musical dream."[478] Written on October 15, 1819, the letter is interestingly about five years after the composer had become fully deaf and, from the wording, seems to suggest that Beethoven, while asleep, was still able to hear music regardless of his physical deafness.

Beethoven also had at least one creative dream inspiration for his compositions while napping in his carriage. In high spirits on September 10th, 1821, Beethoven sent the following letter to one of his publishers, Tobias Haslinger:

> *"Yesterday, in the carriage on the way to Vienna, I was overcome by sleep, naturally enough, since (because of my early rising here), I had never slept very well. While thus slumbering, I dreamed that I made a long journey— to no less distant a country than Syria, then to India, and back to no less than Arabia; finally I reached Jerusalem. The Holy City aroused in me thoughts of the Holy Books and small wonder that the man Tobias now occurred to me, and how natural that our dear Tobias and the pertobiassen[479] should come to mind, and now during my dream journey, the following canon came to me …*

> *"O Tobias! O Tobias! dominus Haslinger! O! O! O Tobias!"*

Beethoven explained that he could not remember the canon melody after waking from the original dream. However the next day on his return trip to Baden in the carriage, he entered a state where he was able to "continue" the previous day's "dream journey", and "through the law of association of ideas", wrote Beethoven, the short musical piece came back to him. He sketched the melody in three voices with the words above.[480,481]

Franz Schubert

"Chalk out a daily routine for spiritual practice and stick to it at any cost. Distractions and obstacles are many. Be ever vigilant."

–Swami Sitaramananda[482]

A contemporary of Beethoven who revered and later met the master, is early 19th century Austrian classical-romantic composer **Franz Schubert** who had an abundance of melodies flow from his dreams.[483] "I compose every morning," claimed Schubert, "and when one piece is done, I begin another."[484] This simple yet remarkably effective strategy of focusing on his creative work from waking until his mid-day meal around 2 p.m. allowed him to become astoundingly prolific and produce over 600 vocal works, 7 full symphonies, operas, sacred music, incidental music, and a large body of chamber and piano music—all before he died at age 31! Schubert even slept wearing his glasses, apparently so he could begin composing as soon as he awoke.[485,486]

Schubert wrote a piece of prose on July 3rd, 1822, entitled *My Dream*, that includes a powerful musical experience about what is at very least a fictional dream, though which may be based on his actual dream experiences. The tale describes the tough life of a man banished twice by his angry father, hinting at difficult elements of Schubert's own life and the challenging relationship he had with his own father, but the tale does not appear strictly literal, and is likely not just purely autobiographical.[487] Near the end, the narrator arrives at the grave of a "pious maiden". Schubert wrote, "And I advanced to the grave with slow steps and concentrated gaze, but before I could have imagined it possible, I found myself in a circle from which there arose spontaneously the most wonderful music, and I felt the bliss of eternity concentrated as it were into a single moment."[488]

Though it is unclear as to whether Schubert dreamt any of the melodies in his composition *Winterreise*, it was published in 1928 by Tobias Haslinger (the same publisher as Beethoven) as an accompaniment for 24 of Wilhelm Müller's poems. The 11th poem, *Frühlingstraum* (*Dream of Spring*), weaves from dreams to waking reality and back a few times.[489] Schubert's music for that poem seems to quite intentionally mirror the transitions from one state of awareness to the other with corresponding musical variations in meter, melody and key, perhaps even offering a musical bridge between the two states, like the bridging of states that can happen during lucid dreams.

Schubert may also have gifted a melody from beyond the grave to fellow German-speaking composer Robert Schumann, as you will see below.

Robert Schumann

Throughout his adult life, romantic era composer **Robert Schumann** would hear auditory 'hallucinations'[490] and occasionally include what he heard inside into his compositions. His wife Clara revealed that her husband reported his inner music as "glorious, and with instruments more wonderful than one ever hears on earth."[491] Later in life however, he reported that he was in the presence of spirits who played for him music that was both "wonderful" and "hideous". Although the spirits shared with him the "most magnificent revelations", they also threatened to send him to hell.

One night, Schumann experienced a powerful dream of an angelic choir singing to him. Upon waking, he quickly inked onto parchment the ethereal music from his subconscious—a choral theme in E flat major.[492] Another source cites Schumann as reporting that either an angel or the late Franz Schubert dictated the theme to him in his dream or hallucination.[493] The piece however also seems based on a musical theme he had used previously multiple times, including just four months earlier in the second movement of his violin concerto.[494] That fateful dream on February 17th or 18th, 1854 not only inspired Schumann's final work *Geistervariationen (Ghost Variations*, initially called *Variations on an Original Theme)*, it also seemed to foretell his close call with death ten days later. Schumann worked on the five variations of the theme that made up *Ghost Variations* in the days following the dream, and finished it on February 28th—the day after he was rescued from an unsuccessful suicide attempt where he leapt partly dressed into the ice-cold Rhine river.[495]

Later, Schumann's wife Clara reported dreaming about her own funeral and the music accompanying it.[496]

Johannes Brahms

Thanks to a dream, 19th-century German composer and pianist **Johannes Brahms** saved months of work that he might otherwise have discarded. Before Robert Schumann had his failed suicide attempt, Brahms became close with him and his wife Clara. In a letter to Clara on January 30th, 1855, Brahms lamented about how he had unsuccessfully "spent all last summer trying to write a symphony."[497] Days later, he had a dream in which he performed his incomplete "unfortunate symphony" (as he called it) not as a symphony but instead as a piano concerto. Brahms explained in a subsequent letter to Clara on February 7th that his perspective in the musical dream was as both soloist and audience, and that he found himself "completely enraptured."[498] The new piece became his first piano concerto, *piano concerto in D minor*, and he abandoned trying to finish the symphony.

Sir Arthur Sullivan

In the 1880s, Sir Arthur Sullivan dreamt a beautiful melody, though unfortunately, he could not remember all the music he dreamt. Nonetheless, he composed what he could remember into a song he titled *The Lost Chord*,[499] which not only became very successful and one of his best-known songs, but is also very likely the first-ever physical recording of music directly inspired by a dream since it was almost certainly the first ever piece of music recorded in England.[500]

Igor Stravinsky

In the summer of 1911, came the dream that sparked the classical composition *The Rite of Spring (Le Sacre du printemps)*. Well-known composer **Igor Stravinsky** revealed his inspiration: "I saw in imagination a solemn pagan rite: wise elders, seated in a circle, watching a young girl dancing herself to death. They were sacrificing her to propitiate the god of spring."

"Very little immediate tradition lies behind, and no theory," Stravinsky said. "I had only my ear to help me. I heard, and I wrote what I heard. I am the vessel through which the *Sacre* passed."[501] Stravinsky crafted the archetypal imagery and highly unusual dancing motions of his dream into the ballet. Along with the sometimes dissonant and frenetic music he composed for it, the ballet was powerful and shocking enough to create an actual riot during the premiere at the Théâtre des Champs-Élysées on

May 29th, 1913. The police had to be called and Stravinsky decided to flee from the theater. The avant-garde production is still widely considered to be one of the most influential musical works of the 20th century and has become a regular work in many ballet companies' repertoires. The music has appeared in Disney's *Fantasia* and elsewhere.

*"The profound meaning of music and its essential aim...is to promote a communion, a union of man with his fellow-man and with the Supreme Being." –***Igor Stravinsky**[502]

Stravinsky also claimed that his *Octet for Winds* began with a dream in 1922. Although in his autobiography he wrote, "I began to write this music without knowing what its sound medium would be—that is to say what instrumental form it would take. I only decided that point after finishing the first part."[503] Stravinsky later described the dream from the night before he started the composition, "I saw myself in a small room surrounded by a small group of instrumentalists playing some very attractive music. I did not recognize the music, though I strained to hear it, and I could not recall any feature of it the next day, but I do remember my curiosity—in the dream—to know how many the musicians were. I remember too that after I had counted them to the number eight, I looked again and saw that they were playing bassoons, trombones, trumpets, a flute, and a clarinet. I awoke from this little concert in a state of great delight and anticipation, and, the next morning, began to compose the Octuor (Octet), which I had had no thought of the day before, though for some time I had wanted to write an ensemble piece—not incidental music like *Histoire du soldat (A Soldier's Tale)*, but an instrumental sonata."[504]

Speaking of his musical theatre piece *A Soldier's Tale,* Stravinsky explained that it includes a key melodic element from a dream he had where a young gypsy woman was repeatedly playing a simple melody on violin to her young son who "was very enthusiastic about the music and applauded it with his little hands".[505] Stravinsky's son Théodore remembers his father's telling of the dream as including how the gypsy woman was very attractive and that she played the short tango motif at the door of her caravan, though reports a slight variation in that he remembers his father saying she was suckling her child.[506] Nonetheless, Stravinsky was very happy to clearly remember the short musical motif and wove it masterfully into the score. He claims it was the only music from a dream that he was ever able to clearly remember upon waking.[507]

The story of the whole piece is based on a Russian folk tale 'The Runaway Soldier and the Devil' by author Alexander Afanasiev. The tale tells the journey of Joseph, similar to Goethe's Faust who sells his soul to the devil in exchange for riches, power, youth and wisdom. Except in Stravinsky's piece, he is lured by the devil to barter his fiddle in exchange for great wealth. Although the musical dream motif is first heard in the score being played by cornet and bassoon, Stravinsky highlights the dream's melody more prominently during the 'Little Concert' scene of the performance where the Soldier plays it happily after being freed from the devil's control by intentionally losing all his recently gained wealth to the devil in a card game. In order to replicate the dream as closely as possible, the composer even included instructions in the score for the violinist to play the musical phrase using the entire length of the bow—the same way he saw the gypsy woman bowing the short melody in his dream.[508]

Giuseppi Tartini

On a related theme of devil and fiddle, Italian composer **Giuseppi Tartini** credited his best known violin sonata, *Sonata in G minor* (more commonly known as *The Devil's Trill*), to a virtuoso performance he heard in a dream in 1713 when he was about 21.[509] Tartini wrote, "I dreamt the devil was playing a violin and the music was so beautiful it moved me to tears. When I awoke, I tried to recreate this music, but the sonata I wrote was never as beautiful as that which I heard in my dream."[510]

In the dream, the devil appeared at the foot of Tartini's bed asking if he could be Tartini's servant. Tartini accepted. The devil seemed to intuitively sense his wishes and easily fulfill them. Then Tartini had the thought to hand the devil his violin to see how well he might play and was amazed as the devil performed an incredible, unearthly sonata. In about 1766, he remarked, "How great was my astonishment when I heard him play with such superiority and intelligence a sonata of such exquisite beauty as to surpass anything I'd ever heard or even imagined. I felt enraptured, transported, enchanted, so much so that my breath was taken away and as a result I awoke gasping."[511]

Tartini was a resident at the Franciscan monastery in Assisi, Italy when he had the dream. The experience appears to demonstrate the process of integrating dark or shadow aspects of the subconscious (such as the devil in Tartini's dream), and how such a process often signifies character development for the dreamer. The integration process also allows great creative energy to flow, such as virtuoso works like Tartini's composition. I therefore suggest that this dream actually marked a great stride forward in Tartini's spiritual development, and since he was by nature an artist, he shared that inner development with the world as *The Devil's Trill.*

"What we achieve inwardly will change outer reality."

–Plutarch

The enchanting melody was not the only element of the dream that Tartini brought forth to our waking world. *The Devil's Trill* pioneered performing techniques that advanced violin playing in new ways during Tartini's era, since it is a difficult piece to play even by modern performance standards. Tartini also later became a great violin teacher and founded a violin performance school. Therefore the dream appears to have been not only a creative inspiration, but also an important life-calling dream, since it offered a doorway that led to Tartini's professional path of service.

Anton Bruckner

19th-century composer **Anton Bruckner** had limited success getting his music known[512] until a dream brought him a career-changing musical theme that he incorporated into the opening movement of his Seventh Symphony. In the dream, Bruckner encountered theatre conductor Ignaz Dorn, a friend from his past for whom he had made funeral arrangements.[513] Dorn whistled[514] the wonderful melody for Bruckner and told him, "this will bring you good fortune". Bruckner awoke, quickly lit a candle and wrote down what he had heard.[515] Starting with its first performance in Leipzig, Bruckner's dream-inspired *Seventh Symphony* did indeed start bringing him much greater success. His student and close friend, Friedrich Eckstein, was very struck by the difference between how Bruckner composed the dreamt theme compared with his previous composing style. Eckstein said this of the dreamt melody, "What a wealth of unimagined beauty was revealed when I saw the very first bars of one newly begun work, the wonderful *Seventh Symphony*: where the string tremolos launch a deeply moving harmonic sequence that arches through a splendid chain of suspensions, bathing the main theme, on horn and cellos, in shafts of radiant sunlight!"[516]

Apparently, it was not the first time that his late friend Ignaz Dorn seems to have visited Bruckner in dreams to help with his compositions. When asked by Austrian music writer August Göllerich (also Bruckner's student) how the final movement of his *Fourth Symphony* came about, Göllerich quoted Bruckner as having replied, "In the last movement, I can't remember myself, just what I was thinking of." However, Bruckner later told another pupil, Max von Oberleithner, that his deceased friend Ignaz Dorn had appeared in a dream and said, "The first 3 movements of the symphony are done. The fourth will go like this …" Dorn then sat at a piano and played the symphony's fourth and final theme for him. Awakening, an excited Bruckner jumped from bed and transcribed the passage he just heard clearly in the dream.[517]

Inspiration for Bruckner's *Te Deum in C major* also came to him in the middle of the night. After an 1885 performance in Vienna, conductor Hans Richter rose with tears of enthusiasm and embraced Bruckner saying that it was on par with something Beethoven might compose. Bruckner surprised Richter by telling him that it was "not from me". The astonished Richter looked at him questioningly, so Bruckner eagerly elaborated, "Yes, that is not from me, it is from [Ludwig] Spohr. In bed one night, Spohr comes in and says to me, 'Bruckner, get up and write [this melody] down!' So I awoke and immediately wrote it out. Now tell me sir, is it then by me or by Spohr?"[518]

Hector Berlioz

French romantic era composer **Hector Berlioz**' work *Symphonie Fantastique* portrays an artist who has an opium-inspired dream. Berlioz revealed that his piece *Le Chant du Bonheur* (*Song of Happiness*) from his Monodrama *Lélio* (which supplemented *Symphonie Fantastique*) came while he was dreaming on the wall of his garden.[519]

In his book *Memoirs*, he also describes another musical dream that he never recorded nor crafted into a composition:

"I dreamed one night that I was composing a symphony, and heard it in my dream. On waking the next morning, I could recall nearly the whole of the first movement which was an allegro in A minor in two-four time...I was going to my desk to begin writing it down, when I suddenly thought, 'If I do, I shall be led on to compose the rest. My ideas always tend to expand nowadays, this symphony could be on an enormous scale. I shall spend three or four months on the work, during which time I shall do no articles, or very few, and my income will diminish accordingly. When the symphony is finished, I shall be weak enough to let myself be persuaded by my copyist to have it copied, which will immediately put me a thousand or twelve hundred francs in debt. Once the parts exist, I shall be plagued by the temptation to have the work performed. I shall give a concert, the receipts of which shall barely cover one half the costs—that is inevitable these days. I shall lose what I haven't got and be short money to provide for the poor invalid [his wife whose health was failing], and no longer be able to meet my personal expenses or pay my son's board on the ship he will shortly be joining.' These thoughts made me shudder, and I threw down my pen, thinking: 'What of it? I shall

have forgotten it by tomorrow!' That night, the symphony again appeared and resounded in my head. I heard the allegro in A minor quite distinctly. More, I seemed to see it written. I woke in a state of feverish excitement. I sang the theme to myself; its form and character pleased me exceedingly. I was on the point of getting up. Then my previous thoughts recurred and held me fast. I lay still, steeling myself against temptation, clinging to the hope I would forget. At last, I fell asleep; and when I next awoke all recollection of it had vanished forever."[520]

Pragmatic considerations are obviously important for anyone, including artists who wish the freedom necessary to pursue their craft because, in many cases, artistic creations may not produce income right away. Berlioz had understandable concerns and admirable reasons for not wanting to transcribe the dreamt symphony. In retrospect however, it may be quite unfortunate that he refused the dream muse's twice-offered creative gift and did not at least write his dreamt composition on paper for later consideration. Recognizing in retrospect the nature of the opportunity he gave up may well be why he included that special repeated dream in his memoirs.

*Though not widely recognized, **seven-year cycles often carry important transitions and opportunities in everyone's life**.*

Although Berlioz' career at the time of the dream seemed at its lowest point, the next seven years of his life became his period of greatest success, with many performances and much acclaim.[521] Although he is respected as a fine composer, it may be that he passed up the inspiration for what could have later become one of his greatest works—a powerful lesson about honoring creative insights and choosing to follow intuitive guidance—especially when it is repeated, and therefore I offer appreciation to Berlioz for sharing about his journey.

"Whatever you can do, or dream you can, begin it. Boldness has genius, power and magic in it." –**William Hutchison Murray**[522]

André Grétry and Daughter Lucile

Belgian-French opera composer **André Grétry** is reported to have crafted compositions from his dreams.[523] His first success in Paris was his comedic opera *Le Huron*. A happy Grétry reported that the night after the opening, his late father, whose deathbed concern was his son's success, came to him in a dream with open arms and the two joyfully embraced.[524]

Grétry's opera *Richard the Lionheart* is deemed not only to be his greatest masterpiece, but also one of the most important French 'opéras comiques' (comedic operas).[525] The composer recounted that before hitting on the opera's melody, he lay on his sofa in "a burning fever"[526] from eleven o'clock at night to four in the morning as he tried to come up with the piece. When Grétry rang for his servant to kindle the fire, the somewhat perplexed servant told Grétry he must be getting cold as he lay there "still doing nothing."[527] Discussing his creative process later, Grétry would say that a composer at work "could make a dozen or fifteen bars of harmony every morning,[528]…but to discover a melody—to put one's hand in the exact spot, the living, hidden spring from which is to issue forth the true accent of nature—that too may need much labor, but it is a different type of labor, and one that has no certainty of any result."[529]

Grétry also wrote about his daughter and student Lucile who, at the tender age of fourteen,[xv] told him she had been dreaming of a certain melody for "a number of days", so he prompted her to get to work on it "right away." Not only did she complete her piece *Mariage d'Antonio* in under an hour, she also shed many tears throughout its creation while she plucked her harp and sang.[530] It was the first opera written by **Lucile Grétry** and her father helped with its orchestral scoring. It was initially performed an impressive forty-seven times at the Comedie-Italienne (Italian-language theatre and opera performed in France) between 1786 and 1791.[531] The young Grétry's promising career unfortunately never had a chance to flourish since she died at age 17 from tuberculosis, part way through her dream-inspired work's very successful initial 47-performance run.

Edvard Grieg

19th-century Norwegian composer **Edvard Grieg**'s piece entitled *A Dream (Ein Traum)* is a musical interpretation of the poem by Friedrich Bodenstedt about a dream that becomes reality and reality that overshadows the dream.

The originality of Grieg's series of compositions entitled *Lyric Pieces* helped attract wide international attention, and seems to hold intrigue especially for foreign musicians who find his harmonies ingenious. Grieg's explanation of *Lyric Pieces* was simple: "My dream world."[532]

[xv] another example of the important seven-year cycle (i.e. 14 = 2 x 7).

Gustav Mahler

Gustav Mahler was yet another European classical composer
whose dreams brought musical revelations. On July 10th, 1896,
Mahler bicycled to the lakeside town of Unterach, Austria with
his friend Natalie Bauer-Lechner. During the trip, he confided to
her that while working on the 6th movement of his third
symphony, he heard the voice of either Beethoven or Wagner call
out to him as he slept, "Let the horns come in three measures
later!" About the dream, Mahler added, "And—I couldn't believe
my eyes—there was the most wonderfully simple solution of my
difficulty!"[533]

Mahler had followed Sigmund Freud's work for some time before
he met the famed psychiatrist for a single, transformational 4-hour
session. Mahler believed that both music and dreams could be
sources of inspiration, as suggested by a comment he made about
his third symphony. "My symphony will be something the world
has never heard before," announced Mahler. "The whole of nature
will be lent a voice in it, and it will impart such deep secrets as
those one might imagine in one's dreams."[534]

Carl Jung – Music Archetypes & Healing

Famed Swiss psychiatrist and author on dreams **Carl Gustav
Jung** believed that universal cultural archetypes can be embodied
in musical form. In 1950, a Parisian music journal invited Jung to
write an article on music and archetypes. He declined the
invitation, yet wrote back, "I can only draw your attention to the
fact that music represents the movement, development and
transformation of motifs of the collective unconscious. In
Wagner, this is very clear and also in Beethoven, but one finds it
equally in *Kunst der Fuge* [by Johann Sebastian Bach]."[535]

Jung later invited San Francisco music therapist and pianist Margaret Tilly to visit him at his home near Zurich. He was so impressed during the meeting by the power of musical motifs to affect his emotions that he exclaimed to Tilly, "This opens up whole new avenues of research I've never dreamed of. Because of what you showed me this afternoon—not just what you've said but what I have actually felt and experienced—I feel that from now on music should be an essential part of every analysis. This reaches the deep archetypal material that we can only sometimes reach in our analytical work with patients. This is most remarkable."[536]

"Music should be an essential part of every analysis."
–Carl Jung

An experience of my own seems to fit with Jung's conclusion. To help with physical pain as well as painful emotions around my heart area, I was offered (and accepted) a treatment by a talented musician and psychologist who employs various sound techniques including voice toning as part of her healing practice. A day later, I awoke from a dream in which I was hearing a melody with four repetitions of the word "coeur-full", each on a different note. I speak French fluently, a language in which not only does 'coeur' means heart, but 'choeur' (pronounced exactly the same way) means choir (i.e. singing). I enjoyed and felt a pleasant peace after the healing/toning session focused around my heart, so the dream suggests to me that the session helped to emotionally "fill my heart", even though there was not any obvious objective way to measure such an effect.

John Coolidge Adams

In 1984, while deeply absorbed in C.G. Jung's writings, post-minimalist composer **John Coolidge Adams** dreamt he was driving across the Oakland-San Francisco Bay bridge when he saw a gigantic super-tanker on the bay suddenly raise its bow into the sky and take off like a Saturn rocket.[537] The dream became the initial inspiration for his orchestral composition *Harmonielehre*, which ended an 18-month composition dry spell and also helped move his career to the next level.[538] The first part of the piece starts and ends with the pounding of E chords creating a 17-minute arch in inverted form with the intention to embody Adam's tanker-rocket dream. However the tanker dream was not the only dream that inspired the piece. Adams divulged that the final part 'Meister Eckhart and Quackie' has both its music and title inspired by a dream he had after the birth of his daughter Emily, who was briefly nicknamed 'Quackie' while she was an infant. In Adams' dream, his daughter was "perched on the shoulder of the medieval mystic, Meister Eckhart, as they hovered among the heavenly bodies like figures painted on the high ceilings of old cathedrals." Adams artistically embodied the dream to create the piece's ending.[539]

Rev. C.E. Hutchison and
Alice in Wonderland's Lewis Carroll

In 1882, Reverend **C. E. Hutchison** of Chichester, England dreamt the following:

> *"I found myself seated, with many others, in darkness, in a large amphitheatre. Deep stillness prevailed. A kind of hushed expectancy was upon us. We sat awaiting I know not what. Before us hung a vast and dark curtain, and*

between it and us was a kind of stage. Suddenly an intense wish seized me to look upon the forms of some of the heroes of past days. I cannot say whom in particular I longed to behold, but, even as I wished, a faint light flickered over the stage, and I was aware of a silent procession of figures moving from right to left across the platform in front of me. As each figure approached the left-hand corner it turned and gazed at me, and I knew (by what means I cannot say) its name. One only I recall—Saint George; the light shone with a peculiar bluish lustre on his shield and helmet as he turned and slowly faced me. The figures were shadowy, and floated like mist before me; as each one disappeared an invisible choir behind the curtain sang the 'Dream music'. I awoke with the melody ringing in my ears, and the words of the last line complete—'I see the shadows falling, and slowly pass away.'"

Hutchison remembered the tune upon awakening but could not recall any more of the words that he had heard, so he asked his friend, renown *Alice in Wonderland* author **Lewis Carroll**, to pen accompanying lyrics for the collaboration that became their appropriately-titled composition *Dreamland*.[540]

Samuel Taylor Coleridge & Charles Tomlinson Griffes

An opium dream by **Samuel Taylor Coleridge** inspired his famous poem *Kubla Khan*. In 1912, over a century later, American composer **Charles Tomlinson Griffes** composed a tone poem *The Pleasure Dome of Kubla Khan* which some sources report also came to him in a dream.[541] What is particularly interesting is that the original concept of the pleasure dome itself also originated in a dream of Chinese emperor Kubla Khan who then sent search parties to locate a site like he had seen in his dream, which ended up being in Shangdu (known better as Coleridge's *Xanadu*). The emperor then decreed that the temple he had seen in his dream be built there. Coleridge's dream about Kubla Khan happened while he was taking opium as medicine and reading about the famed Chinese emperor, yet Coleridge had no way of consciously knowing that Kubla Khan's original inspiration to build his pleasure dome also came in a dream, since the only translations at that time about emperor Khan's dream were in Arabic.

"If a man could pass through Paradise in a dream, and have a flower presented to him as a pledge that his soul had really been there, and found that flower in his hand when he awoke—Ay!— and what then?" –**Samuel Taylor Coleridge**[542]

Jacob Druckman

Pulitzer-prize-winning contemporary and electronic composer **Jacob Druckman** claims that his orchestral composition *Seraphic Games* was inspired by what the composer describes as a very clear and urgent dream of "super angels creating and destroying entire worlds with the detachment of a chess game…it was very beautiful and controlled yet there were these terrifying things happening."[543]

Gunther Schuller

Classical and jazz composer **Gunther Schuller** affirmed that his entire composition *Dreamscape*—number and type of movements, structure, scoring, rhythm, pitch, dynamics, harmonic and melodic decisions and many other details—not only was "composed for" him by his dream, but that the dreamt piece pushed him to compose in ways that he otherwise never would have. He began capturing the dream's details immediately upon awakening and his recall was so remarkably clear that he captured the piece in a "whole ten minutes of precise information."[544]

Bright Sheng

Chinese-American composer, conductor, and pianist, **Bright Sheng**, divulged that he sometimes dreams about his musical works. "Sometimes dreams help, but sometimes they don't," admitted Sheng. After finishing three movements of a new work for the Seattle Symphony, he was "intensely thinking about" how he wanted the final movement to sound, yet was also relaxed. He then dreamt about being at the first orchestral reading of the completed work and following the score of the fourth movement. Awakening in the middle of the night, he quickly grabbed a pad and transcribed the music and notes he just heard and read in his dream. Since he was still excited about it in the morning, he decided to use it in the appropriately-titled composition *China Dreams*, and confirmed that "the first five minutes of the last movement are more or less what I heard in the dream."[545]

William Grant Still

African-American classical composer **William Grant Still** is often referred to as "The Dean" of African-American composers. He was the first African-American not only to conduct an American symphony orchestra, but also to compose a symphony performed by a leading orchestra, as well as to compose an opera performed both on national television and by a major opera company.

Still's daughter Judy recounted how her father had a powerful musical dream vision in which "he heard a whole host of angels sing to him…He realized at that point that the whole universe is really music…And that the angels were the expression of God's sound."[546] The vision was an important epiphany for Still, and not only sounds intriguingly similar to the angel choir dream experiences of African singer-songwriter Joseph Shabalala, it also appears to support the principle suggested by the dream I shared near the start of the chapter 'Seeing Music, Hearing Images' about inner light and sound being alternate aspects of a common underlying energy.

Chapter 10

Ancient and Indigenous Dream Music and Shamanic Power Songs

Cædmon

Seventh century Anglo-Saxon singer and poet **Cædmon** is the earliest English poet whose name is known. He was an illiterate cow-herder at the Streonæshalch monastery[xvi] and knew nothing of music until he learned literally overnight how to sing and create verse during a dream.[547] It was customary at feasts and parties for a harp to be passed around, and for attendees to play it and share a song. Cædmon would always either shake his head when his turn came, or would leave because he did not know how to sing or play. On one such occasion, he left and went to bed ashamed, and dreamt that a man appeared and asked him to sing. Cædmon replied that he could not sing, but the man informed him that he could indeed and told him, "Sing to me the beginning of all things." Cædmon spontaneously then sang forth verses and words he had never heard. Awakening, he reported his experience

---

[xvi] Also known as the Whitby Abbey in what is now North Yorkshire, United Kingdom

initially to a steward, then to Hild, who ran the abbey. She requested scholars to evaluate his surprising new talent and suggested he try composing more divine doctrine into song. He did so successfully and his new creations and miraculous gift impressed Hild so much that she encouraged him to join the brotherhood. Thanks to a combination of the life-calling dream's grace and the vital step of acting on it, Cædmon completely transformed his life. Not only did he become a Christian monk, he also became a successful inspirational bard, composing and traveling to share religious verses and hymns praising God. A number of scholars claim that Cædmon deserves to be called a genius for his innovative creations.[548] His only surviving work is the nine-line poem *Cædmon's Hymn* that honors God and is understood to be the one he first sang during his life-altering dream.

"Intuition tells man his purpose in this life." –**Albert Einstein**[549]

Celtic Traditions

The ancient **Celts** experienced the magical Otherworld as sometimes speaking to them via musical dreams.[550] In one example, a man journeyed on a vision quest to a mountain called Cend Febrat. Sleeping there, he dreamt of the history of every "faery mound" on the mountain. In the dream, he also heard the musical theme of 'his own' song and therefore awakened from the vision blessed as a musician. The dreamer reported, "As I slept (pleasant the manner) therein I met with the theme of my song: there was shown me truly and in full every faery mound that is at Cend Febrat."[551]

The melody for the traditional Celtic song *Sí Beag Sí Mór* (*little faerie hill, big faerie hill*) is said to have arrived in a dream. The song was composed near the end of the 17th century by harpist **Turlough O'Carolan**, who became blind due to smallpox. At about age 21,[552],[xvii] O'Carolan was staying at the home of Squire Reynolds, a respected harpist and poet. Reynolds learned that O'Carolan had not written any original songs and so encouraged him to journey into the countryside to befriend his dream muse. Legend has it that not only did O'Carolan follow the advice and thereby have the musical goal of his 'songquest' bestowed upon him in a dream as he slept near a river, but also that the song helped his career blossom by bringing him renown throughout Ireland.[553]

Ancient Greeks

The **Ancient Greeks** placed great importance on the power and value of dreams for healing among other practical, prophetic, and spiritual purposes, and I share more details about this tradition and their practices in the Techniques chapter.

Regarding music, the ancient hymn *Hypne Anax* is one of the few surviving pieces of music from these ancient traditions and praises Hypnos, the Greek god of sleep who drives away cares, saves souls, and prepares us for death.

[xvii] Yet another example of the important seven-year cycle (i.e. 3 x 7 = 21) mentioned elsewhere in this book.

Musica Universalis

"O Plato! O Pythagoras! Ages ago you heard these harmonies, surprised these moments of inward ecstasy, knew these divine transports! If music thus carries us to heaven, it is because music is harmony, harmony is perfection, perfection is our dream, and our dream is heaven." –**Henri-Frédéric Amiel** [554]

Ancient philosophers such as ***Plato***, ***Cicero*** (in his widely-read story *Dream of Scipio*,[555] based on Plato's *Myth of Er*[556]), ***Pliny***, ***Ptolemy***, and others used the phrases *Musica Universalis* and 'the harmony of the spheres' (now generally known as 'the music of the spheres') to describe how heavenly bodies such as the sun, moon, and planets appeared to move in mathematical ratios like musical frequency intervals between harmonious notes. This philosophy echoes the 'music of the heavens' concept commonly attributed to ***Pythagoras*** who predated Plato by about 150 years. Pythagoras suggested that each planet vibrated to a particular tone[557] and related the movements of the planets to simple mathematical ratios in musical harmonies likes 4ths, 5ths, and octaves (8ths).[558]

"If I were not a physicist, I would probably be a musician. I often think in music. I live my daydreams in music. I see my life in terms of music." –**Albert Einstein**[559]

Australian Aborigines

The **Corroboree** poets of the Australian Unambal place great value on receiving and retrieving songs and chants from "dreamtime". Shamans skilled in such practices can "travel to the Beyond" and "collect songs and chants" which they then teach to the tribe.[560]

Malaysia's Temiar Tribe – Healing Songs

The Senoi (also spelled Sng'oi) **Temiar** tribes of the Malaysian rainforest often receive powerful shamanic healing songs in their dreams. A major technique for healing involves song and trance-dance ceremonies in which the mediums (shamans) sing the sacred melodies and recite texts given to them by spirit guides during their dreams.[561] Like other indigenous traditions, receiving such songs in dreams can also indicate the dreamer's calling as a shaman. Dream songs are also used during rituals by the Temiar to call on spirits.[562]

Zulu shamans

Anthropologist Holger Kolweit researched **Zulu** shamans, also called 'sangomas', hearing from one young shaman when he returned from his vision quest that he had received not one but three songs in a dream. The young shaman reported, *"Now there are things which I see when I lie down. When I left home I had composed three songs, without knowing from whence they came; I heard the song, and then just sang it, and sang the whole of it without ever having learnt it."* [563]

When a young Zulu shaman hears in a dream a song which they have never before heard, they are considered to be initiated by the spirit world, and the tribal elders celebrate the auspicious coming-of-age event. Kolweit also noted that shamans who hear their calling in a dream or vision, sometimes against their own wishes, can have their life and health in upheaval for weeks during which powerful dreams and visions continue to come.

Perhaps the best known Zulu musical artist whose father was an 'inyanga' (traditional African shamanic healer) is master dreamer Joseph Shabalala (highlighted earlier in the book).

North American First Nations

"The Medicine Man, taking his music with him, is passing quietly into the Great Silence, where the old songs were 'Received in Dreams' by inner-plane communication."
–Francis Densmore (friend of Apache leader Geronimo)

Dream songs were also important for American First Nations communities. Songs received during the powerful coming-of-age adolescent vision quest became a key part of the dreamer's life, holding strong emotional power for the dreamer, and so were remembered and sung in challenging times such as war, and also used to evoke the power of his or her own personal spirit.[564] Most songs were inspired by dreams.[565] For some tribes, songs received in dreams were individually owned, often by shamans. The Plain Indians learn songs from beings who appear in dreams, and the songs play a teaching role in the community.[566]

The Mojave song myth from the First Nation tribes of California and Arizona is a collection of songs heard in dreams mixed with plain speech prose. The prose recounts events that the dreamer saw, but did not hear or do, since in the Mojave tradition, the dreamer of a song myth is always a third-person onlooker, not a first person actor.[567] Dream songs still exist for the Yaqui, Shoshone, and Pima-Papago tribes of the region.

For the Yuman Indians "all singing is the result of supernatural dream experiences."[568]

Dream songs were important to treat the sick, with the medicine man often receiving curing songs directly from a spirit in a dream along with treatment instructions.[569]

Craig Sim Webb

Chapter 11

Folk Songs, World Music, and Carols Harvested from Dreamland

Joni Mitchell

As a schoolgirl, folk music legend **Joni Mitchell** fell in love with Rachmaninoff's 'Rhapsody on a Theme of Pagnini', which was on the film 'Story of Three Loves' soundtrack. The young Mitchell soon started dreaming that she could play the piano beautifully.

"In my dreams, my hands would be on the keyboards and I'd be composing these fantastic pieces of music, like *Story of Three Loves*, that I could play and make emotions come out like that." The dreams deeply inspired Mitchell, so she asked her mother for a piano, but her parents couldn't afford it. "I begged, I wheedled, I pleaded, and finally, one winter night, because there was no piano store in North Battleford, this van pulled up with a lot of spinets on the back."[570] Mitchell's dream had called a piano into her life, and ended up growing over the years into an influential and legendary music career that garnered 10 Grammy wins and 18 nominations, among many other accolades.

Mitchell was fortunate to be invited by Paul McCartney to join a bunch of famous colleagues for a party aboard the RMS Queen

Mary. At one point, she was alone with Bob Dylan who asked her what she would paint if she were to paint the room they were in. She replied, "The mirror ball spinning...the women in the washroom...the band." The conversation later popped up in her dream which she then wove together with childhood memories to craft her song *Paprika Plains*.[571]

Pete Seeger

Folk legend and four-time Grammy winner, **Pete Seeger**, dozed off on a plane and awakened remembering the important lyrical line 'long time passing' that helped him write his hit *Where Have All The Flowers Gone?* It was a line he had liked when he read it "a year or two or three" earlier, but it was in that half-awake moment Seeger said, that "all of a sudden" he saw how that line fit together with the lyric 'When will we ever learn?' Highlighting that moment's special insight as a process he seemed to have used at other times, Seeger added, "And you know, when you're dozing, that's when the creative ideas come."[572] His song, released in 1964 on Columbia Records, was inducted into the Grammy Hall of Fame in 2002 in the Folk category, and won a special Grammy award established in 1973 to honor recordings at least 25 years old that have "qualitative or historical significance."

Patty Griffin

Grammy-winning American folk artist **Patty Griffin**, was blessed by the dream muse for the opening line of her song *Servant of Love*, the title track for her 2015 album. "I was reading a lot of magical realism and Latin American fiction at the time I was writing the album," explained Griffin, "and that's about having to accept the magic in life and not even blinking at the bizarre."[573]

Griffin also divulged that her song *Christina* from her 2 CD set *A Kiss in Time* germinated from a dream about unhappy heiress Christina Onassis, daughter of Greek billionaire Aristotle Onassis.[574]

Julia Ward Howe

Writer **Julia Ward Howe** heard the fighting man's song *John Brown's Body* during a public review of the civil war troops outside Washington on Upton Hill, in Virginia. Howe's companion at the review, Reverend James Freeman Clarke, suggested to her that she write new lyrics for the song. She stayed in Washington at the Willard Hotel that fateful night of November 18, 1861, and later shared in her book *Reminiscences* an experience that happened after going to bed as usual and sleeping quite soundly. "I awoke in the gray of the morning twilight; and as I lay waiting for the dawn, the long lines of the desired poem began to twine themselves in my mind," wrote Howe. "Having thought out all the stanzas, I said to myself, 'I must get up and write these verses down, lest I fall asleep again and forget them.' So, with a sudden effort, I sprang out of bed, and found in the dimness an old stump of a pen which I remembered to have used the day before. I scrawled the verses almost without looking at the paper."[575]

Thanks to Howe's half-awake-state-inspired lyrics, the song was renamed *The Battle Hymn of the Republic.*[576]

Christmas Carol Melody Conceived in Dreamland

On Christmas eve, 1865, **Phillips Brooks** visited Israel's Plains of Judea by horseback, where shepherds sat watching their flocks of sheep by night, just as shepherds did on the eve of Jesus' birth many centuries before. Brooks journaled about the evening, and crafted his experience into verse. Three years later, as rector for the Philadelphia Church of the Holy Trinity, he gave the lyrics to the church's organist, **Lewis H. Redner**, to put to music. Once again, it was almost Christmas, and on the Saturday night, under the pressure that Brooks and the choir expected to practise the carol within hours, Redner dreamt of a lovely melody. Describing his experience, Redner stated, "I was roused from sleep late in the night hearing an angel-strain whispering in my ear, and seizing a piece of music paper, I jotted down the treble of the tune as we now have it, and on Sunday morning before going to church I filled in the harmony."[577]

The hymn was finished and performed the following day during the church's Christmas day service in what would become the first-ever playing of the well-known Christmas carol, *O Little Town of Bethlehem.*[578]

King Rama II Dreams Beloved Thai Song

Early 19th century Thai monarch **King Rama II** was a virtuoso instrumentalist on the saw sam sai.[xviii] After an evening playing with the royal mahori orchestra, he fell asleep and dreamt of a heavenly mahori orchestra of angels performing beneath a full moon. Awakening, he remembered the dream's melody and promptly got up to learn it on his saw sam sai. The song seemed

---

[xviii] A bowed, three-string instrument from Thailand.

so important that he woke the royal musicians and had them also memorize it to avoid losing it by daybreak. *The Floating Moon* has now become one of the most beloved songs in all of Thai music.[579]

The Horse-Head Fiddle and Horse-Hair Bow

The group **Huun-Huur-Tu**, from the Tuvan Republic at the southern tip of Siberia, shares traditional indigenous music using specialized overtone singing techniques accompanied by various traditional instruments. A dream seems to have inspired not only the band's traditional song *Lament of the Igil*, but also the invention of an instrument revered by Tuvans, Mongolians, and natives of surrounding regions. The song tells the story of a great slain gray horse that comes to its former master Öskus-ool in a dream and instructs him where to find its dead body and how to create a musical instrument from it. "Hang my skull on an old larch tree, make a musical instrument from its wood," explains the beloved horse to its owner,[580] along with the specific instructions to "carve it with my image, cover it with skin from my face."[581] It then guides him to make strings for the instrument and the soft edge of the bow from the hair of its tail.[582] The dreamer is said to have fashioned the instrument as instructed, creating the first of what is now known as the horse-head fiddle. The Tuvan version of this instrument is called the 'igil'—a two-stringed bowed instrument that produces a sound resembling that of a viola and is the most common accompaniment instrument for Tuvan singers.[583]

A bowed instrument similar to the Tuvan igil is the Mongolian version of the horse-head fiddle called the 'morin khuur'.[xix] It is the national instrument of Mongolia and is considered a symbol of peace and happiness, hence many Mongolians keep one in their homes.[584] The dream-inspired origin of the 'morin khuur'[585] is likely the same as the Tuvan igil since Mongolia borders the Tuva Republic to the south and the two lands have had common rulers in centuries past. Furthermore, the account of the morin khuur's dream-guided invention is strikingly similar[586] to the Tuvan account, except that the deceased horse who visits in the dream also specifically guides his grieving owner to carve a horse head atop the instrument so the owner is reminded of their deep bond each time he sees and plays the fiddle.[587]

Two of the earliest known Western records of bowed instruments with strings as part of the bow are from the late 10th century in countries east of Iberia (vertically-played) and in Iberia (horizontally-played).[588] One or both of these are believed to be the source from which modern bowed string instruments initially developed. The morin khuur's origins also date back about one millennium to the same period.[589] One version still in use that is close or identical to the ones from that era is the ancient Balkan 'gusle', or horse-head fiddle.[590] My aim in pointing out such connections is to suggest that, if the story of the horse-head fiddle is accurate, then the dream-inspired origin of at least the horse hair bow (and perhaps other aspects) of the Central Asian horse-head fiddle may have contributed to modern day bowed string instruments such as the violin, viola, cello, and double bass whose bows are still made with horse hair.

[xix] 'mori' means horse in Mongolian, and interestingly <u>sounds</u> similar to the English word 'mare', a female horse. Synchronistically, 'mori' in Latin means 'die', which is intriguing since Öskus-ool's dream came after his horse died. In Western Mongolia, the morin khuur is also called the 'ikil', which by itself suggests a strong link with the Tuvan 'igil'. Another version of the horse-head fiddle is the Balkan 'gusle', a word that is intriguingly similar in sound to the Czech term 'housle' for violin.

Chapter 12

Little-Known Musical Dreams that Rocked the Modern World – II

Shawn Colvin

Grammy-winning artist **Shawn Colvin** is yet another singer-songwriter who finds creative inspiration in dreams.[591] One of her most intimate and emotional songs is *The Story* from her *Steady On* album. Colvin revealed, "I actually dreamt part of the song, which is something that I've done before. In other words, there have been songs in dreams that I have wanted to remember when I've woken up, but haven't. It's kind of hard to do...I've tried at times, but it hasn't worked out."[592] The song tells of Colvin's youth and tough challenges within her family that still have an impact on her life. Colvin says she receives feedback from many women who resonate with the song since they too felt constrained by the conservative norms of the 1950s.[593]

Colvin's dreaming muse also helped craft *Polaroids* from her 1992 album *Fat City*, a song which tells of pain, confusion and broken promises at the end of a romantic relationship. She was having trouble finishing the tune when a dream came to the rescue to help complete the last verse:

"I had this dream where this couple wasn't walking a plank off of a ship, but they were walking a plank over a huge excavated hole in the ground. And they were totally in love, it was the sweetest damn feeling, you know. And he walked out first and she took a Polaroid, then she walked out and he took a Polaroid as she held up this flash card type of thing that said 'Valentine'. The good will between these people must have been something that I was striving for because I had had relationships with a lot of ill-will (laughs) which just seems so wrong, but it was in my life."[594]

Lenny Kravitz

Multi-Grammy-winner-and-nominee rocker **Lenny Kravitz** is no stranger to harvesting musical dreams, and claimed that many songs from his album *Black and White America* came that way.[595]

In 2017, Kravitz felt his musical direction was at a crosswords. "I was writing and doing stuff but it wasn't feeling right. I just knew that I needed to chill out and really trust the creative process," admitted Kravitz, explaining that he was in the Bahamas, and intentionally quieted his routine and grew more still in order to hear something new "without 'trying'". After about a month, his dreams responded. "I woke up with a song in my head, which is normally how it starts...I have the iPhone by the bed so I can hum the melodies, but I went to the studio and started working on it and realized that this is the beginning of where I want to go...Then the floodgates opened. I dreamt the whole record."[596] Indeed, he reports waking another day at 5a.m. and going directly into the nearby studio since the inspiration felt "very urgent". In an early morning state of creative attunement, he started playing chords, and then having words start flowing from his mouth that surprised him like "Johnny Cash" and "June Carter" including a lyric about just wanting to be held like Johnny Cash did when Kravitz' mother had passed. Kravitz connected the dots to when his own mother died of cancer in 1995 while he was living at Rick Rubin's[xx] Los Angeles house where dream-inspired songwriter Johnny Cash and June Carter also happened to be staying and recording an album. Kravitz recounts how he had been spending time with his mother at the hospital and had just come home for a quick meal break when the call came that she had passed. Moments later, Carter and Cash came around and asked him what was going on, and he told them the tough news. The couple immediately hugged and then consoled him with great compassion, saying thoughful, beautiful things for about 10 minutes. Kravitz honours the timely, heartfelt encounter with Cash and Carter as "such a gift",[597] and aptly titled the new song *Johnny Cash*—a song that flowed from a dream in The Bahamas, where his mother was from.[598]

The dream-woven album, *Raise Vibration*, attained significant international success, especially in Europe, charting Kravitz' work higher than in a number of years including its debut at #4 on the Billboard 200 and climb to #5 on the Top Rock Albums chart.

Janelle Monáe & Producer Nate Wonder

American singer-songwriter and actress **Janelle Monáe** has a love for surrealism and dream-inspired artist Salvador Dali, and

---

[xx] In addition working with Johnny Cash, Rick Rubin produced albums for dream-inspired artists Lady Gaga, Ed Sheeran, LL Cool J, The Cult, Metallica, also interviewed master dream-inspired artist Paul McCartney for the 2021 documentary *McCartney 3,2,1*.

announced that she incorporated many dreams[599] into her album *Archandroid*. "A lot of the music came to me in my dreams. Luckily, I had my iPhone by my bed and I could, you know, just use my recording device and just record what it was that I could remember." Monáe admitted that songs coming in her dreams for the album was a first, and that she had to manage her initial anxiety about remembering the dreamt music and even such specifics as "absolutely gorgeous" string arrangements such as one in the style of John Williams for *Neon Valley Street*. She found ways to calm herself and made sure to quickly "hop up" out of bed since she believes such creative processes to be "very important":

"As an artist, you have to listen to what your Maker is saying." **–Janelle Monáe**

The album received a Grammy nomination and debuted at #17 on The Billboard 200 top US albums weekly chart. Monáe had a feeling the album would do well not only because of her dreams, but also since her producer **Nate Wonder** had dreams while producing the album including of using specific string arrangements.[600]

Carlos Santana

Virtuoso electric guitar icon **Carlos Santana** was deeply moved when he first saw Leonardo Da Vinci's masterpiece Mona Lisa in The Louvre in Paris. Months later, the experience came flooding back when he awoke from a dream with lyrics "fully formed in his mind" for his songs *In Search of Mona Lisa* and *Do You Remember Me*. "It was the first time that I ever woke up and lyrics were there in a tangible way," Santana explained on his web site. "I could just grab them and write the songs."[601]

Don McLean

American singer-songwriter **Don McLean**'s *American Pie* album
reached the top of Billboard's top 200 albums near the start of
1972 and held there for 7 weeks.[602] In 2002, it was inducted into
the Grammy Hall of Fame. Regarding the dream-like story told by
title song's lyrics, McLean writes, "You know how when you
dream something you can see something change into something
else and it's illogical when you examine it in the morning, but
when you're dreaming it, it seems perfectly logical."[603]

McLean, who performed with dream-inspired songwriter Pete
Seeger in the 1960s, divulged in 2003 that his song *The Grave*
from *American Pie* was inspired by a dream where he saw pearls
on a leaf and began to think about how soldiers in a trench may be
in their own grave.[604]

'*Wildfire*'

American singer-songwriter **Michael Martin Murphey** was
inspired for his platinum hit *Wildfire* by dreaming of a ghost
horse. His grandfather had told him tales about the horse when he
was a boy, including how it rescued people in the desert. Murphey
described how he'd been working with his writing partner Larry
Cansler for many days with very little sleep. At about 3 a.m., he
woke from a dream with the lyrics and images in mind.[605] "I
wrote all the images out on a yellow pad that I keep beside my
bed," recalled Murphey. "From the dream, I started to put it
together in lyrical form and patched together a melody."
Eventually, Cansler awoke and joined Murphey to help with the
chords and arrangement, and they finished the song before dawn.
At the time, Murphey did not even have his first recording
contract yet, and it was not until his fourth album that he recorded

the song because his producer, Bob Johnston, was not a fan of the tune.[606] Released the summer of 1975, the song became a chart-topping hit, immediately selling over a million copies and reaching #3 on the Billboard Hot 100, as well as #1 on the Adult Contemporary charts, bringing Murphey a whole new level of success including a gold disc by July.[607] The song has now sold over two million copies in the USA alone.[608]

Bruce Cockburn

Bruce Cockburn is a Canadian artist whose lyrics are inspired by dreams. One evening Cockburn had dinner in Ottawa with a government-employed relative at a time when tensions were high along the China-Russia border. His relative told him, "We could wake up tomorrow to a nuclear war." Cockburn added, "Coming from him, it was a serious statement."[609]

That night, Cockburn had a dream: "I experienced a rerun of a dream I'd had some years before in which lions roamed the streets in terrifying fashion, only this time they weren't threatening at all."[610] In another interview, he continued the story, laughing, "So I woke up the next morning and it wasn't a nuclear war. It was a real nice day and there was all this good stuff going on…it was kind of a peaceful thing. And it reflected a previous dream that was a real nightmare where the lions were threatening."[611] Driving along Ottawa's Queensway highway the next morning, Cockburn drew connections clarifying the meaning of his dream and started writing lyrics for what became his hit *Wondering Where the Lions Are.* The song was Cockburn's only Top 40 hit in the United States, peaking at #21 on the Billboard Hot 100. It was also a Top 40 hit in Canada, and named the 29th greatest Canadian song of all time in the 2005 CBC Radio series '50 Tracks: The Canadian Version'.[612]

Palma Pascale & The Carpenters

Songwriter **Palma Pascale** explained that in October 1973, a dream inspired her to write *Love Me for What I Am*, a song she sold to **The Carpenters** for their platinum-selling *Horizons* album which peaked within the top 10 albums in multiple countries that year. Pascale elaborated how she received the chorus while asleep: "The words 'Love me for what I am, for simply being me. Don't love me for what you expect, or hope that I will be' came in a dream. I remember arguing with myself about waking up to write them down…anything to not have to get up!" Fortunately, Pascale arose from bed and penned the lyrics. Later that day, she finished the song in 45 minutes. She recorded a demo of the song and thought it sounded perfect for The Carpenters, so she contacted them. A couple of weeks later, A&M Records confirmed that Richard Carpenter wanted to record the song. Pascale's dreamt lyrics differed slightly from The Carpenters' recorded version since they requested their lyricist partner John Bettis to tweak the lyrics for Karen's voice."[613]

The Bee Gees

The **Bee Gees** affirm that it is not necessary to read or write music in order to gather it from dreams. "You put a cassette next to your bed," said **Barry Gibb**, describing his simple process, "And you sing into it and you play it back later." He confided that the chorus of *You Win Again* arrived in the manner, "but I didn't have the recorder, so I had to run around the house and find something, because like a dream, those things will disappear." *You Win Again* hit #1 on the UK charts in late 1987 making the Bee Gees the first band to score #1 hits in all three decades of the 1960s, 1970s and 1980s.[614] The dream-sparked song also garnered 1988's coveted British Academy Ivor Novello award for Best Contemporary

Song.

Since none of the Gibb bothers knew music notation, **Maurice Gibb** explained that they collaborated with professional arrangers, including "a wonderful guy called Bill Shepherd for many years…[who] would arrange all our music that we heard."

Both Barry and **Robin Gibb** stated that one of Barry's dreams about singing in falsetto occurred while the group was recording their 1975 hit *Nights on Broadway* and producer Arif Mardin asked if any of the brothers could scream to raise the energy of the song's chorus.[615] Barry's falsetto developed into a key element of the band's signature sound during the 1970s and 1980s, and contributed to the Bee Gees having now sold over 220 million albums worldwide. The group has won 5 Grammys, as well as the Grammy Legend Award in 2003 and the Lifetime Achievement Grammy in 2015, and were inducted into the Songwriters Hall of Fame and into the Rock and Roll Hall of Fame in 1997.[616]

Air Supply

Graham Russell, singer-songwriter and guitarist for Australia's soft rock duo **Air Supply**, claims that he often harvests dreams for songwriting.[617]

In 1975, Graham Russell and Russell Hitchcock were still performing together in the musical 'Jesus Christ Superstar' in Sydney where the duo met, but they were also writing their own songs. One night, the two agreed to go with the best band name idea either could come up with by the next day since they had recorded a new song together that was about to be released. That night, says Russell, "I dreamt there was this massive billboard, like in Times Square, and the lights were flashing all around. And in the middle were two words, and it said 'Air Supply'. It just kept going on and off like a neon [sign]." Russell shared the dream with Hitchcock, saying that he didn't know what it meant, but since they didn't have anything better, they went with it.[618] According to Hitchcock, "It was as simple as that."[619]

The dream also foreshadowed the band's potential and future success in America (i.e. regarding the dream's reference to 'Times Square'), since it has come true in 'time' chronologically-speaking with many hits flashing onto Billboard's Top 100 in the USA, including a #1 hit and 7 other top 10 hits in the early 1980s. It also came true literally, since their dreamt band name Air Supply has appeared several times on actual lighted billboards before performances and even on a huge billboard that Arista Records producer Clive Davis put on Sunset Boulevard in Hollywood when the band's greatest hits album came out in 1983.[620]

REO Speedwagon

"I literally woke up in the middle of the night and I had these three, simple piano chords going through my head," confided **REO Speedwagon** lead vocalist **Kevin Cronin**. In step with the wise strategy followed by many other artists in this book, Cronin decided to reel in the dreamt music more fully and expand it into a song right away, and so he "stumbled" sleepily directly into his home studio. "I sat down and started playing those chords—that was what the song came from."[621] The tune in question is the band's megahit *Keep On Loving You*, that not only rocketed to #1 on Billboard's Top 100, but also propelled its album, *Hi Infidelity,* to become 1981's best-selling rock album and receive a Grammy nomination. The song also attained international success reaching the top 10 in other countries including Canada and UK, and was later certified platinum by the RIAA.

B-52's

The new wave band **B-52's** also received its name from a dream. The group's original drummer, **Keith Strickland** shared that he dreamt "about this lounge band that had a woman keyboard player, and she introduced the band as the B-52's." Upon waking, he realized it was a perfect name for the band.[622]

Kenny Loggins

In the late 1980s, American singer-songwriter and guitarist **Kenny Loggins** was going through marital strife, and he would wake at 5 a.m. each morning and harvest lyrics from emotional dreams about his situation. Not only did the deep introspection help him take the leap of faith required to leave the "distant and adversarial" marriage where Loggins says he and his wife were emotionally "both starving to death", the lyrics also grew into his 1991 title song and album *Leap of Faith*.[623]

Corey Hart Dreams for his Protegé Jonathan Roy

Grammy nominee and multiple Juno Award-winning Canadian pop singer-songwriter **Corey Hart** had top 10 hits *Sunglasses at Night* and *Never Surrender* in the mid 1980s, and then in 2002 started his label, Siena Records. In 2012, Siena signed up-and-coming artist **Jonathan Roy**, son of legendary Montreal Canadians hockey team goalie Patrick Roy. After a few years of working together to hone Roy's style, the young singer experienced "yet another failed date" on the evening of his 26th birthday. Yearning for a deep relationship and a career break through, Roy poured his heart out to his mentor in an emotion-packed email which Hart read just before sleep. In a dream, Hart watched from the right[624] side of the stage as Jonathan performed at a live outdoor festival in Copenhagen, Denmark. A girl approached Hart and introduced herself, "Hi, I'm Daniella—I'm going to be Jonathan's soulmate." Hart awoke, remembering the dream along with a melody, and jumped out of bed to work out the tune on his guitar. "I never write songs this way," explained Hart. "In my entire career, it's the only one that ever came to me in a dream." Released in November 2015, the song spent many weeks in the top 50 and reached #16 on Billboard Canada's national airplay list (which includes international songs). Time will tell whether the dream itself comes true, but the song definitely helped boost Roy's career.[625]

Tori Amos

"Music is the universal language of mankind."

–Henry Wadsworth Longfellow[626]

Around 5:30 a.m.,[xxi] an older African woman came in a dream to American singer-songwriter, pianist, and eight-time Grammy nominee **Tori Amos**. Although Amos was unable to understand the woman's words, she realized that the intonation of the woman's voice was humming a melody. She awoke and recorded the tune she had just heard, and crafted it into her song *1000 Oceans*.[627] The dream song took on a surprise alchemical quality for Amos' husband, sound-recording engineer Mark Hawley,

---

[xxi] I include the time of the dream here since Amos was one of the few who noted it, and also as an example of the principle that the last dream or two on any given night often contain(s) aspects worth acting upon.

whose father died as they were recording the album. Hawley was extremely distraught about losing his dad, and Amos found it difficult to stay emotionally connected with her husband. However, he repeatedly requested that she play the ocean song, and it became a powerful doorway for his grieving and healing, so they decided to shape the song into an anthem for grieving lost loved ones.[628] The song became the final track on Amos' album, *To Venus and Back*, which received a Grammy nomination for Best Alternative Music Album.

Elvis Costello

Grammy winner and Rock and Roll Hall of Fame inductee **Elvis Costello** has worked with artists from The Beatles to Burt Bacharach and numerous other stars. Costello shared that the first line, "I had forgotten all about 'The Case Of The Three Pins'", in his song *King of Thieves* from his *Punch The Clock* album came verbatim from a dream. About the dreamt lyrics, Costello explained, "I still have no idea what it means but it sounds like the beginning of a detective novel."[629]

Costello also shared that his song *Honey, Are You Straight Or Are You Blind?* came to him in a dream:[630] "I had to capture it on a cassette player with just the slapping of my hand on the kitchen counter."[631]

P.F. Sloan

Songwriter **P.F. Sloan** had a wave of success in the mid 1960s. One night in bed, he found himself undergoing a tumultuous inner battle for many hours, wishing he could be free of the music that seemed to be trying to birth through him. As the night went on, though perhaps not exactly in what might normally be called a dream, yet certainly in what seems some type of altered state, Sloan's great turmoil transformed into tears of joy as he "witnessed" lyrics and even saw whole choruses appearing to him. In that one night, he wrote 5 songs: *Eve of Destruction*, *Sins of a Family*, *Ain't No Way I'm Gonna Change My Mind*, *Take Me For What I'm Worth* and *This Morning*.[632] Within the year (1965), three of the songs made it into Billboard's U.S. Hot 100 songs, including *Take Me For What I'm Worth*, *Sins of a Family*, and *Eve of Destruction* which was recorded by artist Barry McGuire and hit the #1 spot since it resonated strongly with the nation's unrest about American military involvement in Vietnam.[633]

"Let all the dreamers wake the nation." –**Carly Simon**[634]

Nicole Atkins' Dream Brings Song & David Byrne Contribution

American singer-songwriter **Nicole Atkins**' shared that *Girl You Look Amazing* was sparked by a dream in which *Talking Heads* lead singer and guitarist David Byrne was singing the song's hook. She woke up in the middle of the night and recorded it on her phone. Not only did the disco-dance beat sound of the song end up shaping the sound of the album, but David Byrne actually ended up contributing to Atkins' crowdfunding campaign for the CD, along with many others including dream-inspired songwriter Bruce Springsteen. Atkins added that dreams have been a constant source of inspiration for her songwriting.[635]

Dan Wilson's 'Secret Smile'

Two-time Grammy-winner **Dan Wilson**, and former lead singer for **Semisonic** said that the band's international hit *Secret Smile* arrived from dreamland and he promptly got out of bed to learn it on piano. Come morning, it sounded too familiar so he thought he'd taken the tune from somewhere,[636] just like the creatorship uncertainty sometimes experienced by other dream-inspired artists. *Secret Smile* was featured in the 'Dawson Creek' and 'Charmed' TV series as well as the movie 'Simply Irresistible', and was one of the band's few songs that placed in the top 40, peaking at #13 and becoming their highest placement on UK charts. It also helped launch a successful songwriting career for Wilson who won the 2007 Song of the Year Grammy for collaborating with **The Dixie Chicks** on their certified-platinum hit 'Not Ready To Make Nice', and shared the 2012 Album of the Year Grammy with Adele for her chart-topper 'Someone Like You'.[637]

Ricki Lee Jones

American singer-songwriter and two-time Grammy winner, **Rickie Lee Jones**, received a gift from the dreaming muse to inspire her song *Infinity* from her 2015 album *The Other Side of Desire*. Jones recalled the dream, "We're traveling on a train and I'm sitting with the band and I'm looking out the window and everything is made of form and shape. Now I'm in a bar and I step into the back and the room expands, and there are people everywhere." An emotional Jones added, "It was a good dream."[638]

Tom Waits & Kathleen Brennan

American singer-songwriter, two-time Grammy winner, and Rock and Roll Hall of Fame inductee **Tom Waits** got motivated to rethink his creative direction by a dream in which he understood that unless he explored new avenues, his music could all too easily end up as unwanted junk at the Salvation Army. "There was my album sitting in a big stack of old records underneath a bunch of old platform shoes and shovels," Waits said, recounting the dream. "I realized I wanted to make something unique, something that you'd want to keep."[639] Waits added that things shifted gradually as "the result of a hundred little decisions" rather than one major change of course.

Waits' wife and songwriting partner **Kathleen Brennan** also harvests creative insights from sleep and dreamt up the idea for their song *Fish in the Jailhouse*.[640]

Los Lobos

Drummer-songwriter **Louie Perez** crafted a powerful dream image of an angel with piano-lid wings into his song *Dream in Blue* that tells the story of a person in a dream who is "almost" able to realize the meaning of life before he wakes up, "but not quite."[641]

While touring with his Grammy Award-winning band **Los Lobos**, he dreamt of band-mate David Hidalgo alone on stage, sitting on a stool, singing and playing guitar. Upon awakening, he remembered the melody and some of the lyrics from the dream, so he called Hidalgo and told him about it. Hidalgo came right over, and their song *Peace* was born.[642]

About his dream-inspired songs, Perez admits they are gifts that "definitely come from somewhere else."[643]

Terence Trent D'Arby

Following a series of dreams in 1995, Grammy-winning artist **Terence Trent D'Arby** adopted the name **Sananda Maitreya**.[644] "I had a recurring dream of walking with my friends, who were angels, and they kept calling out this name which I recognized, but it wasn't until the third dream that I realized it was my name," revealed Maitreya.[645]

The artist also shared that his hit song *Sign Your Name* was also inspired by a dream in the mid 1980s after he saw soul and jazz singer-songwriter-producer **Sade** perform live. In his dream, Sade requested that he compose a song for her.[646] The hit appeared on his debut album *Introducing the Hardline According to Terence Trent D'Arby* which won the 1988 Grammy for the Best R&B Male Vocal Performance and rocketed D'Arby to international fame. The song itself reached the top 10 in at least 9 countries, including peaking at #4 in Billboard's Hot 100.[647]

KT Tunstall

Scottish singer-songwriter **KT Tunstall**'s *Tiger Suit* album is inspired by a recurring dream she has had since childhood of seeing a tiger in her garden and going outside with her brother to stroke it. As the dream continues, she returns indoors and is suddenly gripped by the fear that she could have been killed. She later contemplated that perhaps she and her brother were wearing tiger suits themselves and this is what kept them safe.[648] She relates to the dream in terms of having an invisible armor that she never really knew she had on, including how it protected her from judgment and the public eye.[649] Inspired by her boldness from the dream, she chose to really stretch beyond her comfort zone when creating the songs on her Tiger Suit album.[650],[651]

Third Eye Blind

Stephan Jenkins, lead singer of **Third Eye Blind** and the only member who's been with the band since its 1993 inception,[652] disclosed that their song *Blade* is about one of his recurring nightmare themes of trying to cut through the tension of the dream and get through the nightmare.[653] Appropriately, the original song title when performed live was *Dream Sequence*.[654]

Owl City

Owl City's **Adam Young** often has nightmares, and has made a habit of going into his studio when he awakens and remembers a dream. Young says he attempts to reproduce the dream's "vibe" with lyrics or music. Young divulged that his song *Silhouette* reflects his frequent nightmares,[655] and that his tune *Metropolis* was inspired directly by a Superman dream, with the lyrics growing from his ensuing contemplations about invincibility versus vulnerability and emotional baggage.[656]

The Muse

British rock band **The Muse**'s song *Micro Cuts* is about singer **Matthew Bellamy**'s dream. Bellamy elaborated, "I was having these strange hallucinations of this triangular blade, really silver metallic, razor sharp. I was in this landscape, arid, gray, dead with an endless horizon and I was trying to dodge these blades that were flying about everywhere. They'd go into my head and I could feel them cutting into my brain …. Then I went to the doctor and he told me to drink more water and that was that."[657]

SilverChair

Australian songwriter **Daniel Johns**, lead singer of the band **SilverChair**, explained that many of the band's song lyrics come from their dreams.[658] Regarding the experience of songwriting, Johns' view echoes Sting's perspective, "It's like the feeling you have when you're falling asleep. That half dream state. It feels, to me, the closest thing to that."[659] His song *Anthem for the Year 2000* was inspired by a very vivid dream where the band was performing at a huge stadium and the public address speaker suddenly blew up, so they got the audience to clap their hands. Johns explained that while the music in the dream inspired the song's musical direction, he already had the intention to write an anthemic song and had lyrics in mind that he then completed and combined with the music he dreamt.[660]

Chapter 13

Lucid Dreaming

"Our truest life is when we are in dreams awake."

–Henry David Thoreau[661]

A lucid dream is one in which the dreamer realizes that she or he is dreaming and is often able to consciously interact with the dream while it happens, like in Director Christopher Nolan's movie *Inception*. Lucid dreaming is also depicted in the story lines of music videos such as **The Dave Matthews Band**'s *Dream Girl* music video starring Julia Roberts[662] where she begins to realize during a dream that she can guide it, and also in **Nothing But Thieves**' *If I Get High* music video where a young man manages to connect with his deceased mother via dreamland.[663] In lucid dreams, it is as though our waking mind enters dreamland in real-time, to different degrees, depending on the dream and the level and type of lucidity. Recall of lucid dreams is usually more vivid, and the resulting dream experience is often much more exciting and powerful, since it generally offers the dreamer the option to consciously interact with and affect aspects of the dream to some extent, if they choose to do so.

Even after having personally experienced well over 1000 lucid dreams and having taught thousands of people how to become lucid and make the most of such experiences, I can say that being lucid in a dream is still an amazing experience with so much potential for many things including fun and adventure, answering questions and solving problems in life, learning new skills, spiritual growth, and of course creative inspiration. Pretty much all the benefits possible from dreams can be enhanced with lucid dreaming, including songwriting, as a student of mine confirms:

"The training program went well beyond intellectual knowledge— a real personal experience of lucid dreaming and Lucid Living— and I wrote a new song in no time."

–Class participant Marc Baltzan, M.D. and musician[664]

Lucid Dreaming Research – Sound & Music

One technique to help induce lucid dreams that was explored during early lucid dream research at Stanford University was to stimulate the dreamer's sleeping mind with auditory cues played while they slept. The cues were intentionally played loud enough to enter the dreamer's awareness, yet ideally not so loud as to awaken the person.

Pioneer lucid dream researcher Stephen LaBerge, who I had the good fortune to work with at Stanford, wrote, "We began our experimentation on cueing lucid dreams with perhaps the most obvious sort of reminder: a tape-recorded message stating 'This is a dream!'" Study participants were good lucid dreamers, so the amount of lucid dreams induced was therefore high. In fifteen trials of playing the recorded message, five lucid dreams resulted, and subjects were simply awakened eight times. Twice the sound bite showed up in the dream, yet was not enough to trigger the dreamer's recognition that they were dreaming.

One non-lucid subject even reported expressing his frustration about someone in the dream who kept bugging him with the phrase 'You're dreaming,' a strong hint which he ignored. Added LaBerge, "From this and our subsequent efforts to stimulate lucid dreams with cues, we concluded that we can help people to realize when they are dreaming by giving them reminders from the outside world. But would-be lucid dreamers must still contribute to the effort by preparing their minds to recognize the cues and remember what they mean."[665]

Lucidity for Comparing Brain Activity in Dreams: Singing vs. Counting

LaBerge also ran a study at Stanford to investigate whether left vs. right brain activation in lucid dreams resembles activation patterns during the same activities performed in waking state. Proficient lucid dreamers were asked to count for 10 seconds and then sing for 10 seconds during a lucid dream. Study results suggest that the related brain activation[xxii] was indeed similar to what would be expected in waking state.[666] Combined with additional studies by LaBerge and others since then, this research suggests that when we dream of performing an activity, our brain and body respond much the same way as if we were doing the same activity in waking life, except for the majority of our muscles, which are in most cases rendered inactive while we dream.

This means that we can learn how to intentionally practise mental and physical skills in dreams and reap the benefit in our lives,

---

[xxii] Left- vs. right-brain alpha activity, which was also shown to be inversely related to cortical activation.

because by using lucid dreaming induction techniques, we can to some degree guide the content of what we dream about, especially when we become more fully lucid (i.e. conscious) in a dream. Such skills can include voice or performance training, learning to master an instrument (like Stevie Ray Vaughan and others), crafting new compositions while in direct contact with the subconscious (like Todd Rundgren), mix and/or produce music (as demonstrated in my lucid dream shared early in this book), and many other such skills and benefits. This by no means limits us from practising such skills in our lives also, but it allows us to spend more time doing so if we wish to, and might offer a particularly opportune realm to quite literally and actively "dream" up creative inspirations in their native environment—the subconscious.

Chapter 14

Lucid Dreamer Musical Artists

"While we sleep here [in physical life], we are awake elsewhere."
–Jorge Luis Borges[667]

Creed

Songwriter and **Creed** lead singer **Scott Stapp** revealed that he wrote the song *Higher* about the powerful potential of lucid dreaming. "You're physically asleep, but you're awake in your mind," Stapp explained. After reading a book about monks who have mastered lucidity techniques, Stapp decided to become conscious and transform a recurring nightmare he had about running down a highway, closely pursued by a man with a gun. Normally he would turn left and hide behind a pillar beneath an overpass yet still get shot anyway. However, once he became lucid in the dream, he changed the ending by turning right and escaping. It was the last time Stapp ever experienced the nightmare, which is common for lucid dreamers who shift the ending of a recurring nightmare into a more empowering outcome, and he credits that cathartic dream experience as his inspiration for *Higher*.[668] Released in 1999, the song was the lead single from Creed's second album and ended up becoming a major breakthrough hit for the band, spending 57 weeks on Billboard's Hot 100 and setting a record (at that time) by holding 17 weeks atop Billboard's Mainstream Rock chart. It was also nominated for Billboard's Top Rock Song and MTV's Best Rock Video Awards.

Queensryche

In 1990, American progressive metal band **Queensryche** released *Silent Lucidity*—a power ballad which hit #1 on Billboard's Album Rock Tracks chart,[669] was nominated for a 1992 Grammy as Best Rock Song, and won MTV's Viewer's Choice Award for best video. "It's about what they call lucid dreaming…learning how to master your dreams…being able to steer and control them," explained Queensryche's primary songwriter **Chris Degarmo**.[670] He elaborated in another interview that, "It's inspired by the experiences that I had…I was lucky to experience lucid dreams, in which you are aware that you're dreaming. That brings a tremendous amount of freedom…you can do the things like fly and walk through walls."[671]

While *Silent Lucidity* was Queensryche's biggest hit, it was not Degarmo's only song inspired by dreams. About his song *Queen of the Reich*, Degarmo explained, "I wrote the lyrics to this song after having a nightmare."[672]

Phish

Mike Gordon, solo artist and bassist for the American rock band

Phish, has kept a dream journal since 1977 detailing the imagery, feelings, sounds, music, and experiences he has while asleep. Gordon shares that he has also "done a lot of lucid dreaming over the years," and credits one of his lucid dreams as the subconscious womb where he conceived the Phish song *Susskind Hotel*.[673] He also describes how some visual artists use lucid dreams as a rather unique subconscious studio of sorts where they create their art while in direct contact with their inner world—and he should know since his mother, Marjorie Minkin, is one such artist.[674]

> *"I dream my painting, and then I paint my dream."*
>
> **–Vincent van Gogh**[675]

Gordon shared that his dream life is "very important,"[676] adding elsewhere that "dreams have acted as my road map through my whole career."[677] He acknowledges that dreams have inspired his music "a bunch of times", including for at least one song on every album he's made, and added that they generally offer insights for lyrics, though sometimes musical guitar licks or simply feelings.[678]

One song created thanks to Gordon's dreams is *Andelman's Yard*, which he composed while experiencing recurring dreams about burrowing tunnels in his childhood neighborhood.[679] "It's always a magical feeling, sort of a peak experience dream," explained Gordon.[680]

Sometimes when jamming really well on stage, dream images and feelings come to Gordon, signaling that he's entered a deeper state in the jam.[681] He seems to remember it being South Carolina where, during the concert jam, he suddenly recalled the previous night's dream of being on a hill in the woods near where he grew up, with rocks and grass and Boston in the distance. Gordon said that the feeling was one of being very nurtured, and he recognized the dream as his recurring Andelman's Yard theme in which the neighbor has extra space in their yard where a network of tunnels weave together underground. He suddenly realized, "This is the dream, the way these notes are winding together is this feeling of being nurtured, nestled, maybe because I'm with the guys I've been with so many years." He continued to explain how the dream's tunnels felt womblike since he was nestled deep in the ground in his childhood hometown.[682]

The way that Gordon spontaneously remembered the dream's images and especially feelings while jamming on stage demonstrates an important universal dream principle that can help everyone interpret dreams by quickly offering more clarity about the life situations that dreams correspond with:

Dreams are often linked with waking events that contain the same feelings.

Gordon also wrote his song *The Party* about a long lucid dream that he "described verbatim in the song." Phish learned the tune for their album *Round Room* but removed it before the final album was cut.[683]

Todd Rundgren

"*I have this tendency to dream songs sometimes completely written...All I had to do was to teach myself to remember them, and get up and write them down.*"–**Todd Rundgren**[684]

Songwriter, musician, and producer/engineer **Todd Rundgren** admits that he dreams many of his songs in their entirety. "I dream that I am in the control room, listening to something on the speakers, and it is this piece of music that I have not written yet." Rundgren shared that the scenario is a common dream for him, so he taught himself how to have enough lucidity to choose to wake himself up and remember much of what he just heard in order to record it. "I don't know whether my subconscious has been working overtime writing these songs without my help and then revealing them to me or whether they're transmitted to me by some kind of muse or angel, or whether there is a difference between the two," said Rundgren. He added that, "they're lucid to the extent that I realize that I'm dreaming and wake myself up to write the song down."[685]

He dreamt his song *Horizon* in its entirety while in Nepal. With no recording devices at his disposal, he decided to memorize the song, and managed to do so well enough to record it a few weeks later "pretty much" as he dreamt it.[686]

Among many other songs in his collection, Rundgren also dreamt *Bang The Drum*, a long-time radio favorite which is also featured in DreamWorks' animated movies Shrek (VHS opening), Prince of Egypt (VHS opening), and Antz (trailer), and is played in Lambeau Field after the Green Bay Packers football team scores a touchdown.[687]

Scott Mathews, who first worked with Rundgren on the latter's song *Parallel Lines*, remembers Rundgren telling him that the song "was fully retained from his dream—chords, melody, lyrics, structure, instrumentation."[688]

Prince

Revered singer-songwriter and master guitarist **Prince** divulged that he really enjoyed lucid dreams where he would speak with deceased colleagues and friends, including dream-inspired artist David Bowie.[689]

SOJA

Reggae band **SOJA**'s song *Lucid Dreams* is about lead singer **Jacob Hemphill**'s daytime nap dreams that he guides consciously, and which often bring insight about his night dreams.[690]

~~~

In the Electronic and Ambient Musical Artists chapter, you will find various electronic, avant-garde, and ambient music composers who also use lucid dreams for composing.

Chapter 15

Dreamland Music for "Public Dream" Soundtracks

Movies could be described as 'public dreams' since many people can experience them. Interestingly, the technology that makes movies possible was likely helped to fruition by the "flow of new ideas" that inventor **Thomas Edison** would have "on waking" thanks to intentional naps he frequently took while at work.[691] Edison developed the kinetoscope (which led to the movie projector), the kinetograph (which became the movie camera), and the kinetophone (which linked recorded sound with the kinetoscope's projected image to create movies).

"Movies are like dreams in the middle of the day."

–**Hugo** (from the movie *Hugo*)[692]

Not only are a number of movie plots and TV shows dream-inspired, such as *Avatar*,[693] *The Terminator*,[694] the *Twilight*[695] movie series, ABC's *Extreme Makeover*[696] and various others, but dreams have delivered music that has entered various film, TV, and computer gaming soundtracks as well.

Soundtrack Composer Howard Shore

"You want to get into the subconscious…and then you will get into the subconscious of the audience." –**Howard Shore**[697]

Canadian soundtrack and classical composer **Howard Shore** has scored over 80 films, including The Lord of The Rings Trilogy and The Hobbit, and has won three Academy Awards.

Shore shared that his score for the 1988 film *Dead Ringers* came "all from a dream." He is convinced of the value of dreams for songwriting, and intentionally takes a lot of naps.[698]

TV Host & Songwriter Steve Allen

American TV personality and prolific songwriter **Steve Allen**'s best-known hit *This Could Be the Start of Something Big* was conceived in a dream. Written in 1954 for the (original) TV production called The Bachelor, it then became the opening theme for The Tonight Show and was described by Allen as "the most commercially successful" song he ever wrote. That gives his dream inspiration an impressive top position, since Allen was an extremely prolific professional songwriter who wrote over 4000 songs! Allen tells the story, "I awakened from my sleep having just dreamed that catchy melody and four or five lines of lyrics…I went to the piano and played the tune." He explained that the song's central idea was "all there" in his dream, and that he completed it after waking.[699]

Allen also revealed that some of the nineteen songs he wrote for Irwin Allen's TV mini-series *Alice in Wonderland* came to him while he was asleep. He added, "That's happened to me all my life…I often hear music in dreams."[700]

Another of his songs, *I Had a Dream Last Night About My Old Piano*, as suggested by the title, came to the composer in the same manner.[701]

Mac Davis

To kick off a long and successful country music artist career which included a gold record and being named the Academy of Country Music's 1974 *Entertainer of the Year,* American singer-songwriter and TV personality **Mac Davis** wrote songs for Elvis. Davis later hosted *The Mac Davis Show*, a variety show on NBC. The inspiration for his fourth yuletide TV special, a musical titled *A Mac Davis Special—Christmas Odyssey: 2010*, "actually came from a dream I had about Christmas," said Davis. "I dreamed that it had become commercial and all of its real meaning was gone." Davis' dream seems to offer a foretelling hint about commercial trends associated with the Christmas holidays today. The show centered around the dream's theme, airing on NBC on December 19, 1978,[702] and starred Davis alongside well-known entertainers of the era: Bernadette Peters, Paul Lynde, and Ted Knight.[703]

Computer Gaming Composer Yasunori Mitsuda

Japanese computer gaming soundtrack composer **Yasunori Mitsuda** described how he often receives inspiration for his music in dreams and sleeps in his studio while leaving all his recording equipment on so he is able to capture and develop his dream melodies immediately upon awakening. Compositions inspired by his dreams include *Bonds of Sea and Fire* from the game *Xenogears*, and the ending theme *To Far Away Times* for the *Chrono Trigger* game soundtrack[704] which brought him to tears when he first saw it incorporated into the game. The *Chrono Trigger* soundtrack was Mitsuda's first composing project, yet he feels that it not only helped mature his composing talents,[705] it also significantly affected his career and his life.[706] The piece was first performed live by the Tokyo Symphony Orchestra in 1996, and has since been performed on numerous occasions internationally as well as included in various soundtrack albums.[707]

Chapter 16

Dreaming Instrumentalists, Conductors, Librettists, Hosts & Producers

'*Volare*' – Italian Dream Duo Fly to Stardom

On a warm Sunday in July 1957, Italian artist and actor **Franco Migliacci** fell asleep at home after a few glasses of Chianti wine[708] that he enjoyed while admiring prints of works by Russian-French painter Marc Chagall. Migliacci had been awaiting his friend **Domenico Modugno** for a trip to the seashore. Modugno showed up late, which in retrospect seems fortuitous. Either dreaming or in an altered state on the edge of waking, Migliacci saw the paintings with distortions; in Chagall's 'Le Coq Rouge' ('The Red Rooster') he saw a yellow man floating in the air, and in Chagall's 'Le peintre et le modèle' ('The painter and the model') he noticed that half of the painter's face was blue. Migliacci had combined the two dreamy inconsistencies and started crafting lyrics about a man painting himself blue and flying. He excitedly shared them with his friend after Modugno finally arrived. The duo decided to drop their seashore trip, and together composed during the next few days their hit *Nel Blu, Dipinto Di Blu* (*In the Sky, Painted Blue*), also often known as *Volare* (*To fly*).[709] Shortly after Migliacci turned 28,[xxiii] the song placed at #1 on Billboard's Hot 100 for five non-consecutive weeks in late 1958 and became Billboard's #1 single that year. Out of three Grammy nominations at the first Annual Grammy Awards show, it also won the first-ever Grammys awarded for Record of the Year and Song of the Year, beating out nominee favorites Frank Sinatra, Perry Como, Peggy Lee, and others in both categories.[710] The song has since been covered by scores of musicians internationally, including The Gypsys Kings as well as dream-inspired artists Paul McCartney, David Bowie, and Louis Armstrong.

Louis Armstrong

While touring the Dakotas in the winter of 1947, American trumpeter, singer, composer, and jazz music icon **Louis 'Satchmo' Armstrong** reeled in a dream that became his song *Someday You'll Be Sorry*. "This thing kept runnin' 'cross my mind, like dreamin' a musical comedy. And this 'Someday' was the theme of this show," recounted Armstrong. "We was asleep...But I got up in my pajamas and got me a piece of paper and pencil out. I say, 'I'm gonna lose it if I don't write it down'...the next day I had it, and we looked at it...and everybody liked the tune."[711]

[xxiii] Another example of the important 7-year cycle (i.e. 4 x 7 = 28) shown elsewhere in this book.

Chick Corea

With twenty-eight Grammy wins and seventy-five nominations, it is perhaps not surprising that virtuoso pianist and composer **Chick Corea** confided that he has, like so many other artists, gotten inspiration for his music in dreams. "I found myself waking up in the middle of the night with a complete song in my head," reported Corea. He continued that he awoke and "wrote it down at the piano", and then "touched it up the next morning". He emphasized how the tune that arrived to him via special delivery from the subconscious was a "very pretty, emotional melody...every time I play it I get teary-eyed."[712]

Music Dream Comes Calling for Lightning-Strike Survivor

Orthopedic surgeon **Tony Cicoria** had no skill nor special interest in music beyond sometimes listening to rock and roll...until he was hit by a bolt of lightning[713] in August 1994 at age 42.[xxiv] He had just gotten off a call on a public phone when the lightning struck him in the face. He went into cardiac arrest, and had the experience of floating above his body, being surrounded by a blue and white light, and feeling a profound sense of peace and well-being.

As Life would have it, the person in line behind him waiting to use the phone was an intensive-care-unit nurse who soon resuscitated Cicoria using CPR.[714] Other than burns on his face and left foot (where the lightning had entered and exited his body), and a bit of sluggishness and slight memory difficulty which doctors investigated without finding anything unusual, his

---

[xxiv] Another instance of the 7-year principle (i.e. 42 = 6 x 7)

life returned mostly back to normal. A few weeks after the medical tests, the memory problems and sluggishness disappeared, he suddenly started longing to hear piano music, and before long felt an urge to play and then to compose for piano. Cicoria revealed that it was a dream that sparked what he describes as his new "insatiable passion" for piano. "The first time was in a dream. I was in a tux, onstage, playing something I'd written," recounted Cicoria.[715] "So I listened to the music… and it had a loud ending, and it was rather abrupt, and it woke me up. It was 3:15 in the morning, and I went to the piano to try to plunk out some tones that I recognized, but I had no idea how to write, and no idea how to really play, so I went back to bed.

"The next day when I got up to practise, and from that moment on whenever I sat down at the piano, the music would start to play [in my head], and it would play exactly the way I heard it in the dream." In life, Cicoria had never previously tried to write music. However the piano piece "became like a little two-year-old who's very incessant, and if I didn't sit down at the piano and try to do something with this music, it would interfere in my regular activities—I'd start to hear it when I was trying to work, or trying to do something else." So over the following days and months, he sat at the piano "every day", and slowly notated the piece in his own short hand "that didn't really look like music but it at least had the ideas down, and I threw them in a drawer thinking someday I'll do something with this." A few years later, he found a teacher to help him properly write out what became his composition *Lightning Sonata*.[716]

Cicoria is now an accomplished pianist and performs both well-known and original compositions (including his *Lightning Sonata*), sometimes to sellout audiences.

In dreams, the face is a universal symbol for our identity (i.e. generally how people recognize each other), feet are linked with the life and career path we walk, and the left side of the body is generally associated with our creative/intuitive side. I bring this up here, because life can be interpreted as a dream, which is one of the practices of the Lucid Living approach that I developed and teach. In that framework, the body can act as one of our strongest universal symbols. If Cicoria's experience is viewed as a dream, it would make symbolic sense that a strong surge of new energy (symbolized by the lightning) entered into his identity (symbolized by his face). It also fits that such energy could manifest (lightning exiting into the ground) a corresponding life/career path change (symbolized by his foot) that would integrate more intuition and creativity (symbolized by the fact that it exited his *left* foot). The symbolic perspective on the lightning strike event mirrors what indeed happened in his life as the dream of piano music flooded into his heart and mind, and then out into his life as his new passion and creative outlet.

As a tracker of synchronicity and 'sound symbolism' associations such as homonyms, I can't help but notice that Cicoria's surname is a direct sound match for just previously mentioned pianist Chick Corea's full name, and that both men just so happen to be dream-inspired piano composer-instrumentalists.

"They who dream by day are cognizant of many things which escape those who dream only by night." –**Edgar Allan Poe**[717]

Béla Fleck and the Flecktones – Dreamtime Teamwork

American banjo player, arranger, and thirteen-time Grammy winner **Béla Fleck** reported that the song *P'lod*, recorded by his bluegrass/jazz/fusion instrumental group **Béla Fleck and the Flecktones**, originated in a dream of their percussion player

Future Man who explained that the band's saxophone player **Jeff Coffin** taught it to him during the dream.[718] The song appeared on the group's 11th album *Hidden Land*, helping the group to win the 2006 Grammy for Best Contemporary Jazz Album.[719]

Guitar Slim with Ray Charles as Producer

Guitar Slim revealed that the biggest hit of his career, *The Things That I Used to Do,* came in a dream where the devil auditioned it for him, reminiscent of Giuseppi Tartini's dream where the devil also performed what became his most known composition.[720] Twenty-three-year-old **Ray Charles** arranged and produced the song, which held the #1 spot for 6 of the 22 weeks that it spent on Billboard's R&B charts. The album became the best-selling R&B album of 1954 with over a million copies sold,[721] and the song was inducted into the Rock and Roll Hall of Fame as one of the 500 songs that shaped rock and roll.[722]

A Dream Arranged Success for The Flamingos

Properly arranging a song is usually key for its success, and is the way dreams helped 1950s doo-wopp vocal group **The Flamingos** land their biggest hit, a cover of the 1934 classic *I Only Have Eyes For You.* Tenor singer and guitarist **Terry Johnson** had been trying to come up with an arrangement all day, and had even explored ideas on his guitar in bed before sleep. "I had the guitar on my chest, and I fell asleep." recounted Johnson. "I heard the song in my dream. I heard it just as you hear it now, with the 'doo-wop-she-bops' and the beautiful harmonies and the chord structure."[723] The song was inducted into the Grammy Hall of Fame in 2003, and its success played an important roll in the group being inducted into the Vocal Group Hall of Fame in 2000, the Rock and Roll Hall of Fame in 2001, and the Doo-Wopp Hall of Fame in 2004.

Dream Lands Hollywood Singer Role

1930s singer **Rowene Williams** claimed that she always followed her dreams and hunches, and reported that a dream specified the 3 songs to sing that helped her beat out twenty thousand other girls in a 1934 nationwide contest, thereby landing her a lead vocalist role on CBS' **Hollywood Hotel** radio series opposite actor Dick Powell.[724] The show was the first major network show to broadcast from the West Coast.[725]

Multi-Instrumentalist Rahsaan Roland Kirk

American jazz multi-instrumentalist **Rahsaan Roland Kirk** was twice inspired to change his name due to dreams. A first dream motivated Kirk to swap two letters of his birth name 'Ronald'.[726] In 1970, another dream inspired him to add 'Rahsaan' to the beginning of his name.[727]

"I constantly think about music," Kirk revealed in 1963. "When I go to sleep, I actually dream about music and hear things which I try to play during my waking hours."[728]

Kirk was perhaps best known for his amazing ability to play multiple wind instruments at the same time. Perhaps this is partly why he was one of Jimi Hendrix's musical heroes[729] and highly-respected by various other well-known artists. One such artist is saxophonist Jeff Coffin from the Grammy-winning and dream-inspired group Béla Fleck and the Flecktones. Coffin also learned to play two saxophones simultaneously, a skill for which he offers "a nod to the late great saxophonist Rahsaan Roland Kirk."[730] The spark for Kirk's then-original talent came, as you might guess, in a dream. Kirk became blind at age 2 as the result of a poorly done medical treatment, but the challenge did not stop his dreams. When he was about 23,[731] Kirk dreamt of playing his tenor sax, his recently acquired and customized saxello (a 'manzello'), and his straight alto sax (a 'stritch') all at the same time. Not only did he soon learn the avant-garde dream skill, he also self-taught himself circular breathing to be able to hold long notes. During the rest of his life, Kirk expanded this special talent of simultaneously performing on multiple instruments to include other instrument variations.[732]

Multi-Instrumentalist Taj Mahal

During his 50-year musical career, American blues artist and multi-instrumentalist **Taj Mahal** has been nominated for nine Grammys and won twice, both times for Best Blues Album. The legendary singer-songwriter shared that his stage name came to him in dreams he had over a period of time from childhood to his late teens[733] about Gandhi, India, and social tolerance.[734]

John McLaughlin – Dreamt Track List and Liner Notes

Composer and Grammy-winning guitarist **John McLaughlin** revealed that the track list and description for his album *To the One* arrived in a dream in October 2010—a year during which he had no intention of recording anything new. "The liner notes and track titles came to me as a kind of dictation," recalled

McLaughlin. "I had to get up in the middle of the night and write everything down." McLaughlin added that "only after seeing the notes in the morning" did he realize the impact of the dream, and came to realize that it was calling him and his band **4th Dimension** to record an album about experiences he'd had in music and in his inner life since 1965, when he first heard John Coltraine's album 'A Love Supreme'.[735] In 2011, *To the One* received a Grammy nomination for the Best Contemporary Jazz Album.

Conductor David Blum

Writer and widely-traveled and respected orchestra conductor **David Blum** sketched many of his dreams with pastels and found therein powerful spiritual insight and growth, especially during his challenging two-year journey with cancer that is beautifully depicted in the excellent documentary film *Appointment with the Wise Old Dog*.[736] One example of a musical dream that came during his struggle with cancer was a dream where Mozart's Clarinet Concerto was playing too quickly. As a conductor, the symbolism of an overly fast musical tempo brought Blum the important insight that he needed to conduct his own life more slowly.[737]

The Famous People Players & Liberace

The **Famous People Players** is a black light puppetry theater company that tours internationally and employs people with physical and intellectual disabilities. The non-profit organization was founded by Canadian **Diane Dupuy** after she dreamt that if she started it, Liberace would discover it.[738] Dupuy actively wrote letters to Liberace who finally saw the group perform their original piece *Aruba Liberace.* The famous pianist was so enthusiastic that he brought them to Las Vegas in 1975 and included them as part of his show. For ten years the troupe performed with Liberace both in Las Vegas and internationally, and now has a large repertoire of productions.[739]

Radio/TV Host Michelle Dawn Mooney

Radio host and former NBC TV news anchor **Michelle Dawn Mooney** told me on-air during a radio interview where I was an invited guest expert on dreams, that she sometimes researches her shows ahead of time—in dreams. "I've actually booked guests in my dreams," admitted Mooney, adding that she writes the dreams down so as not to forget practical insights like "I want to have so and so on because I remember booking them in my dream."[740]

Producer Stephen Powers

Grammy-winning music producer **Stephen Powers** says a dream guided him to take a job as Director of Agape Media International. The dream was strongly confirmed hours later when he received a spontaneous morning email from Agape's choir director, Rickie Byars. Although the two had not communicated for some time, the dream, followed by her email right after it, heartily encouraged him to take on the role.[741]

Music Executive Russ Regan

The musical recordings that veteran music executive **Russ Regan** has been involved with have collectively sold over 1 billion copies worldwide. While president of 20th Century Records, a dream spurred Regan to make the cult movie *All This and World War II* in which WWII Fox News Footage was scored with a soundtrack of numerous superstar artists singing Beatles' tunes. Unfortunately, the project was never released and still resides in the 20th Century Fox vaults.[742]

Multi-Instrumentalist John Zorn

While working on his album *The Big Gundown: John Zorn Plays the Music of Ennio Morricone*, arranger and multi-instrumentalist **John Zorn** experienced "the first dream in his life that was pure music." Zorn awoke in the middle of the night and wrote down the music he had just dreamt. The music was so striking that it motivated Zorn not only to change the arrangement he soon planned to record for Morricone's *The Big Gundown* soundtrack, but also to highlight the dream muse's gift by making that track both the title and lead track so that the dreamt music became the introduction for the entire album.[743]

The album was a career breakthrough for Zorn, and its 15th anniversary edition was endorsed by the famed soundtrack composer, Ennio Morricone, who commented, "This is a record that has fresh, good, and intelligent ideas. It is realization on a high level, a work done by a maestro with great science-fantasy and creativity…Many people have done versions of my pieces, but no one has done them like this."[744]

Chapter 17

Electronic & Avant-Garde Artists: Soundscapes from the Subconscious

Brian Eno

Ambient music composer **Brian Eno** has also produced bands such as The Talking Heads and dream-inspired artists U2 and David Bowie. Eno claims that his composition *On Some Faraway Beach*, was inspired by dreams. All the dreamt words that he incorporated into the composition, he explained, were initially scribbled in the dark right when he woke up. Regarding composing using dreams as inspiration, Eno added, "you don't feel any responsibility for what you do, which is important to me."[745]

Robert Rich

Another electronic/ambient music composer and performer of note is lucid dreamer **Robert Rich,** who has not only used dreams to inspire his music, but also holds overnight 'sleep concerts' to enhance and induce altered states in the audience. Rich suggests the concerts may be akin to a modern version of extended shamanic rituals found in other cultures. During the night, he subtly weaves pre-recorded ambient clips with live keyboards, guitar, flute, and sometimes other instruments creating slowly changing soundscapes to encourage what he calls "activated sleep". Audience feedback suggests that the concert setting and music affect not just the more commonly known REM-period 'sleep stage 1' dreams, but also and perhaps even more so, other sleep states such as the hypnagogic and hypnopompic dreaming states that occur on the border of falling asleep and awakening, respectively.[746]

Rich helped with the Stanford University pioneering lucid dream research led by scientist Dr. Stephen LaBerge. I also had the good fortune to be part of the Stanford research and work with these two pioneers.

As an undergrad in 1985, Rich had a powerful lucid dream: "In the dream, I was at the venue Shared Visions in Berkeley where I had given sleep concerts, and I was sitting in a circle with 8 or 9 others discussing dreams and shamanism. We were showing each other paintings, and one of the paintings was a landscape by [the artist] Monty Klarwein [depicting the nearby] Santa Cruz Mountains. I suddenly realized I was dreaming and at that moment, I felt a shove from behind and I fell forward and flew right into the painting. Knowing that it's a dream, I find myself flying over the Santa Cruz mountains right by the coast. I feel this ecstatic, tearfully energized state of being where I'm feeling the ecstasy of the land coming up towards me—the plants, the chaparral, the hills. There's a knowing in the land when we live here, when we have our feet in the soil—it was talking to me, and I was hearing music. This music was floating clouds of air, tuned air. That lasted for maybe 20 seconds... absolute ecstatic feeling. I woke up and that sound was indelibly etched into me." Rich crafted the experience into his composition *The Walled Garden* on his album *Numena*.[747]

Aphex Twin

Irish-born composer and electronic musician **Richard David James**, more widely known by his stage name **Aphex Twin**, has been described by UK's *The Guardian* as "the most inventive and influential figure in contemporary electronic music."[748] James says that all the music on his 1994 album *Selected Ambient Works Volume II* was inspired directly or influenced by lucid dreams.[749] James has also drawn inspiration from dream-inspired colleague Brian Eno, and explains that right after waking, he tries to create music that captures the sounds he's just heard in dreams.[750]

Karlheinz Stockhausen

Avant-garde, experimental electronic music composer **Karlheinz Stockhausen** experienced flying dreams throughout his life. In 1991, Professor Hans Landesmann of the Salzburg Festival commissioned Stockhausen to compose a string quartet.[751] Stockhausen was originally not interested to write the piece, but then he dreamt he was flying above four helicopters, each carrying a member of a string quartet. In the dream, he could see into and through the transparent helicopters.[752] Stockhausen elaborated, "In the dream, I saw the musicians playing—and in my mind as though with multiple vision—I could keep them all in view at the same time even though they were in different helicopters."[753]

Inspired by the dream, Stockhausen made sketches and plans, and then in 1992-93 he composed and finished the piece.[754] By this time, he had also experienced several more dreams related to the composition including one about a swarm of bees and a violinist, about which Stockhausen commented, "The buzzing made by lots of bees is a magic sound to me."[755]

The composition and performance piece *Helikopter-Streichquartett* (*Helicopter String Quartet*) became the third scene of his opera *Mittwoch aus Licht* (*Wednesday from Light*), though it has also been performed independently from the opera. For the performance, a string quartet separates into four helicopters flying independent flight paths over the countryside near a concert hall. Each in their respective helicopters, the players listen through headphones to a specialized 'click track' that keeps them all synchronized but which the audience doesn't hear. Their playing is then mixed together along with the sounds of the helicopters, much like the sound in Stockhausen's dream of a violinist and a swarm of buzzing bees. The result is played through speakers to the live audience in the concert hall, along with real-time streamed videos of the four performers.[756]

Stockhausen's 1971 musical theater composition *Trans* is also the embodiment of a dream.[757] On the morning of December 10th, 1970, he jotted down this dream: "Dreamt orchestral work…orchestra sits in series…sound wall opens with different intervals at periods of about twenty seconds, allowing music behind this wall to come through—brass and woodwinds mixed— and I hear low instruments that are the fundamentals; in timbres they're colored like organ mixtures. With each low melodic line of one of the lower instruments there are several instruments in parallel, playing softer and coloring this low sound…at the same time I hear the sound of a weaving chair."[758]

Music in the Belly is another dream-inspired piece by Stockhausen. When his daughter Julika was 2 years old, he joked with her that she had music in her belly because her stomach was making strange gurgling sounds. She started laughing about the idea, and her laughter escalated to the point where she began to choke. Eventually, he got her to stop laughing by crying her name repeatedly at her and carrying her to her room. The event made an emotional mark on Stockhausen, because he dreamt of pulling three music boxes out of the belly of a man with the head of a bird that he called Miron. The dream inspired Stockhausen to research music boxes for a week, and he learned that no original music had ever been composed for them, which was surely an exciting discovery for a composer who liked to create avant-garde works. Stockhausen took his recorded dream imagery and music box motifs from the dream and crafted them into his 1975 musical theater composition *Music in the Belly*.[759] In the play, Miron is attacked by three automatons that cut open his belly and find three music boxes. A short while later, Stockhausen also created nine more music box melodies to combine with the three from the dream, and the collection of songs became *Tierkreis*, a composition originally written mostly for music boxes (along with some percussion) which has become one of his most widely known and performed works.

On an interesting related note, curator **Claudia Gould** dreamt about creating an art installation of music boxes. *The Music Box Project* included electroacoustic music from composer and pioneer **John Cage,** as well as other artists, and took eight years to complete before it went on exhibit at The Equitable Gallery in December 1994.[760]

György Ligeti

In 1923, classical and electronic composer **György Ligeti** was born in Transylvania, Romania, also the fictional birthplace of Dracula, so it is interesting that when Ligeti was just a boy, he experienced a terrifying nightmare that stuck with him much of his life. "I dreamt that I couldn't find a way to my cot, my safe haven, because the whole room was filled up with a dense, confused tangle of fine filaments," recounted Ligeti. "It looked like the web I had seen silkworms fill their box with as they change into pupas. I was caught up in the immense web together with both living things and objects—huge moths and beetles of every kind trying to reach the flickering flame of a candle." Ligeti also remembered other disgusting images such as huge dirty pillows with their rotten filling falling out through cuts in their coverings, mucus balls, food gone cold, and other "revolting rubbish". Each struggle of the entangled creatures reverberated throughout the dense web, but although a few occasionally got free, they would soon get caught again and their buzzing would slowly fade. Ligeti elaborated that "an indescribable sadness hung over these shifting forms and structures, the hopelessness of passing time and the melancholy of unalterable past events."[761]

This upsetting nightmare remained clear to Ligeti even as an adult, so in 1961 he drew upon its haunting images, sounds and feeling to create his eerie-sounding composition *Atmosphères* which was featured 7-years later on the soundtrack of Stanley Kubrick's 1968 blockbuster film *2001: A Space Odyssey*.

Kaija Saariaho

Contemporary Finnish composer **Kaija Saariaho** used dream research about how sleeping body movements affect or interrupt dreams as the inspiration for her electronic music composition *La Grammaire des Rêves*[762] (*The Grammar of Dreams*). The piece incorporates upper range voices, 2 flutes, harp, viola and cello, and poetic texts from surrealism co-founder poet Paul Éluard. That the composition includes surrealistic poems is very appropriate since the aim of the entire surrealist movement was to "resolve the previously contradictory conditions of dream and reality into an absolute reality, a super-reality."[763]

Current 93/David Tibet

Electronic music artist **David Tibet** of **Current 93** often has dreams that inspire his lyrics. For his album *Black Ships Ate the Sky*, Tibet said the album title came to him first as a phrase and that he then "started having a lot of very intense dreams and a lot of text would come in."[764]

Current 93 has also written songs "based on the idea of the lands where dreams went when they died" including *The Dreammoves of the Sleeping King* and another piece on the band's *In Menstrual Night* album.[765]

Wendy Mae Chambers

Avant-garde composer **Wendy Mae Chambers** first gained public attention for her work *Music for Choreographed Rowboats*, where 16 musicians performed the score in rowboats as the Columbia University crew team rowed them around New York's Central Park Lake. Chambers inspiration for the performance was a dream she had with "tubas as passengers in pedal boats." The only boats on Central Park's lake were rowboats so she adjusted the choreography accordingly.[766]

Her piece *The Car Horn Organ*, along with the musical instrument invention she created, was also born in a 1983 dream where she heard "an incredible symphony with these massive

beautiful chords, totally sustained and shifting into other chords."
When she woke she realized the dream music was actually an
auditory incorporation into her dream of real car horns in a nearby
traffic jam on New York's Brooklyn-Queens Expressway.[767]
Being an avant-garde artist, she contemplated the dream and
decided to create an organ made out of 25 car horns from General
Motors, Fiat, Datsun, Volkswagen, a Cadillac C-trumpet, and an
"ahooogah" horn. The unique invention was christened as an
instrument and first put into service in a parking lot performance
of The Star Spangled Banner and New York, New York. It was
later featured on NBC's 'Live at Five', Fox TV's 'Good Morning
NY', 'The Tonight Show with Jay Leno', in the April 1999 issue of
Smithsonian Magazine, and numerous other media.[768]

Snake of Deep Waters is another composition sparked by one of
Chambers' dreams in which she heard music, apparently written
by someone else, and was asked what she thought about it.
"Static," she replied in the dream, "and somnambulistic."[769]

Chapter 18

Other Artists Inspired by the Dream Muse

There exist many more tales of dream-inspired musical creations and professional decisions than I have room to include in this book, however here is a brief mention of a few other songs, titles, names, and music business choices that are based on dreams:

- **Little Richard**, American singer and musician and one of the pioneers of rock and roll with a career spanning six decades, actually took a seven-year[xxv] hiatus from his rock and roll career after a dream motivated him to do so.[770] During that time, he became an ordained minister.

- Country singer-songwriter **LeAnn Rimes** has won numerous awards, including 2 Grammys, and was ranked #17 on Billboard's top artists of 1990-2000. Rimes shared that she received her track and album title *Spitfire* in a dream.[771]

- Scottish historical folk-rock singer-songwriter and guitarist **Al Stewart** dreamt the chorus to his song *Post World War Two Blues*.[772]

[xxv] Another example of the important seven-year life and career cycle.

- Canadian singer-songwriter **Michael Bublé** reported that the inspiration for one of his hits (most likely his song "Home", according to radio host Neil Hedley) came to him all of a sudden in the shower right after waking.[773]

- Country singer-songwriter **Cam**'s hit *Burning House* is about a very emotional "big dream" where she rescued a former boyfriend from a house on fire.[774]

- Latin-jazz percussionist and songwriter **Bobby Matos**, whose musical career spans more than five decades, credited a dream for bringing the melody of his "swinging mambo jazz" piece *Early Morning Song*.[775]

- **Metallica** bassist **Robert Trujillo** awoke at 4 a.m. from a dream that offered him the concept for the animated short, music-related film *Tallica Parking Lot*.[776]

- Singer-songwriter and guitarist **Pete Yorn**'s song *Break Up*, a duet with well-known actor **Scarlett Johannsen**, arrived in a dream. After an unusual week of insomnia, said Yorn, "I finally passed out and it came to me in a dream. I woke up and the whole thing was in my head, fully formed."[777]

- Two-time winner of ASCAP's Top Television Composer and two-time Grammy-nominated feisty indie rock artist **Liz Phair** literally dreamt up the title for her 1998 album whitechocolatespaceegg (#35) while she was pregnant with her son.[778]

- Multi-platinum, Grammy-nominated songwriter **Shelly Peiken**, who has composed two #1 hits in the U.S. (*What A Girl Wants* and *Come On Over Baby* performed by Christina Aguilera), has also written a (currently) unreleased song that she received in a dream.[779]

- American singer-songwriter **Vanessa Carlton** harvested her album title *Be Not Nobody* from a dream.[780]

- On season 10 of NBC's nationwide talent TV show *The Voice*, star coach Christina Aguilera turned around to accept 18-year-old contestant **Lacy Mandigo** only as Mandigo sang her audition song's last note – exactly as Mandigo had dreamt would happen. "I had a dream last night that you turned around for me," the ecstatic Mandigo told Aguilera, "and it was on the last note."[781]

- On TVA's *La Voix Junior* (the French-Canadian version of *The Voice* for young artists), 14-year-old singer **Laurie Pouliot** told judges right after her blind audition cover of Adele's *Remedy* that she had a dream the week before where celebrity coaches Alex Nevsky and Marc Dupré turned around. Just like in the dream, they two men did turn their chairs, and the 3rd coach Marie-Mai did not.[782] During blind auditions the following week, 12-year-old **Arina Mireille** sang a beautiful version of Edith Piaf's *La Vie en Rose*, and all three coaches turned around their chairs with the hope of having the young singer join their team. In discussing her performance, she also told the judges that she had a recent dream, where she saw all three of them turn around.[783]

- **Shirley Lawrence** was a soprano singer hoping to meet a baritone "man of her dreams". She had a lucid dream in which a princess sat on a float in a pond in a lush woods as a hand maiden brushed her hair. Suddenly, a beautiful baritone voice resounded from the woods singing "you are my music" (and other lyrics), and the princess soon saw that the voice belonged to a handsome prince who emerged from the woods on a white horse. The two then joined in a sweet duet. The dreamer loved the words and music, and being lucid, she asked the dream to please let her remember the lyrics and melody so she could record them when she awoke. The song then repeated within the dream, and Shirley did indeed remember the tune clearly upon waking and recorded it. She entered the recording in a composer's contest and won first place as a ballad. Shortly thereafter, she met Jeff Lawrence—apparently a precognitive dream and surrealistic fairy tale come true, since Lawrence had the same baritone voice that Shirley heard in the dream. The two married and sang the duet from the dream "in a contest of winning numbers", and then performed together across California for about nine years. In 2016, the dream-depicted duo celebrated their 50th wedding anniversary.[784]

- Soul and gospel singer-songwriter **Rickie Byars** harvests dreams to write her songs.[785]

- Singer-songwriter and guitarist **Bill Callahan** transformed a "horror movie" type of nightmare about flying a plane and looking down at the ground into the lyrics for his song *Small Plane* from his album *Dream River*[786] which was featured in FOX's TV series 'Backstrom'.[787]

- Nashville songwriter **Jim Owen** researched the life and music of country legend Hank Williams for 23 years. He also toured doing a one-man road show about Williams' life. "The idea came from a dream my wife had," recounted Owen. "She dreamed I was at the Grand Ole Opry singing in Hank's voice. It never left my mind."[788]

- In the mid 1990s, folk singer-songwriter **Dave Carter** started dreaming song hooks and melodies and incorporating the dreams into his compositions. As a computer programmer, he also had and followed a mystical vision that encouraged him "chuck everything and devote himself to music."[789]

- British singer-songwriter **Richard Hawley** shared that a slew of songs from his 2001 *Late Night Final* album were harvested from dreamland. Around the time blues singer-songwriter John Lee Hooker died, Hooker appeared in Hawley's dream with a black raven on his arm and it inspired Hawley's song *Long Black Train*. Another dream about astronaut Neil Armstrong sparked *Cry a Tear For The Man on The Moon* from the same album.[790]

- American contemporary composer **Edgar Stillman Kelley**, who taught music at Yale and in Berlin, reported that he was having trouble creating a good motif for the galloping horses of a composition he wrote for a production of Shakespeare's *Macbeth*. Kelley recalled that nothing he could come up with seemed fitting for storm-hoofed chargers until a dream brought him a subconscious inspiration for the theme. Kelley also claimed that other creative ideas had come to him during sleep in the same way, including a German poem and music to accompany it.[791]

- Contemporary composer **Daniel S. Godfrey** claims to have received the solution to a composition problem while he slept.[792]

- Inspired by a dream of his parents dancing, contemporary composer **Bruce Adolphe** created the musical work *Dream Dance*.[793]

- **The Fleshtones** lead singer **Peter Zaremba** credits a dream for the band's song *Hipster Heaven*. In his dream, the group was performing atop a colorful "Magic Bus" in a field, and laughing like crazy. He awoke laughing.[794]

- Sir Paul McCartney apparently inspired songwriter **Jake Shears** of **Scissor Sisters**, appearing in one of his dreams to discuss songwriting. The dream inspired Shears appropriately titled song, *Paul McCartney*.[795]

- Modern rockabilly-punk singer-songwriter-guitarist Jim Heath, a.k.a. **Reverend Horton Heat** leapt up from bed to write his cult hit *Show Business* exactly as he heard it in a dream.[796]

- French singer-songwriter **Melody Prochet** got the title of her band and debut album *Melody's Echo Chamber* from a dream. "I had a dream in which my bedroom's acoustics changed into infinite echo mode," said Prochet, quite amused. "When I talked, my voice resounded endlessly. It woke me up."[797]

- Harpist and singer-composer **Maryse Thuot** had her entire musical path sparked at age 23 by a "vibrant and real" visionary dream where she saw herself playing a beautiful harp in a celestial setting while hundreds of tiny, peaceful snakes gracefully slithered around her and gently weaved between the harp strings. Later the same day, she happened across an ad offering harp lessons. Because of the dream, she decided to go for a lesson, even though she had never previously considered playing harp. The following day, she touched a harp for the first time, and that night, the exact same dream of little snakes recurred. She interpreted the returning dream as guidance, so she continued harp lessons. For three decades, she has shared original harp melodies and world music internationally.[798]

- Canadian fiddle player **Émile Benoît**, who wrote over 200 songs, awoke in the middle of the night from a dream which felt so important that he promptly phoned his sister and asked her to record through the line as he played a fiddle piece he had just heard in a dream. The melody became his aptly-titled *Emile's Dream.*[799]

- "I often hear music in my sleep," reported pianist **Yelena Eckemoff**, whose musical dreams sometimes motivated her to get up and write them down, because on other occasions where she tried to memorize just-dreamt music while staying in bed, it had vanished by morning. Eckemoff explained that the inspiration for her piece *Quasi Sonata* came during sleep: "I woke up like at two in the morning hearing some persistent tune, got up and went to my piano room where I remained the rest of the night and wrote the entire piece." She also clearly recalled another new dreamt melody, but didn't record it after waking and then forgot about it. And just as Billy Joel's dreamt melody for *Just The Way You Are* returned to again nudge him towards bringing it to life, Eckemoff revealed how her dreams repeated the tune that became *Pep* from her CD *A Touch Of Radiance.* "To my surprise," recounted Eckemoff, "I dreamed about it again the next night. And the next day, I sat at the piano and played it as if it was already done."[800]

- **Robin Easton** claimed she was an "absolute failure" at childhood musical lessons, with no interest in music until she had a series of dreams in which ballet dancers moved to grand orchestral music in a large concert hall. The dreams both spooked and invigorated her. She enjoyed them yet felt too old for ballet and didn't read music, so she remained perplexed and dismissed the dreams. One day, she and her husband were moving furniture at her mother's home when she felt an urge to play piano. "I looked at the piano," Easton recalled, "and I knew…what all the dreams were about." And play she did, from start to finish what became her first song, *The March of Courage and Peace.* Her husband listened surprised, since she had never mentioned knowing how to play piano in the sixteen years they'd been together. He also had a hard time believing her claims that she did not know how to play, so the episode unsettled them both. However, Easton continued to explore her newfound piano gifts. She initially performed only for a few friends, but they soon convinced her to share her talents more publicly, so she recorded the album *Miracles, Dreams and Memories* for which some of the songs were harvested from her dreams.[801]

- Anthropology professor **Curtiss Hoffman** had a passing interest in musical dreams until he experienced a large spike in recall of nocturnal musical inspirations. The dreams not only motivated him to return to playing the crumhorn, a renaissance double-reed instrument, but also sparked him to compose a cantata he was hearing in dreams. He studied how to create a cantata, and as if in response, many more musical dreams came, adding details for what became his *Gilgamesh Cantata.*[802]

- The British band **10cc** was named thanks to a dream by the group's producer Jonathan King. "Jonathan had a dream about seeing a sign above the Hammersmith Odeon the night before he came to meet us," confirmed 10cc co-founder **Kevin Godley**. "The sign said, '10cc The Best Band In The World'."[803]

- Mexican rockers **Jaguares** got their band name from a dream by lead singer Saul Hernandez in which he was playing inside a Jaguar's mouth.[804]

- British composer **Simon Jeffes**' concept and name for his band **Penguin Cafe Orchestra** came from a feverish dream he had while suffering from food poisoning in Southern France.[805]

- **Qntal** is another band name mined during the night. Lead singer Sigrid Hausen dreamt of the letters in flames written on a ball.[806]

- Irish rocker **Alex Trimble** from **Two Doors Cinema Club** admits that he was inspired to write the song *Sleep Alone* by "really crazy dreams" he had the morning after smoking cannabis to fall asleep.[807]

- A synesthesia example of music blended with visual plant symbolism came in the dream of an unnamed dreamer about a "garland of flowers intertwined with horizontal lines" that were arranged on an ordinary musical stave to form a melody. Upon awakening, the dreamer remembered some of the music as well as the positions of the flowers on the stave and was able to transcribe it into a 3-line song fragment.[808]

- Shock rocker **Marilyn Manson** claims that *Little Horn*[809] and *Tourniquet*, like most of the songs from his *Antichrist Superstar* album, originated in dreams.[810]

- Punk rocker **Poison Ivy** from **The Cramps** dreamt her stage name.[811]

- **Tech N9ne** credits a dream for his song *Hiccup*.[812]

- **Bob Segarini** of the 1970s American rock group **The Wackers**, signed to Elektra Entertainment, dreamt the song *Such A Good Thing* "from beginning to end, almost every word." He then ran downstairs and played it for his two band mates who were jamming at the time.[813]

- The band name and debut album title for American rockers **Maids of Gravity** was inspired by a group that singer/guitarist **Eddie Ruscha** saw playing in a dream.[814]

- **Lothar and the Hand People**'s Richard Willis dreamt about an enslaved race called the Hand People who were saved by a hero named Lothar.[815]

- British alternative rock band **Wolf Gang**'s album *Suego Faults* was named after a utopian place dreamt of by lead singer Max McElligott.[816]

- British singer **Thea Gilmore** recollects a "bizarre" dream in 2001 in which she knew she had written a song called *Josef's Train*. Said Gilmore, "I had no idea why the title had appeared or who Josef was, but I figured it must mean something so I decided to write the song."[817]

- Elvis tribute performer **Jack Smink**, who plays Elvis songs at numerous venues including Florida's Disneyland, was inspired for his original song *Just One More Time* by a dream where he was in an open field and saw visions described by the song's lyrics and awoke with the song title in mind.[818]

- **Hudost**'s singer and guitarist **Jemal Wade Hines** reported that the main guitar riff for the band's song *All My Guitars* came from his dream.[819]

- Songwriter/actor **David Archuleta**'s dreams inspired his song *Elevator*.[820]

- Canadian singer-songwriter **Garnet Rogers**, brother of Canadian folk music legend, Stan Rogers, received the lyrics for his song *Painted Pony* from a dream. After awakening from his nap, Rogers says the lyrics were "dictated to me as fast as I could write it. I really like getting those ones that arrive like telegrams." He performed the song that very night.[821]

- **Raquel Bignucolo** had a dream that sparked her career shift from painting, writing and teaching to singing and songwriting. Singing to an empty audience in her dream, she wrote her first song in its entirety. It was her country ballad *Our Masterpiece Unseen* which made the semi-finals in the 2007 UK songwriting contest along with two of her other songs, one of which made the finals.[822]

- The lyrics for *Millions* by **Gerard Way** of **My Chemical Romance** arrived in one of his dreams.[823]

- American rapper **Burnell Washburn**'s song *Mountain Ears* blends a recurring dream set in the Utah mountains and a dream encounter with a beautiful woman.[824]

- Electronic artist **Dntel**'s song *This is The Dream of Evan and Chan* is a dream download.[825]

- Danish alternative rocker **Jonas Bjerre** of **Mew** often finds inspiration at night, and wrote *The Zookeeper's Boy* from a dream. He elaborated, "I don't always know what the lyrics are about, they're just images that I come up with and I just write them, it's sort of surreal."[826]

Craig Sim Webb

Chapter 19

Techniques

If you rarely or never remember dreams, or wish to remember more, I heartily encourage you to read **Appendix 1**, which offers a number of **tips for boosting dream recall**. Remembering dreams is a primary door that needs to be open in order to start welcoming them into your life and thereby receive the insights and potential benefits they offer. Boosting recall will also help a great deal with other dream skills like dream incubation and lucid dreaming, since increasing recall is like improving our *innernet* connection.[xxvi] The improved *innernet* connection will increase the link between your waking and dreaming mind in both directions. It will also boost intuition during the daytime, so there are multiple significant benefits in exchange for a little focus.

The majority of people actually find dream recall fairly simple to increase, even if they don't remember any dreams to begin with. Recall grows simply by becoming interested and spending a little more time with dreams, including recording and contemplating them. I like to encourage people to think of this process as 'befriending' dreams, and as you will hopefully soon discover, it can become a very worthwhile friendship indeed. The techniques described in Appendix 1 have been a great help for many people.

[xxvi] My invented word 'innernet' and the related concept is explained near the start of the book.

Enjoying music before sleep may not only inspire musical dreams, it could also increase the amount of dreaming. Research shows that listening to music before sleep seems to have the effect of increasing the amount of REM sleep which is largely associated with visual dreaming.[827]

Nightmares

If you are just starting to remember dreams (or starting to remember somewhat more dreams than usual), you might have a nightmare. This is not uncommon, since the deeper psyche that speaks through dreams may try to catch your attention with an upsetting or scary dream. That is usually a good thing as long as you are prepared to explore and deal with it, so if you experience strong nightmares or recurring upsetting dreams, I encourage you to read Appendix 2: *"Bad" Dreams or Nightmares? Lucky You!*

A Little History

As mentioned previously, the ancient Greeks placed great importance on the power and value of dreams for healing, as well as for other practical, prophetic, and spiritual purposes. From about 1300 BCE until approximately 600 ACE, sacred dream healing temples called asclepieia (plural of asclepieion) were built and used in ancient Greece and regions surrounding the Mediterranean. There are 320 documented temples mostly located in Greece, but also in as far away places as Spain and Italy to the west, Bulgaria to the north, Northern Africa to the South, and Asia Minor to the east.[828] Those seeking healing, inner guidance, and revelations would make pilgrimages to the asclepieion temples, such as one of the main sites in Epidauros/Epidavros,

Greece, with the hope that the Greek god Asclepius may appear in a dream and help them on their quest.

"The prime objective of all initiatory music in the Temples of Antiquity was to bring about physical purification and renewal, mental stimulation and alertness, spiritual exhilaration and illumination." **–Corinne Heline**[829]

The process of inviting dreams about a specific question or topic (such as for creative inspiration) is generally called dream incubation in modern culture, and was obviously effective, since the Asclepian tradition lasted nearly two millennia in its original form. Even the current medical symbol for the World Health Organization, the Greek Medical Association, American Medical Association, Canadian Medical association and other such organizations acknowledge the Greek god Asclepius by using the symbol of a single snake around his staff at the center of their emblem. The Hippocratic Oath that medical students take when becoming physicians also begins by honoring the Greek gods including the healer Asclepius: "I swear by Apollo, the healer, Asclepius…"

Why and how dreams may bring remarkable new insights is suggested by a 1999 scientific study which demonstrated that when certain conscious brain functions are inactive, as they are during sleep, our creative potential is increased.[830]

Intentional Dreaming

In an experiment involving a few of my students, 7 out of 8 were able to intentionally invoke a dream containing music on their first try simply by suggesting it to themselves before sleep, and 2 of the 8 had not just one but a series of three dreams that night containing music. This rather surprising success rate on the first attempt suggests that music dreams may be available simply for those who request or intend them.

I joined the musical dream intention experiment myself that week and recalled 5 or 6 dreams containing music, 3 or 4 of which came on a single night. One experience was a lucid dream with a long Sanskrit mantra chant. I realized during the dream that I would not remember how to pronounce it when I awoke. After I woke, I sang the chant into the voice recorder that I keep beside my bed for recording musical dreams, and indeed I could only remember some of the chanted words, though I believe I did accurately remember the melody.

In another of my dreams that night:

> *A young artist is attempting to paint on canvas a melody that is playing. His work is only partly finished but looks very interesting at that stage as though he was starting with a basic blueprint of the music which I seem to know he will afterwards flesh out. The colors include light teal and I think yellow, and some darker colors including blue. The strokes are straight, tiny, colored line segments that are rounded at the end and interweave with each other forming a mesh of sorts.*

The day after the dream, I learned that a student in the class who is a painter also dreamt of music, and another class mate suggested he try painting the melody—before either of them knew about my dream. The experience suggests, as seen earlier with composer Shirish Korde and others, that musical and visual dream elements can overlap and blend. It is also an example of how I am often able to 'tune in' to my students at other levels by dreaming about them, sometimes learning during the dream specific facts about their life that I have no other way of knowing at the time, but which I later verify to be true. For over two decades, I have had the good fortune to offer training programs about dreams and work with thousands of dream explorers around the world. My experiences show that it is not only possible, but actually fairly common for people to tune into others this way through dreams, especially those people we have an emotional connection with. As a mentor, I usually tune in to aspects of students' lives that can help them learn principles or skills, or advance along their professional or personal development path.

If you have never experienced this type of perception before, I do not ask you to necessarily believe in it outright. I rather encourage you to keep an open mind that it might be possible. The example above is much like connecting with a friend by calling or texting or emailing them, but on an inner rather than physical level. You can explore such inner communications yourself by diplomatically and privately checking during the day with friends or family that you dream about to see if any aspects of the dream seem connected with events or emotional situations in their lives. Of course, not all characters in dreams directly represent the waking person that they resemble, since many times the connection is symbolic. However, as long as you use your best judgment about what and when to share, you will likely find that such investigations will not only soon surprise you with waking connections, but may also offer helpful insights for you and for those who you dream about. This has been true for the many explorers I have had the privilege to train as they develop their own skills towards mastery of what I call Applied Dreaming.

Technique: Dream Up Your Own Masterpiece or Virtuoso Performer Skills

A proof-reader for this book got intrigued by the possibility of having a musical dream simply by setting an intention to do so before sleep, since he had never experienced such a dream. To his surprise, he awoke remembering a familiar melody and specific line of lyrics that closely described an unpleasant experience from two nights prior. Interestingly, he and the song's well-known singer-composer have the exact same first name, exemplifying the name association principle I stated previously about ways dreams can link with waking events. He was intrigued, but wanted an original melody, so I encouraged him to focus on that specifically before sleep. That night, he was again successful at experiencing a musical dream, though this time it was an original melody, thanks to that he had more clearly set his intention specifically for that.

So, if you wish, you can offer yourself the suggestion before falling asleep to dream on a topic such as music and to clearly remember such dreams as well as anything else that might be important and helpful. This is generally called **dream incubation**. It can help to actually write your intention atop a blank new page in a dream journal that you keep near your bed. Ideally, phrase it as though it is already happening and include the feelings you would like to experience when the intention comes true. For example, an intention to experience musical dreams might be phrased something like this:

> *"I feel grateful to be clearly remembering more dreams, and excited that such experiences will tonight or sometime soon include dreaming of excellent music (and lyrics) that I can record when I awaken and gladly share later with others."*

Thoughts have a certain momentum in the mind, so it can also really help to immerse yourself completely for an hour or two before sleep in music, or in whatever other subject you wish to dream about. Also helpful, is to read about the topic in the evening or right before sleep, such as reading stories about musicians you admire and their accounts of dream-inspired works. **Important:** make sure to have some recording device handy near your bed for when the muse comes calling!

DreamLand Invitations and Collaborations

You may also expand your creative collaborations by inviting friends or experts to join you in a dream, perhaps even a famous composer, singer, or instrumentalist you admire, regardless of whether they are alive or not. Although it may be fun and motivating to directly invite others to join you in dreams, you do not necessarily need to speak or write to them for the process to work. You can simply make such a suggestion privately in your mind, and see what dreams bring. If you dream of them, you can communicate with them to see if they had 'any dreams of interest' before telling them about the unspoken invitation for a 'dream meeting' that you offered them. Surely this will bring fascinating experiences that can inspire others, so please consider sharing them with me at: *music@craigwebb.ca*

Becoming Lucid Through Intention

The intentional dreaming technique described above for experiencing musical dreams can also serve as a simple yet effective way to invoke lucid dreams. Only the specifics of the intention needs to change. To experiment with this, hold a clear intention in mind before sleep along the lines of:

"I feel excited that tonight or some time soon, I will experience a dream during which I realize I'm dreaming while I'm dreaming."

It is also helpful to have in mind beforehand (and include in your pre-sleep self-suggestion) an experiment that you would like to try when you become lucid in your dream. Experiment examples include flying, looking into your own heart, asking questions to the Dream Weaver (i.e. the part of your deeper self that creates dreams), and many other amazing possibilities.

Inspirations from Hypnagogic Micro-Naps

Variations of a technique for having short hypnagogic micro-naps have been used by many creative thinkers and artists, including Sting, David Bowie,[831] composers Richard Wagner, Johannes Brahms, Giacomo Puccini, author/composer Robert Louis Stevenson, authors Charles Dickens, Mark Twain, Leo Tolstoy, and Aristotle, writers/poets Johann Wolfgang von Goethe and Edgar Allan Poe, inventor Thomas Edison, surreal artists Paul Klee and Salvador Dali, multi-millionaire businessman and speaker/author Clement C. Stone,[832] and surely many others.

Leonardo Da Vinci also napped while working creatively,[833] though with a more extreme routine than most since he is reported, in certain periods at least, to have taken quarter-hour naps every 4 hours, sleeping a total of only about 90 minutes during a 24-hour period.[834] During such experiences, Da Vinci likely got powerful subconscious insights for inventions such as those that show up in his sketchbooks, including designs for multiple musical instruments such as his viola organista (circa 1488-1489) and clavi-viola (1503-1505),[835] among others. Da Vinci was not only an inventor and painter, he was also a talented musician. He is reported to have made from silver a horse-head-shaped fiddle[xxvii] called a 'lira da braccio' (arm lyre) that he presented to the Duke of Milan as a gift from the Lord of Florence, and to have played it so masterfully that he won a musical contest in the Milanese court.[836]

David Crosby of Crosby, Stills and Nash revealed that he also harvested the interesting mental state just after nodding off and before fully falling asleep for creative inspiration. "In that little window," explained Crosby, "something will leap up, and I will wind up grabbing for the lamp and frantically writing pages and pages of lyrics."[837]

Composer Johannes Brahms offered specific guidance for composers to improve their craft, including this technique: "The dream-like state [that can be very helpful for creative inspiration] is like entering a trance-like condition—hovering between being asleep and awake; you are still conscious but right on the border of losing consciousness, and it is at such moments that inspired ideas come. Then it is of the utmost importance to put the ideas down on paper immediately. Then they are fixed and cannot escape, and when you look at them again, they conjure up that same mood that gave them birth. This is a very important law. Themes that occur this way are usually ones that will endure."[838]

Make sure to register on **DreamsBehindTheMusic.com** (near the bottom fo the page) for other helpful techniques, tips, and tools.

[xxvii] Where Da Vinci got the idea for his silver horse-head fiddle is a mystery, though possibly from seeing a Central Asian horse-head fiddle or hearing the legend of how it was created from a dream.

Salvador Dali

"You must resolve the problem of 'sleeping without sleeping'...it is a repose which walks in equilibrium on the taut invisible wire which separates sleeping from waking."

–Salvador Dali[839]

To get inspirations for his work, master of surrealism painting Salvador Dali used a special technique that he called "slumber with a key" which he said he learned from Capuchin monks. Dali would sit in a chair (preferably a Spanish-style bony armchair, claimed Dali) with a heavy metal key pressed between his thumb and forefinger and held above an overturned plate.

Dali explained, "The moment the key drops from your fingers, you may be sure that the noise of its fall on the upside-down plate will awaken you, and you may be equally sure that this fugitive moment when you had barely lost consciousness and during which you cannot be assured of having really slept is totally sufficient, inasmuch as not a second more is needed for your physical and psychic being to be revivified by just the necessary amount of repose."[840]

Elbow Technique for Surfing the Edge of Sleep

I developed and have taught for a couple of decades a simpler version of Dali's technique whereby one rests an elbow on the arm of a chair or on the bed, with the same arm's hand raised vertically above the elbow and balanced in a relaxed way so that very little effort is required to keep the forearm and hand vertical. At the moment of sleep onset, the muscles of the arm relax and the hand falls, awakening the dreamer. Following in the footsteps of Sting, Dali, Edison, Brahms, and other successful dreamers, you may well find some powerful creative inspirations as you surf the border between wakefulness and sleep. Keep in mind that such insights are mostly just seeds and that you need to act on them to bring them into our world and grow them to their full creative fruition.

Craig Sim Webb

Appendix 1 – How to Boost Dream Recall

How to Boost Dream Recall for a Wealth of Awaiting Treasure

Your dreams can be a natural wellspring of creative inspiration. They can help you craft new artistic works, solve problems at work and in your relationships, heal emotional wounds and even physical illnesses, learn new skills, and explore the vast inner realm of profound experiences for far greater spiritual fulfillment—all while allowing you to explore and have fun during the third of life that we all spend asleep. If these possibilities sound interesting, you need not just take my word for it. Begin remembering dreams better tonight and start experiencing for yourself the fascinating adventures and powerful hidden benefits your subconscious is trying to offer you every night. The following paragraphs will explain proven techniques for recalling more dreams, likely starting within a week or less.

The main barrier to recalling and benefiting from dreams is that waking and dreaming memory are not connected nearly as well as they could be with greater intention, practise and focus. Making a relatively consistent effort to remember and especially to record your dreams will help your waking mind align with and integrate your dream experience. ***It is also an excellent way to increase imagination and intuitive abilities, which are both intimately linked with dreams.*** This alone should provide strong incentive.

1) IT IS IMPORTANT TO WANT IT: First and foremost, you must feel that it will be useful to you, if not extremely valuable. Without this intention, motivation will soon disappear. More importantly, the desire acts as a subjective magnet, which draws your dreams into your normal memory.

2) FOCUS and ATTENTION: Understand that dream recall is an inherent, natural human trait. That is why young children are quite in touch with their dreams, as are many native cultures. Some of these native cultures even share their dreams with each other daily and base important life actions upon guidance they receive from them. ***Dream recall is like a mental muscle—the more you use it, the stronger it becomes.*** Without exercise, it may shrink, but it is there if you decide to work it out again. So if your recall is poor, trust that it will come in time, and the trust itself will actually help because expectation is a powerful subjective tool.

3) BEDTIME PRACTICE: Before sleep, reread your dreams from at least the night before, if not the previous few nights. This allows you to begin to connect with your dream memory, and is also an opportunity to interpret your dreams and spot connections to the day's events. Then, as you go to bed, clearly request (rather than command) yourself to remember any dreams when you awaken in the morning or during the night, especially ones that would be beneficial to you. Also, ***remind yourself that recall is a simple, natural process that happens by itself anyway.*** You can also suggest to yourself to spontaneously awaken when you need to, <u>without using an auditory alarm</u>, since any strong external perception such as a loud noise can inhibit recall. This method works well with practise, but you may initially wish to set your alarm for 15 minutes after your suggested wake-up time, just to be safe. **<u>Whenever you awaken, keep your eyes closed</u>** (or shut them if already open) and **<u>remain as motionless as possible</u>**. If you move after waking, quickly return to your earlier body position. Gather as many images, impressions, feelings, body sensations, or initial waking thoughts as you can. A helpful technique is to think of it like fishing. Gently, cast out your intention to remember a dream, and wait a little to see what comes. As soon as you get anything, no matter how brief or vague it may *at first* seem, rise and *immediately* record (i.e. write, draw, paint, etc.) it in a journal, or speak (or sing) it into a tape recorder which you keep by your bed. You will be surprised at how much more you remember once you take the actual step to begin writing/speaking/drawing/painting/singing/etc.

4) ENVISION: A few times during the first few weeks of focusing on recall, take a quiet, meditative moment and imagine your dream journal's pages filled with many dreams written down, including accompanying drawings, images, melodies if you wish, and other notes and associations you have added about them. See this as clearly as you can in your mind's eye and make sure to *feel pleased* (at least during this visualization exercise) that your dream recall is very good and becoming even better.

5) BE PLAYFUL, PATIENT, and PERSISTENT: Although most people start having success in the first week or two, dream recall is a mental muscle which may require some time to get back into shape. Try to maintain a relaxed and playful attitude of looking forward to your dreams while being willing to let them come all in good time. *Trying too hard or being too serious can be limiting factors.* Dream recall and motivation tend to come and go naturally in cycles and also depend upon what else is going on in your life, on how much sleep or exercise you get, seasonal factors, etc. [841] **Once you begin a period of focusing on recall, stick with it for *at least* a few days, because consecutive nights can have an additive effect.**

6) A WEEKLY STUDY GROUP with a shared interest in dreams is unmatchable for sustained motivation, inspiration and plenty of intriguing surprises and insights.

Learn more at: **www.AppliedDreaming.com**

Appendix 2 – "Bad" Dreams or Nightmares? Lucky You!

Why would anyone *want* anxiety dreams?!

Though perhaps not obvious, almost all nightmares and recurring dreams provide an extremely valuable service to the dreamer. If we block them, we are likely missing their immediate benefit. If we remember but ignore them, we miss their vital messages— both very unwise strategies indeed that serve to perpetuate or worsen the situation, much like putting a Band-Aid over the oil light on our car because we find it annoying or upsetting.

For some people, unpleasant dreams recur identically; for others, the content changes yet the theme repeats, such as scenes of falling, being pursued or attacked, late or unprepared for an exam or presentation, unable to move or scream, or having teeth crumble or fall out. These types of anxiety dreams usually recur and are mainly associated with the dreamer's failure to recognize and solve related life conflicts or lessons.

The majority of nightmares therefore, like a bitter but necessary medicine, represent opportunities for healing through much-needed emotional release. They also warn of current behaviors that need adjustment if we don't want such unpleasant dreams to repeat or worsen. Sometimes, such imbalances resolve themselves as the dream percolates into waking thought and we unknowingly respond and make changes in our life. Yet if we ignore such subconscious warnings repeatedly, then life often speaks 'louder' to get our attention, bringing related events, which I call 'daymares', into our waking hours. These daymares show up as sickness, accidents, relationship difficulties or other unfortunate circumstances that force us outright to deal with the issue at hand.

So, we truly are lucky to have such nightmares, since they provide a natural 'pressure-release' therapy for the psyche, and an early warning and potential solution if we try to understand and act upon the valuable insights they offer. The goal is still to put an end to anxiety dreams, but by evolving them into more beneficial scenarios, not by blocking, ignoring or denying them.

Fortunately, there exist non-pharmaceutical nightmare treatments that are remarkably effective. Two of the most useful techniques are dream re-scripting and lucid dreaming. The lucidity approach is demonstrated by a woman I worked with who was often tormented by nightmares:

"After many recurring nightmares where I'm pursued by a terrifying figure, I learned lucid dreaming and had the following dream: I'm in a frantic car chase with the pursuer right behind me. Swerving into a parking lot, I bolt out of the car with him hot on my heels. Suddenly, the scene seems familiar and I realize that I'm dreaming though the lot and trees still seem more real than ever. Drawing up every ounce of courage, I swirl to face my pursuer, repeating to myself that it's only a dream. Still afraid, I scream, 'You can't hurt me!' He stops, looking surprised. For the first time I see his beautiful, loving eyes. 'Hurt you? I don't want to hurt you. I've been running after you all this time to tell you that I love you!' With that, he holds out his hands, and as I touch them, he dissolves into me. I awake filled with energy, feeling great for days. The nightmare never returned." (M.R., San Jose, CA)

So instead of wishing you sweet dreams, I will go one step further, with your greatest fulfillment in mind, and wish you truly pleasant nightmares!

~

www.DreamsBehindTheMusic.com

End Notes

[1] Nancy Grace, Making Dreams Into Music: Contemporary Songwriters Carry On an Age-Old Dreaming Tradition, section 1 in Dreams: A Reader on Religious, Cultural and Psychological Dimensions of Dreaming, edited by Kelly Bulkeley, Palgrave Macmillan (2001).

[2] Frederic Seaman, The Last Days of John Lennon, New York: Random House (1996), p. 171.

[3] Paul Zollo, Songwriters on Songwriting, Da Capo Press, 2nd edition (2003), p. 7.

[4] Robert Hilburn, *Joy Makes a Return*, LAtimes.com (2001-12-16).

[5] The Power of Dreams: The Creative Spark, Discovery Channel TV series & video, part 3, first segment, Discovery Communications (1994).

[6] Corinne D. Heline, Healing and Regeneration Through Music, Literary Licensing, LLC (2013, original edition 1952).

[7] Jorge Luis Borges, Ruth L. C. Simms, Other Inquisitions, 1937-1952, University of Texas Press (1964), p. 11.

[8] Larry Page, *Larry Page's University of Michigan commencement address*, Google channel, YouTube.com (2009-5-4), at time: 6min7sec.

[9] Ibid.

[10] As one indicator among others, see:
https://trends.google.com/trends/explore?date=today 5-y&q=spiritual growth

[11] William Hermanns, Einstein and the Poet: In Search of the Cosmic Man (1983), p.16.

[12] Oliver Sacks, Musicophilia, Knopf (2007-10-16), p. 308.

[13] Elliot J. Huntley, Mystical One: George Harrison : After the Break-up of the Beatles, Guernica Editions (2004), p. 156.

[14] Dhani Harrison, George Harrison: Living in the Material World (documentary film by Martin Scorsese), Grove Street Productions & Spitfire Pictures & Sikelia Productions (2011-10-4). At time: 1min18sec.

[15] Sacks (Musicophilia), p. 311.

[16] Mallory Simon, *Jackson shared bond with 'very dear friend Diana Ross'*, CNN.com (2009-7-3).

[17] Erin Bates, *How Billie Eilish's Design Team Turned Her Dreams (and Nightmares) Into Realities*, Livedesignonline.com (2019-7-18).

[18] H.C. Schonberg, Horowitz: His Life and Music, New York: Simon & Schuster (1992), pp. 171-172.

[19] David Dubai, *David Dubai: Dreams & Creativity*, The Snapshots Foundation Channel, YouTube.com (2012-5-28), at time: 0min49sec.

[20] Heinz Prokop, Eine schopferische Produktion des Unbewussten [A creative product of the unconscious]. Musik und Medizin (1979), 2, p. 52.

[21] Told to me directly by Mr. Higman at Pop Montreal (2013-9-27).

[22] Brian Hill, Gates of Horn And Ivory: An Anthology of Dreams, Taplinger (1968), pp. 22-23.

[23] Tina Maples, Jayhawks, Dream Theater, Cowboys heat up the fest, The Milwaukee Journal (1993-6-30), p. B7.

[24] A thank-you coupon is available for readers of this book by sending in a photo or scanned copy of your book receipt.

[25] Andy Wimmer, Happy movie, Wadi Rum Films, Inc. (2011), at time: 1h7min.

[26] Sri Chinmoy, *Illumination-Fruits*, Agni Press (1974).

[27] Zollo, p. 7.

[28] Calvin S. Hall & Robert L. Van De Castle, Content Analysis of Dreams, New York: Appleton Century Crofts (1966).

[29] Valeria Uga, Maria Chiara Lemut, Chiara Zampi, Iole Zilli & Piero Salzarulo, *Music in Dreams*, Conscious Cognition (2006-06-21), 15(2):351-357 (also Epub. 2005-10-21).

[30] *Coast to Coast radio* (2010-8-23), hour 1.

[31] Ibid.

[32] Richard Bach, shared in a private email interview (2015-12-9).

[33] Timothy Foote, *It's a Bird! It's a Dream! It's a Supergull!*, TIME Magazine (1972-11-13), pp. 60-66.

[34] *Richard Harris*, 16th Annual Grammy Awards (1973), Grammy.com

[35] *Neil Diamond*, 16th Annual Grammy Awards (1972), Grammy.com

[36] Neil McCormick, U2 by U2, Harper Collins (2009-12-1), p. 196.

[37] Hans Commenda, Geschichten um Anton Bruckner (Stories of Anton Bruckner), Verlag H. Muck, Linz / Donau (1946), p. 76.

[38] Simha Arom, The Origins of Music, edited by Nils Lennart Wallin, Björn Merker & Steven Brown, MIT Press (2001), p. 27.

[39] Danilo Kiš. Hourglass. New York: Farrar, Straus & Giroux (1990), pp. 148-149.

[40] Prokop, p. 51.

[41] Roger Shepard, Externalization of Mental Images and the Act of Creation, article published in Visual Learning, Thinking, and Communication, edited by B. S. Randhawa & W. E. Coffman, New York: Academic Press (1978), p. 177-179.

[42] Deirdre Barrett, The Committee of Sleep. New York: Crown Publishers (2001), p. 69.

[43] Isabelle Peretz & K.L. Hyde. What is specific to music processing? Insights from congenital amusia. Trends in Cognitive Sciences (2003), 7, p. 362.

[44] Oliver Sacks, The man who mistook his wife for a hat and other clinical tales, New York: Harper & Row (1987), pp. 18–19.

[45] N. Angier. Sonata for humans, birds and humpback whales. New York Times (2001-01-09), p. D5.

[46] L. Stewart, V. Walsh, U. Frith & J. Rothwell, Transcranial magnetic stimulation produces speech arrest but not song arrest (2001). Appears in R. J. Zatorre & I. Peretz (Eds.), The biological foundations of music. Annals of the New York Academy of Sciences: Vol. 930. New York: New York Academy of Sciences (2001), p. 434.

[47] Laurain F. King & Doreen Kimura, Left ear superiority in dichotic perception of vocal nonverbal sounds, Canadian Journal of Psychology (June 1972), vol. 26, p. 111-116.

[48] Sources vary in their selection of translations, such as one source that represents the Chinese symbol for music as 'mínyuè' which is composed of the two Chinese characters 'min' (people) and 'le' (happy/music) together, essentially meaning "happy people."

[49] John R. Clark Hall, The Concise Anglo-Saxon Dictionary, New York: Macmillian & Co, (1916), p. 77.

[50] M. Besson & D. Schön, Comparison Between Language & Music, Annals of the New York Academy of Sciences (June 2001), 930:232-58.

[51] *Baddeley's model of working memory*, Wikipedia.org (retrieved 2014-11-17), section: Phonological loop.

[52] Carolyn Gregoire, *This Bizarre Trick Will Get A Catchy Song Out Of Your Head*, HuffingtonPost.com (2015-4-25).

[53] Vogelsang, L., Anold, S., Schormann, J., Wübbelmann, S., & Schredl, M. The continuity between waking-life musical activities and music dreams, Dreaming Journal, *26*(2), 132-141 (2016).

[54] Laetitia Elizabeth Landon, The Complete Works of L. E. Landon, Phillips, Samson (1867), p. 185.

[55] Don Piper, *90 Minutes in Heaven: A True Story of Death & Life*, BakerPublishingGroup channel, YouTube.com (2007-3-2), at time: 1min43sec.

[56] A Select Library of the Nicene and Post-Nicene Fathers of the Christian Church: The confessions and letters of St. Augustin, with a sketch of his life and work, Christian literature Company (1886), p. 514.

[57] *Happy 30th, 'Stranger'!*, USAToday.com (2008-11-7).

[58] The Power of Dreams: The Creative Spark, Discovery Channel TV series & video, part 3, 3rd segment, Discovery Communications (1994).

[59] Leopold Stokowski (addressing the audience at Carnegie Hall), First Lady Spends a Busy Day in City; Attends Concert for Retired Union Members and a Dinner in Evening, The New York Times (1967-5-11), p. 49.

[60] Richard Wagner, Richard Wagner's Prose Work, volume 2, Kegan, Paul Trench, Trübner (1893), p. 317 (translated from Wagner's essay: *Opera and Drama*).

[61] Hazrat Inayat Khan, *The Sufi Message of Hazrat Inayat Khan: The Mysticism of Sound, Music, The Power of the Word, Cosmic Language*, Library of Alexandria.

[62] One source reports that about 1 in 9000 people experience this form of synesthesia: http://www.daysyn.com/Types-of-Syn.html

[63] Seth / Jane Roberts, The Early Sessions, Book 4, Session 155 on 1965-5-17, New Awareness Network, Inc. (1998-6-1).

[64] Seth / Jane Roberts (The Early Sessions, Book 4), Session 154 on 1965-5-12, p. 30.

[65] Maureen Seaberg, Tasting the Universe, New Page Books (2011), p. 89.

[66] Maia Kedem, *Billie Eilish explains her synesthesia and how it influences everything she does*, Audacy.com (2021-8-10).

[67] Jeremy Hobson, *FINNEAS, Billie Eilish's Brother, Steps Out From Behind The Scenes With 1st Solo Album*, WBUR.org (2019-11-5).

[68] Lady Gaga, *Lady Gaga's interview in Singapore*, Jayohenjee channel, YouTube.com (2010-1-6), at time: 2min18sec.

[69] Lorde, LordeMusic.Tumblr.com (retrieved 2015-12-11). Reprinted: Alyssa Ladzinski, *Lorde Talks Curly Hair, Synesthesia & and Wanting to Be a Comedian in Tumblr Chat*, MusicTimes.com (2015-10-17).

[70] Ed Wright, A left-handed history of the world, Pier 9 / Murdoch books (2007), p. 208.

[71] Tori Amos & Ann Powers, Tori Amos: Piece by Piece, Crown/Archetype (2008-12-10), p. 123.

[72] Maureen Seaberg (Tasting the Universe), p. 174.

[73] Maureen Seaberg (Tasting the Universe), pp. 179-180.

[74] György Ligeti, Ligeti in conversation, Eulenburg Books (1983), p. 58.

[75] Ryan Dombal, *What the Hell is Synesthesia and Why Does Every Musician Seem to Have It?*, PitchFork.com (2014-1-31).

[76] John Jurgensen, *Coldplay and Chris Martin Open Up for New Album*, Wall Street Journal, WSJ.com (2015-11-18).

[77] Richard E. Cytowic & David M. Eagleman, Wednesday is Indigo Blue: Discovering the Brain of Synesthesia, MIT Press (2009), p. 93.

[78] Kanye West, Kanye West Behind the Scenes Interview, KanyeWestShow channel, YouTube.com (2011-7-16), at time: 4ming55sec. (Retrieved: 2016-2-2).

[79] article in Neuen Berliner Musikzeitung (1895-8-29); quoted in: Friedrich, Mahling, Das Problem der 'Audition colorée: Eine historische-kritische Untersuchung, Archiv für die Gesamte Psychologie; LVII Band, Leipzig: Akademische Verlagsgesellschaft M.B.H. (1926), p. 230. Translation by Sean A. Day.

[80] Gavin Edwards, Is Tiny Dance Really Elton John's Little John?: Music's Most Enduring Mysteries, Crown/Archetype (2010-2-10), pp. 21-22.

[81] Maureen Seaberg, *Synesthetes: "People of the Future"*, PsychologyToday.com (2012-3-3).

[82] Daniel J. Levitin, *Neural Correlates of Musical Behaviors – A Brief Overview*, Music Therapy Perspectives, Vol. 31 (2013), p. 16.

[83] Prokop, p. 50.

[84] Carl Alfred Meier, The Unconscious in its Empirical Manifestations, Boston: Sigo Press (1984), p. 11. Original letter in German: Heinrich Schenker, *Ein verschollener Brief von Mozart und das Geheimnis seines Schaffens*, Zu Mozarts 175, Geburtstag, Kunstwart VII (1931), p. 661.

[85] *Beyoncé*, Grammy.com

[86] Beyoncé, *part 1 of Self-Titled*, Facebook.com (posted 2013-12-13).

[87] Stephanie Theobald, Queen B, Harper's Bazaar (September 2011), p. 254.

[88] Beyoncé Breaks Vacation to Record Dream Album, WENN (2006-6-9).

[89] Barrett, pp. 75-76.

[90] Judy Bachrach, Glimpsing Heaven:The Stories and Science of Life After Death, National Geographic (2014-9-2), p. ~150.

[91] Roger Knudson, Significant Dreams: Bizarre or Beautiful?, Dreaming, Vol. 11, No. 4 (2001).

[92] Fyodor Dostoevsky, The Dream of a Ridiculous Man, translated by Constance Garnett, Library of Alexandria (1916), quote appears at the end of part II. Reprinted at: wikisource.org

[93] David Ryback, Ph.D. with Laetitia Sweitzer, Dreams That Come True: Their Psychic and Transforming Powers, Random House (1990-1-1), p. 14. / This statistic is also confirmed in a number of informal audience polls I have briefly made during live presentations.

[94] Edgar Cayce, reading 136-7, spoken word transcribed by Gladys Davis in Dayton, Ohio, Virginia Beach: Association for Research & Enlightenment (1925-7-1).

[95] Clary Croft, Still the Song Lives On CD, Wedge Island Publishing (2001).

[96] *Annie M. Pride - 1894*, Marine Heritage Database (online, retrieved 2013-12-20).

[97] Told to me directly by songwriter Clary Croft at *Festival interculturel du conte du Québec* (2003-10-19).

[98] Frederic Seaman, The Last Days of John Lennon, New York: Random House (1996), p. 171.

[99] Sam Kemp, *"One of John's favourite songs": The mind-bending track that John Lennon wrote in a "dream"*, Faroutmagazine.co.uk (2024-3-31).

[100] John & Yoko, The Interview by Andy Peebles, BBC Radio 1 (1980-12-6). Distributed on BBC Records, CD 6002, CD #2, track 7.

[101] Philippe Margotin & Jean-Michel Guesdo, *All The Songs: The Story Behind Every Beatles Release*, Hachette Books (2014-2-4), p. ~500.

[102] Geoffrey Giuliano, Lennon in America: Based in Part on the Lost Lennon Diaries, 1971-1980, Rowman & Littlefield (2001), p. 103.

[103] Giuliano, pp. 205-206

[104] Giuliano, p. 39.

[105] Ed King, Muscle Shoals documentary movie, directed by Greg 'Freddy' Camalier (2013), at time: 1h45min30sec.

[106] Richard Buskin, *Lynyrd Skynyrd 'Sweet Home Alabama' | Classic Tracks*, SoundOnSound.com (January 2008).

[107] Gary Rossington, *Lynyrd Skynyrd's Fatal Planbe Crash | On This Day*, Facebook.com (2024-10-20).

[108] JoJo Billingsley, interview on Freebird Outreach YouTube channel, YouTube.com (posted 2010-5-10), at time: 3min21sec.

[109] film written by Jared Cohen including interview segments of Lynyrd Skynyrd drummer Artemus Pyle, *Street Survivors: The True Story of the Lynyrd Skynyrd Plane Crash* (2020). At times: ~30m (Allan Collins) and ~32m (Cassie Gaines).

[110] Jojo Billingsley, interview by Rod Zimmerman on WKEQ (2008-7-31). Reposted at: *The Jo Jo Billingsley Interview*, Rod Zimmerman channel, YouTube.com (posted 2009-8-5), at time: 4min37sec.

[111] Paul Welch (Lynyrd Skynyrd sound technician), *Lynyrd Skynyrd plane crash survivor - Paul Welch*, Freebird Outreach YouTube channel, YouTube.com (posted 2012-10-21), at time 2min45sec.

[112] Jon Mulvey, *Mark Linkous interview*, NME.com (1996-6-8).

[113] J. Randy Taraborrelli, Diana Ross: A Biography, Citadel (2014-5-27), p. ~120.

[114] Ibid.

[115] Paul Zollo, Patti Smith on How She Writes a Song, Lithub.com (2016-11-8).

[116] Dave Thompson, Dancing Barefoot: The Patti Smith Story, Chicago Review Press (2011-8-1), pp. 41-42.

[117] Thompson (The Patti Smith Story).

[118] Victor Bockris & Roberta Bayley, Patti Smith: An Unauthorized Biography, Simon & Schuster 1999, p. 56.

[119] Thompson (The Patti Smith Story).

[120] Patti Smith, Sleepy nod to William Blake, pattismith.substack.com (2024-8-13), at time: 3m22sec.

[121] *Even As a child, I felt like an alien*, The Guardian (2005-5-22).

[122] Victor Bockris and Roberta Bayley, Patti Smith: An Unauthorized Biography, Simon and Schuster (1999), p. 129.

[123] Thompson, p. 251.

[124] J.L. Creed, *Sources Chrétiennes*, New York: Clarendon Press (1984), p. 39. Translation of: Lactantius, *De mortibus persecutorum*, 44, 5 (circa 313-316 CE) /

Also appears in: Eusebius, Eusebius' Life of Constantine, Clarendon Press (1999-9-9), p. 209.

[125] in Deuteronomy 18:10 and Leviticus 19:26

[126] P Music Group, *Grammy Nominee Charlie Wilson to Receive Spirit of Los Angeles Award*, Yahoo! Finance, Finance.Yahoo.com (2014-1-30).

[127] Gary Graff, *Charlie Wilson to Hit Studio, May Record Own Version of Kanye West's 'Bound 2'*, Billboard.com (2014-1-9).

[128] Ellis Amburn, Dark Star: The Roy Orbison Story, Carol Publishing Group (1990).

[129] Alan Clayson, Only the Lonely: Roy Orbison's Life and Legacy, St. Martin's Press (1989).

[130] Bono (interview), Roy Orbison: In Dreams, produced by Nashmount Productions' and Gregory Hall; directed by Mark Hall; written by Maryse Rouillard. Originally broadcast on Bravo! TV's NewStyleArts Channel (1999), interview at time: 1h10m40sec.

[131] *Mystery Girl*, Wikipedia.org (retrieved 2015-11-4), section: History.

[132] Robert Hilburn, *Joy Makes a Return*, LAtimes.com (2001-12-16).

[133] McCormick (U2 by U2).

[134] David Kootnikoff, Bono, A Biography, ABC-CLIO (2012), pp. 83-84.

[135] John Jobling, U2: The Definitive Biography, Macmillan Publishing (2014-10-7), p. 195.

[136] A Sort of Homecoming, Disney+, at time: 1h04m20sec.

[137] David Letterman, Dave Letterman on the sweet song Bono and the Edge wrote for him, Yahoo! Entertainment (2023-3-16).

[138] *U2*, Grammy.com

[139] Bono & Michka Assayas, Bono: In Conversation with Michka Assayas, Penguin (2006), p. 178.

[140] *Jimmy L. Webb*, Grammy.com

[141] Zollo, p. 164.

[142] *Legend Glen is no punk*, The Daily Express, UK (2008-12-29).

[143] *Highwayman (song)*, Wikipedia.org (retrieved 2015-3-26).

[144] Gayle Thompson, *47 Years Ago: Johnny Cash Proposes to June Carter*, TheBoot.com (2015-2-22).

[145] Alex Redekop, *Rear-view mirror: Johnny Cash's hit-making dream*, music.CBC.ca (2015-5-4).

[146] Otto Kitsinger, album liner notes for Anita Carter – Ring of Fire, Bear Family Records BCD 15434 (1989).

[147] Steve Turner, The Man Called Cash, New York: Thomas Nelson (2004), p. 99.

[148] Op. cit. (Kitsinger)

[149] Roseanne Cash, from the lead and title song on her album The Wheel, Columbia Records (1993).

[150] David Kamp, *American Communion, Vanity Fair* (October 2004), p. 6.

[151] Johnny Cash interview, The Larry King Show (November 2002).

[152] Johnny Cash, liner notes for American IV: The Man Comes Around, Universal (2002).

[153] Johnny Cash, liner notes for Kris, Willie, Dolly & Brenda, Monument Records (1982).

[154] C. Eric Banister, Johnny Cash FAQ: All That's Left to Know About the Man in Black, Hal Leonard Corporation (2014-8-1), p. ~40.

[155] Scott Mathews, shared in a private email interview (2015-8-1).

[156] Scott Mathews (email interview).

[157] Win Butler, *Bridge School 2013 Benefit Concert*, President Pizza channel, Youtube.com (2013-10-26).

[158] Howard Reich, *How Barry Manilow Writes his Songs*, The Chicago Tribune (2001-6-24).

[159] Chuck Taylor, Bette…Intimately, Billboard magazine (2003-10-18), p. 1.

[160] Lincoln Barnett, Lindsay & Crouse, LIFE Magazine (1946-11-11), pp. 120 & 122.

[161] Caryl Flinn, *Brass Diva: The Life and Legends of Ethel Merman*, University of California Press (2007), p. 66.

[162] Barnett, p. 122.

[163] Gabrielle H. Cody, The Columbia Encyclopedia of Modern Drama, Volume 1. Columbia University Press (2007), p. 821.

[164] Douglas Everett, original source unknown.

[165] Steve Turner, *A Hard Day's Write: The Stories Behind Every Beatles Song* (3rd ed.). New York: Harper (2005).

[166] More recently, McCartney shared that "after about two weeks I claimed it." [*Sir Paul McCartney Sings Blackbird Live at Rollins College*, Rollins College channel, YouTube.com (2015-1-8), at time: 9min20sec.]

[167] Craig Cross, *The Beatles: Day-by-Day, Song-by-Song, Record-by-Record*. Lincoln, NE: iUniverse, Inc. (2005), pp. 464–465.

[168] *The Beatles Anthology*, San Francisco: Chronicle Books (2000), p. 175.

[169] Mark Lewisohn, The Complete Beatles Recording Sessions.

[170] Steve Turner.

[171] Reports of how many times *Yesterday* has been covered vary widely from about 200 to over 3000. The wide variation may depend on how 'covered' is defined, including whether meaning re-recorded, performed, or otherwise. Although it seems likely that *Summertime* by George Gershwin and Dubose Hayward is likely the *Most Covered Track* of all-time (*Guinnessworldrecords.com*, 2018), it is safe to say that Yesterday is amongst the top few covered songs of all time.

[172] *500 Greatest Songs of All Time*, RollingStone.com

[173] Paul McCartney, The Right Words at the Right Time, edited by Marlo Thomas. New York: Atria Books (2002), p. 219.

[174] Barry Miles, *Many Years From Now*, Vintage-Random House (1997), p. 20. Also: Bob Spitz, *The Beatles*. Little Brown (2005), pp. 73-76.

[175] Bob Spitz, *The Beatles*, Little Brown (2005), pp 88-90. Also: *The Beatles Anthology*, Chronicle Books (2000), p. 19.

[176] *Let It Be*, Paul McCartney interview on Sold on Song, BBC (2008-11-11).

[177] McCartney, pp. 217-219.

[178] *500 Greatest Songs of All Time*, RollingStone.com

[179] Keith Badman, The Beatles: Off The Record 2 – The Dream is Over: Off The Record, Omnibus Press (2009-12-15).

[180] Robert Palmer, Paul McCartney Rocks Hard Again, Star News, North Carolina, (1986-8-31), p. 4G.

[181] Jessica Catcher, *Paul McCartney's Newest Dancing Buddy Is a Robot*, Mashable.com (2014-5-16).

[182] *Paul McCartney: 'John Lennon and I had the same premonition about The Beatles' success'*, NME.com (2012-2-12).

[183] Billy Joel Visits The Howard Stern Show, VideodromeVaultRadio channel, SoundCloud.com (2010-16-11), at time: 11min58sec. (Retrieved: ~2016-3-3).

[184] Op. cit. (*Billy Joel Visits The Howard Stern Show*), at time: 1h06min42sec

[185] The Power of Dreams: The Creative Spark, Discovery Channel TV series & video, part 3, 3rd segment, Discovery Communications (1994).

[186] Op. cit. (*Billy Joel Visits The Howard Stern Show*), at time: 1h06min48sec.

[187] Op. cit. (The Power of Dreams: The Creative Spark).

[188] Walter Berry, Billy Joel to recoup Cash on Tour, Lawrence Journal-World (Lawrence, Kansas, 1990-11-18), p. 2D. (Original article from Associated Press)

[189] Op. cit. (The Power of Dreams: The Creative Spark).

[190] Op. cit. (*Billy Joel Visits The Howard Stern Show*), starting at time: 1h12min34sec.

[191] The Power of Dreams: The Creative Spark, Discovery Channel TV series & international video, part 3, 3rd segment, Discovery Communications (1994).

[192] *Talk to Billy Joel*, The Herald Sun (Australia) online blog (2006-7-17).

[193] *Happy 30th, 'Stranger'!*, USAToday.com (2008-7-11).

[194] Timothy White, *Billy Joel Is Angry*, Rolling Stone Magazine (1980-9-4).

[195] Maureen Seaberg (Synesthetes: "People of the Future").

[196] Sting (Lyrics), p. 154.

[197] Op. Cit. (Grace, Bulkeley).

[198] *Sting*, Grammy.com

[199] Hunter Davies & Giles Smith, *Interview / Sting: How we mock our most serious star, our national Friend of the earth. Shouldn't he be a protected species? Or at least a Respected one?*, Independent.co.uk (2011-10-22).

[200] Fred Bronson, *Hot 100 55th Anniversary: The All-Time Top 100 Songs*, Billboard.com (2013-8-2).

[201] Sting, Lyrics, Random House Publishing Group (2009-7-16), p. 75.

[202] *The Dream of The Blue Turtles*, Sting.com (various article excerpts about the blue turtles dream).

[203] Sting reported twenty-two years earlier that his perspective in the dream was from his bedroom window, and that he looked out the garden (ref: Jonathan Taylor, *Sting's LP Dream-influenced*, see below).

[204] Sting, Lyrics, Dial Press (October 2007).

[205] Jonathan Taylor, Sting's LP Dream-influenced, Los Angeles Daily News (1985-8-16).

[206] Sting (Soundbites).

[207] Sting, confirmed in a private email interview (2016-2-4).

[208] Taylor (Los Angeles Daily News).

[209] Tim Allis, *Chatter*, People Magazine, Vol. 28, No. 16 (1987-10-19). Original interview in London's Sunday Express Magazine.

[210] Sting (Lyrics), p. 33.

[211] Sting (Lyrics), p. 154.

[212] Sting, Nothing Like the Sun album liner notes for the song The Lazarus Heart, A&M Records (1987).

[213] Sting, The Mystery and Religion of Music, Billboard Magazine, Commentary Page (1994-5-28), p. 5.

[214] Dave Itzkoff, Sting and Paul Simon Will Tour Together, The New York Times (2013-11-4). Reprinted at: NYTimes.com (2013-11-5).

[215] Paul Zollo, *Paul Simon on Songwriting: I Know What I Know*, Americansongwriter.com (2018-10-5).

[216] Paul Cowan, Paul Simon Today vs. The Paul Simon of Yesterday, Lakeland Ledger newspaper (1976-7-31), p. 6D.

[217] Paul Simon, Paul Simon literally dreamed up his newest album, Seven Psalms, Q with Tom Power, CBC.ca (2023-9-13).

[218] Paul Simon, *Paul Simon contemplates faith, death, and the existence of God*, Q with Tom Power, Youtube.com (2023-6-20), at time: 6m40sec.

[219] Op. cit. (Paul Simon contemplates faith, death and the existence of God), at time: 14m29sec

[220] Chartmasters.org, including digital sales and streaming (retrieved 2025-8-31).

[221] Joseph Shabalala, Ladysmith Black Mambazo: Journey of Dreams, directed by David Lister, ILC (1988), at time: 3min50sec.

[222] Ladysmith Black Mambazo: Journey of Dreams, directed by David Lister, ILC (1988).

[223] Joseph Shabalala, Ladysmith Black Mambazo: Journey of Dreams, directed by David Lister, ILC (1988), at time: 18min56sec.

[224] The Power of Dreams: The Creative Spark, Discovery Channel TV series & video, part 3, first segment, Discovery Communications (1994).

[225] Joseph Shabalala (Ladysmith Black Mambazo: Journey of Dreams), at time: 18min56sec.

[226] Member of Ladysmith Black Mambazo, shared in a private email interview (2016-2-4).

[227] Singing to the Rhythm of Dreams, TIME Magazine (1987-8-10), p. 37.

[228] Member of Ladysmith Black Mambazo, shared in a private email interview (2016-2-4).

[229] Joseph Shabalala (Ladysmith Black Mambazo: Journey of Dreams), at time: 28min58sec.

[230] Singing to the Rhythm of Dreams, TIME Magazine (1987-8-10), p. 37.

[231] *Ladysmith Black Mambazo*, Grammy.com

[232] The Power of Dreams: The Creative Spark, Discovery Channel TV series & video, part 3, first segment, Discovery Communications (1994).

[233] *ARASHI Awarded Global Album of 2019 for Their 20th Anniversary Compilation 5×20 All the BEST!! 1999-2019*, ifpi.org (2020-3-19).

[234] *Billie Eilish - Spotify Top Songs*, kworb.net (retrieved 2025-8-31).

[235] Billie Eilish, *First Look: Zane Lowe Interviews Billie Eilish and Finneas, Apple Music channel*, Youtube.com (2019-2-25). At time: 1m39sec.

[236] Carolyn Droke, *Billie Eilish Opened Up About How Experiencing Sleep Paralysis Inspired Her Music*, Uproxx.com (2020-2-10).

[237] Joe Taysome, *Listen to Billie Eilish's haunting isolated vocal on 'Everything I Wanted'*, Faroutmagazine.co.uk (2020-9-25).

[238] Erin Bates, *How Billie Eilish's Design Team Turned Her Dreams (and Nightmares) Into Realities*, Livedesignonline.com (2019-7-18).

[239] Michael Jackson, Moonwalk, Crown/Archetype (2010-10-27), p. 4.

[240] *Michael Jackson*, Wikipedia.org (retrieved 2015-5-6).

[241] Michael Jackson (Moonwalk), p. 196.

[242] William Carlton, Write a Song - Risk a Lawsuit, The Montreal Gazette (1985-1-17), page E1.

[243] Gerri Hirshey, Michael Jackson: Life as a Man In the Magical Kingdom, Rolling Stone Magazine (1983-2-17). Reprinted at: RollingStone.com

[244] *Michael Jackson: The Peter Pan of Pop*, Newsweek (1983-1-9).

[245] Joe Jackson, *Only Yesterday*, JWJackson.com (2014-6-24). (Retrieved 2016-3-3)

[246] *Joe Jackson Pacemaker Surgery After 3 Heart Attacks*, TMZ.com (2016-7-27).

[247] 500 Greatest Songs of All Time: 2|*The Rolling Stones (I Can't get No) Satisfaction*, RollingStone.com.

[248] As of 2025-8-31, Satisfaction is #31 on Rolling Stones top 500 songs list.

[249] Stacey Anderson, *When Keith Richards Wrote (I Can't Get No) Satisfaction In His Sleep*, RollingStone.com (2011-5-9).

[250] *Keith Richards Celebrates His 71st Birthday With A New Album & A Documentary*, 1059sunnyFM.CBSlocal.com (2015-9-18). (Retrieved 2016-3-3)

[251] Jack Dickey, *Taylor Swift on* 1989, *Spotify, Her Next Tour and Female Role Models*, Time.com (2014-11-13).

[252] Taylor Swift, interview on Live with Kelly And Michael (2014-11-26), at time: ~2 minutes before end.

[253] Taylor Swift, *Taylor Swift NOW: The Making Of A Song (I Did Something Bad)*, EJ Dulay channel, YouTube.com (2018-10-20).

[254] Taylor Swift, Conversations interview, ET Canada (2013-7-5).

[255] Taylor Swift (interview), *So This is What Taylor Swift Dreams About*, Capital 96 FM (2015-2-25)

[256] Ed Sheeran, End Game | Behind The Scenes, Taylor Swift channel, Youtube.com (2018-2-9). At time: 60sec.

[257] Lady Gaga, *Lady Gaga: I have nightmares I'll Die Before I Get My Ideas Out*, Metro.co.uk (2011-5-10).

[258] Larry King interview (just before 2010-6-1).

[259] Lady Gaga, *Lady Gaga Relives Illuminati Dreams*, ThatGrapeJuice.com (2010-6-24).

[260] Aimée Lutkin and Samuel Maude, *Everything to Know About Lady Gaga's New Album Mayhem*, Elle.com (2025-3-6).

[261] James Factora, *After Losing Her Way, Gaga Says Mayhem Brought Her Back to Herself*, Them.us (2025-3-6).

[262] Rolling Stone Magazine, Issue 1108/1109 (July 8-22, 2010).

[263] *Sexxx Dreams (song)*, Gagapedia (retrieved 2025-10-27).

[264] Lady Gaga, @ladygaga channel, X.com (formerly Twitter.com), 2013-9-2 at 10:44pm.

[265] Derrick Rossignol, *Lady Gaga Explains the Dream Fan She Wrote 'Joane' For in Equisite Detail*, Uproxx.com (2017-8-28).

[266] Teddy Swims, *Teddy Swims - Bad Dreams (Story of My Song)*, Teddy Swims channel, YouTube.com (2025-3-24).

[267] Rebecca Schiller, *Shawn Mendes Talks Justin Timberlake-Inspired 'Lost in Japan,' Says He's Really of 'In My Blood': Watch*, Billboard.com (2018-3-23).

[268] Jimi Hendrix, (interview on) The Dick Cavett Show (1969-9-9).

[269] Steven Roby, *Hendrix on Hendrix: Interviews and Encounters with Jimi Hendrix*, Chicago Review Press (2012-10-1), p. ~53. Original interview by Bob Garcia from Open City, done during afternoon concert rehearsals in The Hollywood Bowl (August 24-30, 1967).

[270] Harry Shapiro & Caesar Glebbeek, *Jimi Hendrix, Electric Gypsy*, pp. 524-526. Original interview by John King for New Musical Express (1967-1-28).

[271] Jimi Hendrix, *Jimmy Hendrix: Voodoo Child*, directed by Bob Smeaton (2010), at time: 27min16sec.

[272] *Jimi Hendrix "Purple Haze" Lyrics*, Rock and Roll Hall of Fame (1966).

[273] Monika Dannemann, *The Inner World of Jimi Hendrix*, St. Martin's Press (1996-10-1), p. 44.

[274] Janie Hendrix & John McDermott, Jimi Hendrix: An Illustrated Experience, Atria Books (2007-10-9), p. 59.

[275] Anne Erickson, Jimi Hendrix's Friend Says Red Wine Caused His Death, UltimateClassicRock.com (2011-6-27).

[276] *Cyanosis*, Wikipedia.org (retrieved 2015-1-15).

[277] *Jimi Hendrix "Purple Haze" Lyrics*, Rock and Roll Hall of Fame (1966).

[278] *The RS 500 Greatest Songs of All Time*, RollingStone.com (2009-1-25).

[279] The 100 Greatest Guitar Songs, Rolling Stone Magazine (2008-5-28).

[280] Dannemann.

[281] Jimi Hendrix (interview by Meatball Fulton), Meatball's Podcast: number 10, iTunes.com (added to iTunes 2000-12-31), at time: 14min03sec.

[282] Angel (Jimi Hendrix Song), Wikipedia.org (retrieved 2015-8-4).

[283] Richard Bach, Illusions: The Advetures of a Reluctant Messiah, Dell Publishing (1989), p. 174.

[284] Armando Gallo, Peter Gabriel, Omnibus Press (1986).

[285] Spencer Bright, *Peter Gabriel: An Authorized Biography*, London: Headline Book Publishing, PLC (1989).

[286] In a private email with Bobby Braddock's daughter Jeep, songwriter & radio host for Sirius' Jacie & Jeep show where I was an invited guest (2013-1-22).

[287] David Dalton, Carl Perkins 1932-1938, Gadfly (July 1998).

[288] Jerry Naylor, *Rockabilly Legends*, p. 137.

[289] Carl Perkins and David McGee, *Go, Cat, Go!*, Hyperion Press (1996), p. 187.

[290] The Atlantic (December 1970), p. 102.

[291] Nick Spitzer, *The Story of 'Blue Suede Shoes'*, All Things Considered, NPR (2000-2-7).

[292] Ibid (Spitzer).

[293] *Blue Suede Shoes*, Wikipedia.org (retrieved 2014-9-3), Section: List of Recorded Versions.

[294] Zollo, p. 373.

[295] Ibid.

[296] Zollo, p. 377.

[297] Scott Young, Neil and Me, Mclelland & Stewart (2009-10-27), p. 173.

[298] According to WTMY 1280 AM radio host Sherman Baldwin when he interviewed me on 2010-10-22.

[299] Neil Young, comments made to audience at Bayfront Center Arena, St. Petersburg, FL (1973-2-3).

[300] Susan Stamberg, 'California Dreamin,' Present at the Creation, NPR Morning Edition (2002-07-08).

[301] Paul McCartney, *Paul McCartney Inducts Brian Wilson into the Songwriter's Hall of Fame*, Brian Wilson Channel, YouTube.com (2012-10-23).

[302] Brian Wilson, Pet Sounds Box Set liner notes introduction, Universal Music Canada (1997).

[303] Peter Ames Carlin, Catch a Wave: The Rise, Fall, and Redemption of the Beach Boys' Brian Wilson, Rodale (2006), p. 81.

[304] Brian Wilson, Pet Sounds Gold Disc liner notes introduction, Audio Fidelity (2009).

[305] *The Times All Time Top 100 Albums*, The Times (of London) (1993-November/December).

[306] *New Musical Express Writers Top 100 Albums*, NME (1993-10-2).

[307] *Mojo: The 100 Greatest Albums Ever Made*, Mojo Magazine (August 1995).

[308] *500 Greatest Albums of All Time*, RollingStone.com (2012-5-24).

[309] *Best Songs of All Time*, RollingStone.com (2025-8-31).

[310] Martin Celmins, *Peter Green: Founder of Fleetwood Mac*, Castle Communications (1995).

[311] Johnny Black, *The Shape I'm In: Peter Green*, Mojo (Sept. 1996).

[312] Jordan Potter, *Christine McVie and the "spiritual" experience of writing 'Songbird'*, FaroutMagazine.co.uk, (2022-12-1).

[313] Dave Simpson, *Fleetwood Mac's Christine McVie: 'Cocaine and champagne made me perform better'*, TheGuardian.co.uk (2022-6-9).

[314] Keaton Bell, *Stevie Nicks Just Wants to Keep Telling Stories*, Vogue Magazine / Vogue.com (2020-10-20).

[315] Amy Kaufman, *The Moonlight Confessions of Stevie Nicks*, The Los Angeles Times / LAtimes.com (2020-9-30).

[316] Mesfin Fekadu, *On Edge of 72, Stevie Nicks Just Wants to Sing a Song Live*, Associated Press (2020-10-8).

[317] Op. cit. (Keaton Bell)

[318] Jeff Apter, The Dave Grohl Story, Omnibus Press (2009-11-5), p. ~30.

[319] Alex Young, *Another Round: Foo Fighters – "Everlong"*, ConsequenceOfSound.com (2011-3-15).

[320] Washington Chris Nelson, *Foo Fighter Dave Grohl Directs A Video*, MTV.com (1997-4-11). Original source: New Musical Express Magazine.

[321] *25 Things You Don't Know About Me: Dave Grohl*, US Weekly (2011-4-13).

[322] *Pharrell Williams on Juxtaposition and Seeing Sounds*, NPR.org (2013-12-31).

[323] Jake Stone, *I Spent Last Night With Pharrell Williams, And All I Got Was An Inspiring Discussion About Gender Inequality*, Junkee.com (2014-6-3).

[324] Maureen Seaberg (Synesthetes: "People of the Future").

[325] *Black Eyed Peas - Will.i.am's Dream Music*, Bang Showbiz (2012-2-24).

[326] *will.i.am dreamed up I Gotta Feeling*, DailyStar.co.uk (2012-2-23).

[327] WENN, *will.i.am Dreamed Up I Gotta Feeling*, theWest.com.au, The West Australian (2012-2-23).

[328] *52nd Annual GRAMMY Awards Winners*, Grammy.com

[329] *The Top 20 Billboard Hot 100 Hits of the 2000s*, Billboard.com

[330] *Apple announces most-downloaded iTunes songs of all time*, Independent.co.uk (2011-9-17).

[331] Most Downloaded Songs of All Time, chartmasters.org/most-downloaded-songs-of-all-time (retrieved 2025-8-31).

[332] Fergie, *Fergie on her son Axl Jack*, TheEllenShow channel, YouTube.com (2013-11-19), at time: 1min10sec. Original appearance: The Ellen Degeneres Show, CBS (2013-11-20).

[333] Fergie (Slash & Fergie - Sweet Child O' Mine + INTERVIEW)., mp3Tunes.mobi/download?v=FauHsI7A0nc

[334] Chris Vinnicombe, *Slash solo album interview: the track-by-track guide*, MusicRadar.com (2010-3-4).

[335] Fergie (Slash & Fergie - Sweet Child O' Mine + INTERVIEW).

[336] *The Everly Brothers discography*, Wikipedia.org, section: 1950s. / Also: "The song is the only single ever to be at No. 1 on all of Billboard's singles charts simultaneously, on June 2, 1958." (*All I Have to Do Is Dream*, Wikipedia.org, retrieved 2015-11-16).

[337] Pat Monahan, *interview on VH1's TrueSpin* (uploaded 2008-7-13), / See also: wiki.answers.com

[338] Jayne Moore, *Pat Monahan Of Train Discusses The Group's Fifth Album, For Me, It's You*, SongwriterUniverse.com (2006-3-2).

[339] Anya Leon, *Pat Monahan: How We Chose Our Son's Name*, People.com (2012-4-17), appears in video at time: 10sec.

[340] Train - Vacation featuring Rock Monahan (from The Dressings Room Sessions), Train channel, YouTube.com (2022-7-15)

[341] Lorde, posted on lordemusic page, Facebook.com (2013-12-3, 4:02pm).

[342] Chris Payne, *LL Cool J Song Debut: "Billie Jean Dream"*, Billboard.com (2009-8-10).

[343] *Drake's Leaked "Fireworks" Addresses Rihanna Relationship*, Billboard.com (2010-5-28).

[344] *Talking Shop: Katy Perry*, BBC News (2008-8-26).

[345] *The Rumpus Interview with Jill Sobule*, TheRumpus.net (2009-7-30).

[346] Op. cit. (Katy Perry, BBC News).

[347] *Katy Perry - I Kissed a Girl*, Capitol Music channel, YouTube.com (2008-6-10), at time: ~2min45sec.

[348] Amy Davidson, *Meghan Trainor Interview*, DigitalSpy.co.uk (2015-1-23).

[349] Ryan Kristobak, *Miley Cyrus Debuts New Track 'The Twinkle Song' About a Friend's Dead Cat*, HuffingtonPost.com (2014-12-8).

[350] J. Randy Taraborrelli, Madonna: An Intimate Biography, Simon and Schuster (2001-9-27), p. 144.

[351] Bill Conger, *Dolly Parton Talks About Her Album Blue Smoke, And Writing Her Songs "Home" And "You Can't Make Old Friends"*, Songwriteruniverse.com (2014-6-2).

[352] Dolly Parton, *Don't Make Me Have To Come Down There*, Instagram.com (2023-1-19).

[353] Christina Vinson, *Blake Shelton Shares Serious Video for Savior's Shadow*, Theboot.com (2016-5-19).

[354] Cindy Watts, *Blake Shelton finds grace in God, Gwen Stefani*, TheTennessean.com (2016-5-19).

[355] David Buckley, R.E.M. | Fiction: An Alternative Biography (2012-5-31), p. ~250.

[356] Christopher Bollen, *Michael Stipe*, Interview Magazine (2011-5-4).

[357] Adam Block, The Secret Behind The Songs, Parade Magazine (1993-9-5), p. 22. Originally from: David Wallechinsky & Amy Wallace, The People's Almanac Presents The Book of Lists: The 90's Edition, Aurum (1994).

[358] Stephen M. Deusner, *R.E.M*, Pitchfork.com (2008-3-23).

[359] Evan Schlansky, *Great Quotations: Bruce Springsteen*, AmericanSongwriter.com (2011-11-7).

[360] Jacquie Swift, TheSun.co.uk (2009-2-6).

[361] metrowebukmetro, *The Fray's Conversation with God*, Metro.co.uk (2009-1-30).

[362] Cristina Santiago Montiel, *Isaac Slade's Biography and Facts*, EverythingAboutTheFray.blogspot.ca (2013-7-28).

[363] Ayala Ben-Yehuda, *Rock band the Fray masters "Anatomy" of a hit*, Reuters.com (2008-11-16).

[364] Adrian Thrills, *The Frays Isaac Slade Reveals how Bruce Springsteen helped save his marriage*, TheDailyMail.co.uk (2009-1-15).

[365] Brian May, Queen – A Night at the Opera, In the Studio With Redbeard (syndicated radio interview) (1989).

[366] *Queen | The Prophet's Song*, wiki tab, Last.fm (retrieved 2015-8-10).

[367] *The Making of The Prophet Song (Classic Album)*, Queensville channel, YouTube.com (posted 2012-3-12), at time: 4min46sec.

[368] *The Prophets Song*, Queenpedia.com (retrieved 2015-8-10).

[369] Mark Blake, Born Again, MOJO Magazine (October 2008). Reprinted at: http://freddiemqueen.forumfree.it/?t=32349502

[370] Bill DeMain, *Waterloo Sunset*, Music & Musicians Mag / MMusicMag.com (January 2013).

[371] *500 Greatest Songs of All Time*, Rolling Stone.com (retrieved on 2025-8-31).

[372] Russell Hall, *The Kinks' Dave Davies Talks about His New Album, Gibson Guitars and a Possible Kinks Reunion*, Gibson.com (2014-11-18).

[373] Dinah Shore, *The Dinah Shore Show* (1976-1-3).

[374] David Buckley, *David Bowie: the complete guide to his music*, London: Omnibus (2004), p. 16.

[375] Craig Copetas, *Beat Godfather Meets Glitter Mainman: William Burroughs Interviews David Bowie*, Rolling Stone Magazine (1974-2-28).

[376] Tony Wilson, *Don Wants to Spin a Film Legend*, Melody Maker (1968-7-6), p. 5.

[377] *Hurdy Gurdy Man*, Wikipedia.org (retrieved 2015-1-14), section: Lyrics.

[378] Brian Hinton, Celtic Crossroads, Sanctuary Publishing, Ltd. (2003-3-31), p. 109.

[379] James Earl Ray, Wikipedia.org

[380] David Ritz and Ray Charles, Brother Ray: Ray Charles' Own Story, Da Capo Press (2009-3-17), p. ~230.

[381] Geoff Barton (interview with Alex Lifeson & Neil Peart), This Man Has Nightmares, Sounds magazine (1978-9-30).

[382] Neil Peart, The Game of Snakes and Arrows / Prize Every Time, originally published at: Rush.com, p. 3.

[383] Snakes And Arrows album liner notes, Atlantic Records (2007).

[384] *Q&A: Thom Yorke Talks Dreams, Creative People, Fitting Format*, by David Sinclair, Rolling Stone Magazine (1997-12-25).

[385] Thom Yorke, Radiohead message board (1999-12-19).

[386] Dave Thompson, Smoke on the Water: The Deep Purple Story, ECW Press (2004), p. 127.

[387] Roger Glover, *in a private email* to TheHighwayStar.com staff on 1996-8-20.

[388] Harold de Muir, *Everything We've Ever Done Has Been Selfishly Motivated: AN INTERVIEW WITH Robert Smith of THE CURE*, East Coast Rocker (1987-7-22).

[389] Andy Price, *Dreams, red wine and the desire to explore - Robert Smith's songwriting approach in his own words*, MusicRadar.com (2025-3-20). Reprinted at: Yahoo.com

[390] Larry O'Reilly, Three Heavy Metal Bands Pour On The Iron At Civic Arena, The Pittsburgh Press (1983-8-16), p. B-6.

[391] The Number of the Beast (album), Wikipedia.org (retrieved 2015-10-27).

[392] Gary Hill, The Strange Sound of Cthulhu: Music Inspired by the Writings of H. P. Lovecraft, Lulu.com (2006), p. 44.

[393] Black Sabbath: An Illustrated Biography, Sao Paulo: Universo dos Livros (2013).

[394] Jocelyn Y. Stewart, Lula Mae Hardaway, 76; Stevie Wonder's Mother Helped Him Write Lyrics, Los Angeles Times / LaTimes.com (2006-6-10).

[395] Stevie Wonder, *Stevie Wonder talking at Dreamforce with Marc Benioff*, Deanna C. C. Peluso channel, YouTube.com (posted on 2010-12-14, event date was 2010-12-8).

[396] Piet Levy, *Stevie Wonder talks about that top-secret White House party, Michael Jackson, more*, The Journal Sentinel / jsonline.com (2015-6-25).

[397] Stevie Wonder, keynote speech, ASCAP *I Create Music* Expo (2017-4-15).

[398] Jennifer Vineyard, *Jennifer Lopez Says New Single Came From Marc Anthony's Dream*, MTV.com (2006-9-12).

[399] Dario Rubio, *Ya está en la radio nuevo sencillo de Jennifer Lopez*, Netjoven.pe (2007-5-23).

[400] Joe Nick Patoski & Bill Crawford, Stevie Ray Vaughan: Caught in the Crossfire, Little, Brown and Company (1993), p. 130.

[401] Michael Ventura, Texas Flood album reissue liner notes, Sony Music (2009).

[402] Keri Leigh, Stevie Ray: Soul to Soul. Lanham: Taylor Trade Publishing (1993).

[403] Scott Freeman, *Midnight riders: The story of the Allman Brothers Band* (1st ed.), Boston: Little, Brown & Company (1995).

[404] *Little Martha*, Wikipedia.org (retrieved 2015-3-3), section: Song Origin.

[405] Gerald M. Gay, *Ziggy Marley sounding a spiritual tone*, Arizona Daily Star (2006-8-10).

[406] Joseph K. So, *Olga Kern: Celebrating the Music*, Scena.org (2012-2-16).

[407] Olga Kern, *News*, OlgaKern.com (2014-9-9).

[408] Sarah Bryan Miller, Pianist Kern to make St. Louis Symphony Orchestra debut, STLToday.com (2010-11-21).

[409] Nanette van der Laan, Teen Wins Piano Competition, TheMoscowTimes.com (1993-2-8).

[410] Op. cit. (Sarah Bryan Miller).

[411] Op. cit. (Nanette van der Laan).

[412] Op. cit. (Sarah Bryan Miller).

[413] Olga Kern, News, OlgaKern.com (2014-9-9).

[414] Boris Nelson, Pianist Van Cliburn steps back slowly into the limelight, The Toledo Blade (1989-7-2), p. D1.

[415] Sarah Bryan Miller.

[416] David Rohde, From Beethoven to Rachmaninoff to Billy Joel: An Interview with Superstar Pianist Olga Kern, DCMetroTheaterArts.com (2015-11-12).

[417] Ben Finane, Soaring Melodies, Listen magazine (Spring 2015). Reprinted at: Steinway.com

[418] Olga Kern, *About*, OlgaKern.com/about/

[419] *2nd movement from Violin concerto by Alma Deutscher (9): Romanza*, AlmaDeutscher YouTube channel, YouTube.com (2015-2-3).

[420] *Cindarella. Opera by Alma Deutscher (b.2015). Act 1*, AlmaDeutscher YouTube channel, YouTube.com (2015-7-27).

[421] John Stevens, *Meet Little Miss Mozart: The miniature musician aged seven who has composed her own opera*, TheDailyMail.co.uk (2012-10-21).

[422] Bob Weir, *As Trump Trails Biden In The Polls, Bob Weir Rallies First-Time Voters | The Beat with Ari Melber*, MSNBC channel on Youtube.com (2020-10-30). Starting at time 5m40sec.

[423] Sammy Hagar, Hear SAMMY HAGAR's EDDIE VAN HALEN-Inspired New Song, 'Encore, Thank You, Goodnight.', Blabbermouth.net (2025-4-25).

[424] Paul Elliott, "This was 100% a communication from the beyond": Listen to the song that Sammy Hagar Claims to have written with Eddie Van Halen in a dream, Musicradar.com (2025-4-25).

[425] Marina Watts, Sammy Hagar's New Song 'Encore. Thank You. Good Night.' Was Inspired by a Dream About Eddie Van Halen, People.com (2025-4-25).

[426] Op. cit. (Paul Elliott).

[427] Wes Orshoski, Sinead O'Connor 'Sexys Up' Irish Traditionals, Billboard Magazine (2002-10-8). Reprinted at: www.Sinead-OConnor.com

[428] Mike Posner, interview with the artist, SXSW conference (2017-3-18).

[429] according to user edgeturbo03, Barenaked Ladies – Leave, SongMeanings.com (2006-03-02).

[430] Ray Waddell, Rodney Crowell Looks Back On 'The Houston Kid', Billboard Magazine (2001-2-10), p. 14.

[431] James Montgomery, *Florence and The Machine Reveal Inspirations Behind the New Album*, MTV.com (2011-6-10).

[432] Black Eyed Peas - Will.i.am's Dream Music, Bang Media International (2012-2-24). Reprinted at: ElleCanada.com

[433] *Florence Welch*, Wikipedia.org (retrieved 2015-7-19).

[434] Jason Bracelin, Killers' Second Album Strikes Higher Chord, Las Vegas Review-Journal (2006-10-13). Archived at: Web.Archive.org

[435] An excited Brandon Flowers talks NME through The Killers' new LP 'Sam's Town', NME (2006-10-6).

[436] Glenn BurnSilver, *How a Dream of Louis Armstrong Inspired Dr. John's Latest Album*, The New Phoenix Times (2014-8-6).

[437] Gil Bailie, *Violence Unveiled: Humanity at the Crossroads*, New York: Crossroad Publishing Company (1995), p. xv. (sometimes falsely attributed to Harold Whitman or Harold Thurman Whitman).

[438] Rory Block, under 'Interview' tab at RoryBlock.com (retrieved 2015-6-15).

[439] Rory Block, liner notes for *Confessions of a Blues Singer*, Rounder Records (1998).

[440] Rory Block, liner notes for Ain't I a Woman, Rounder Records (1992).

[441] Formerly called the W.C. Handy Awards up until Block's most recent award win.

[442] Earl Robinson & Alfred Hayes, Songs of Joe Hill sung by Joe Glazer, New York: Folkways Records (1954), track 1.

[443] Lori Elaine Taylor, *Joe Hill Inc.: We Own Our Past*. Indiana University Press (1993), p. 26.

[444] *The Lost Forest Fones, episode 1*, TeganAndSaraMusic channel on Youtube.com (2008-5-2), at time: 3min57sec.

[445] Megadeth defends music Dawson College gunman loved, CBC.com (2006-9-28).

[446] Liz Ramanand, Dave Mustaine on the Making of Megadeth's 'Public Enemy No. 1' video, LoudWire.com (2012-1-27).

[447] (fan site) http://megadeth.rockmetal.art.pl/lyrics_cryptic.html (retrieved 2015-8-4).

[448] Seniqua Sherman, Timbaland Says Tink Is "The One", Because Aaliyah Said So In A Dream, GoodFellaMedia.com (2015-3-22).

[449] *Georg Solti*, Grammy.com

[450] Prokop, p. 49.

[451] Dr. Waldemar Schweisheimer, p. 546.

[452] Richard Wagner, My Life. 2 vol., New York: Dodd, Mead & Co. (1912), p. 603. German version: M. Gregor-Dellin, ed.: *Richard Wagner: Mein Leben*, Munich (1963), 2/1976; Eng. trans., Cambridge (1983) [1st authentic edition]).

[453] *Georg Solti*, Grammy.com

[454] John Culshaw, Ring Resounding: The Recording of Der Ring Des Nibelungen, Random House, (2012-10-18), pp. 215-219.

[455] *Georg Solti*, Grammy.com

[456] Paul C. Horton, Review of *Psychoanalytic Explorations in Music: Second Series* (ed. Stuart Feder), American Journal of Psychiatry, vol. 156 (July 1999), pp. 1109–1110.

[457] Bryan Magee, Aspects of Wagner, Oxford: Oxford University Press (1988).

[458] Diaz de Chumaceiro, Cora L., Richard Wagner's Life and Music: What Freud Knew, a paper included in Feder, Stuart, Karmel, Richard L., Pollock, George H.'s, Psychoanalytic Explorations in Music, Second Series, Madison, CT (1993), pp. 249-278.

[459] T. Picard, Dictionnaire encyclopédique Wagner, Paris: Actes Sud (2010; in French).

[460] Richard Wagner, Beethoven, Originally published by E. W. Fritzsch, Leipzig (1870; reached a second edition before the end of same year). Translation into English by William Ashton Ellis.

[461] Arthur Schopenhauer, *Die Welt als Wille und Vorstellung* (German for: The World as Will and Idea), volume 2, Brockhaus (1844), p. 391.

[462] Stanley Krippner, Access to hidden reserves of the unconscious through dreams in creative problem
solving, Journal of Creative Behavior (1981), vol. 15, pp. 11–22.

[463] Richard Wagner, The Master Singers of Nuremberg, translation by Peter Branscombe, Essen: Kaiser (1974), p. 195.

[464] After much discussion with an experienced German-English translator, I initially added the word 'verse' to keep this stanza truer to the original German version and removed the word 'that' to preserve the rhythmic meter without disturbing the meaning. Then, considering that not only was Wagner writing an opera, which is sung, and that by sharing this line, instructor Hans Sachs is encouraging his student Walther to write the verses of a <u>song</u>, I decided to change 'verse' (used it its plural form) to 'songs'.

[465] Dr. Waldemar Schweisheimer, It Came in a Dream, The Etude Magazine, Volume LXII, No. 9, Philadelphia: Theodore Presser Co. (September 1944), p. 515. This is a very slight variation on the English translation of part of Richard Wagner's Die Meistersinger von Nürnberg, Act III, Scene II. (note: after much discussion with an experienced German-English translator, I added the word 'verse' to keep the stanza truer to the original German version and removed the word 'that' to preserve the rhythmic meter without disturbing the meaning. Considering that not only was Wagner writing an opera, which is sung, and that by sharing this line, instructor Hans Sachs is encouraging his student Walther to write the verses of a <u>song</u>, the word 'verse' might even be better, in modern day, if replaced by 'song'.)

[466] 'Interpretation' can mean either the mental process of translation, or the creative embodiment of an idea by a singer, poet, actor, or other artist. However, the common modern day meaning of 'interpretation' when used after the word 'dream' is usually much closer to the intellectual understanding of the dream, a lop-sidedness quite possibly be related to the invisible effect which has taken place for over more than a century now since the publication of Sigmund Freud's landmark classic The Interpretation of Dreams and the process of psychoanalysis related to it that Freud pioneered. Note that Wagner wrote the opera well before Freud's work ever appeared.

[467] Wagner (Master Singers of Nuremburg), pp. 233-235.

[468] Wagner (Master Singers of Nuremburg), p. 203.

[469] Wagner (Master Singers of Nuremburg), p. 205.

[470] James Joyce, Portrait of a Young Artist, New York: B. W. Huebsch (1916), p. 217.

[471] Georges Borach, Conversations with James Joyce, translation by Joseph Prescott, College English 15 (March 1954), p. 327.

[472] *Georg Solti*, Grammy.com

[473] Alice Herz-Sommer, The Lady in Number Six: Music Saved My Life, Produced by Malcom Clarke, Nicholas Reed, and Christopher Branch (2014-1-16).

[474] Luckett, Richard. *Handel's Messiah: A Celebration*. London: Victor Gollancz (1992), p. 86. Prior citation: Horatio Townsend An Account of the Visit of Handel to Dublin (1852), p. 93, citing (original:) Laetitia Matilda Hawkins, Anecdotes, Biographical Sketches and Memoirs vol. 1 (1822).

[475] The Harvard Magazine (December 1862), p. 141.

[476] Ed Hird, Rediscovering Händel's Messiah, Deep Cove Crier (April 1993).

[477] Bettina von Arnim, Goethe's Correspondence with a Child, Longman, Orme Brown, Green and Longmans (1839), pp. 210-211.

[478] Maynard Solomon, American Imago, XXXII, 1975: *The Dreams of Beethoven*, pp. 113-144. Reprinted in The Psychoanalytic Quarterly (1977), p. 46:349.

[479] 'pertobiassen' is the word used originally by Beethoven in his letter which appears to be a verbal noun he created along the lines of a word play that roughly means "the use of the name Tobias in and/or for a composition" (according to a colleague skilled at translation from German to English).

[480] Alexander Wheelock Thayer, Thayer's Life of Beethoven, Princeton University Press (1967), p. 778.

[481] It has been suggested that the canon was not an entirely new idea to Beethoven since a sketch of it appeared at the start of his desk sketchbook 'Artaria 197' [Artaria 197, Staatsbibliothek, Berlin] as well as its companion 'Pocket Sketchbook of Late 1821' [Beethoven, Pocket Sketchbook of Late 1821, Ms. 51 Nr. 3, Ms. 99 and Ms. 80, Bibliothèque Nationale, Paris]. However the canon's appearance at the start of 'Artaria 197' is out of place since it's squeezed into some free space on the first page of the book, so it seems quite likely then that the canon was added there later. That the canon came as a spontaneous inspiration to the composer seems strengthened by how the piece suddenly interrupts improvements to his Credo of the Missa Solemnis near the middle of the pocket sketchbook [William Drabkin, *The Songs and Sketches for the Allegro molto from Beethoven's Op. 110*, Beethoven Forum, Volume 14, No.1, University of Illinois Press (Spring 2007), p. 59].

[482] email newsletter, sivanandayogafarm.org (circa 2014). Quoting: Sri Swami Sivananda.

[483] Alfred Hoche, Das träumende Ich (The Dreaming I), Fischer (1927), pp. 102-103.

[484] Edmondstoune Duncan, Schubert, J.M. Dent & Co. (1905), p. 26. Original source: Schubert's Diary, Sofie Muller, Vienna (1832).

[485] Duncan, p. 82.

[486] Patrick Kavannaugh, Spiritual Lives of the Great Composers, Grand Rapids, MI: ZondervanPublishing House (1996), p. 66.

[487] Maynard Solomon, Franz Schubert's 'My Dream', American Imago 38 (1981), pp. 137-154.

[488] Duncan, pp. 111-113.

[489] Wilhelm Müller, Dream of Spring (translation by Celia Sgroi), gopera.com/lieder/translations/schubert_911.pdf (retrieved 2016-3-3).

[490] Schumann recounted such episodes as increasingly vivid, as happening not just during sleeping dreams, and finally as simplifying into a lone high A note that he no longer enjoyed, like an incessant tinnitus. It seems possible, due the increasing level of the hallucinations, that Schumann may have developed neurosyphilis or some other neurological or psychological disorder, or the very slight chance of even a brain tumor or minor epilepsy that affected his temporal lobes since similar auditory hallucination experiences have been reported by modern day people with such problems [Op. cit., Musicophilia, pp. 21-23 & 56).]

[491] Robert Jourdain, Music, The Brain, and Ecstasy: How music Captures Our Imagination, New York: William Morrow (2008-4-1).

[492] Wolf-Dieter Seiffert, *Preface to Thema mit Variationen (Geistervariation)*, Munich: G. Henle Verlag (1995).

[493] Victoria Tischler (editor), Mental Health, Psychiatry and the Arts: A Teaching Handbook, Radcliffe Publishing (2010), p. 124.

[494] Wolf-Dieter Seiffert, *Preface to Thema mit Variationen (Geistervariation)*, Munich: G. Henle Verlag (1995).

[495] *Geistervariationen*, Wikipedia.org (retrieved 2014-11-1), section: History.

[496] Prokop, p. 50.

[497] David Lee Brodbeck, Brahms: Symphony, Issue 1, Cambridge University Press (1997-1-23), p. 4.

[498] Jan Swafford, Johannes Brahms: A Biography, Knopf Doubleday Publishing Group (2012-1-11), pp. 138-139.

[499] G. Johnson, Music in Dreams, in Virginia W. Bass' Dreams Can Point The Way, Miracle Publishing Company (1984-10-1).

[500] Ian Bradley, Lost Chords and Christian Soldiers: The Sacred Music of Arthur Sullivan, Hymns Ancient and Modern Ltd. (2013-7-31), p. 109.

[501] *Then The Curtain Opened: The Bracing Impact Of Stravinsky's 'Rite'*, NPR.org (2013-5-25).

[502] Igor Stravinsky, Poetics of Music in the Form of Six Lessons, Harvard University Press (1970), p. 18.

[503] Igor Stravinsky, An Autobiography, Simon & Schuster, Inc. (1936), p. 103.

[504] Igor Stravinsky & Robert Craft, Dialogues and a Diary, London: Faber and Faber (1968), p. 39.

[505] Igor Stravinsky & Robert Craft, *Conversations with Igor Stravinsky*, Garden City, New York: Doubleday & Company, Inc. (1959), Question 14.

[506] Théodore (Igor's eldest son) & Denise Strawinsky, Stravinsky: A Family Chronicle 1906-1940, Music Sales Group (2004), p. 49. Translated from 1999 French edition: *Au coeur du foyer: Catherine et Igor Strawinsky, 1906-1940.*

[507] Op. cit. (Conversations with Igor Stravinsky).

[508] Op. cit. (Conversations with Igor Stravinsky).

[509] Here again we see that important events such as transformational dreams, and in this case likely a life-calling vision, happen at ages divisible by 7, i.e. Tartini's age of 21 = 3 x 7.

[510] The Power of Dreams: The Creative Spark, Discovery Channel TV series & video, part 3, Discovery Communications (1994).

[511] Jerome J. le Français de Lalande, (translated from interview in French with Tartini in:) Voyage d'un Français en Italie (1770), pp. 189-190.

[512] By the time Bruckner began composing his Symphony No. 6, only three of his symphonies had even been performed [*Symphony No. 6, Anton Bruckner*, Wikipedia.org (retrieved 2014-8-4), section: Historical Context.]

[513] Elisabeth Maier, The Bruckner Journal. Vol. 4, issue no. 1 (March 2000).

[514] In his work Stories of Anton Bruckner, Hans Commenda tells a variation of this dream where Bruckner heard a violist play the start of the 7th, as opposed to Göllerich/Auer's account that it was whistled by Dorn. Max Auer later wrote a biography of Bruckner (separate from the collaborative version with August Göllerich) saying that in the dream, Dorn "dictated" the opening of the 7th to the sleeping Bruckner.

[515] August Göllerich & Max Auer, Anton Bruckner ein Lebens- und Schaffensbild (4 volumes), 4 editions: 1922-1936 Regensburg / Bosse (1936). Vol. 4/2, p. 99.

[516] *Anton Bruckner, Symphony No 7*, Hyperion Records, HyperionRecord.co.uk, 7th paragraph (retrieved 2014-4-4).

[517] Op. cit. (Göllerich-Auer), Vol. 4/1. pp. 345-6. (quoting Max von Oberleithner's My memories of Anton Bruckner, G. Bosse, 1933).

[518] Commenda (Geschichten um Anton Bruckner / Stories of Anton Bruckner), p. 76.

[519] Hector Berlioz & Ernest Newman, Memoirs of Hector Berlioz: From 1803 to 1865, Comprising His Travels in Germany, Italy, Russia and England, Courier Corporation (1932), p. 160.

[520] Hector Berlioz, The Memoirs of Hector Berlioz (translated by David Cairns), New York: Everyman's library (2002).

[521] David Cairns, Berlioz: Volume Two: Servitude and Greatness, 1832-1869. University of California Press (2003), p. 466.

[522] William Hutchison Murray, The Scottish Himalayan Expedition, Dent (1951), p. 7. Incorrectly quoting (or inaccurately paraphrasing) Johann Wolfgang von Goethe, however the quote stands well on its own.

[523] Dr. Waldemar Schweisheimer, It Came in a Dream, The Etude Magazine, Volume LXII, No. 9, Philadelphia: Theodore Presser Co. (September 1944), p. 515.

[524] André-Ernest-Modeste Grétry, Mémoires, ou Essai sur la musique, self-published by Grétry (1789), p. 186.

[525] Amanda Holden, Nicholas Kenyon, Stephen Walsh, The Viking Opera Guide, Viking (1993).

[526] Pierre Lasserre, The Spirit of French Music, London: Forgotten Books (2013), p. 28-29. (Originally published in 1921). Reprinted at: Archive.org

[527] André-Ernest-Modeste Grétry, (Mémoires, ou Essai sur la musique), p. 466.

[528] Ibid.

[529] Pierre Lasserre.

[530] André-Ernest-Modeste Grétry, Voyages, études et travaux de A.-M. Grétry, C. Delagrave (1889), p. 192.

[531] Robert Adelson (editor), Abstract for Lucile Gretry's Mariage D'Antonio, A. R. Editions, Inc. (2013).

[532] Richard Taruskin, Music in the Nineteenth Century: The Oxford History of Western Music, Oxford University Press (2009-6-24), p. 820.

[533] Natalie Bauer-Lechner, Erinnerungen an Gustav Mahler, p. 48.

[534] Record/CD liner notes for Mahler: Symphony No. 3 (performed by The London Symphony Orchestra conducted by Sir Georg Solti).

[535] C.G. Jung, C.G. Jung Letters, 1906-1950, Princeton University Press (1973), p. 542.

[536] Margaret Tilly, The Therapy of Music (1956), from *Jung Speaking* (anthology), eds. William McGuire & R.F.C. Hull. Princeton: Princeton University Press (1977), p. 275.

[537] John Adams, *Hamonielehre*, Earbox.com (retrieved 2015-1-7).

[538] Will Myers, *Eine Kleine Nachtmusic* (2012-10-11).

[539] Op. cit. (John Adams)

[540] Stuart Dodgson Collingwood, The Life and Letters of Lewis Carroll, chapter 5, New York: The Century Co. (1899). (*Dreamland* sheet music & lyrics published by Oxford University Press).

[541] *Griffes and 'The Pleasure Dome of Kubla Khan"*, NPR (2006-2-10).

[542] Jorge Luis Borges, Ruth L. C. Simms, The Flower of Coleridge in Other Inquisitions, 1937-1952, University of Texas Press (1964), p. 10-11.

[543] Chris Pasles, *Druckman Looks to Heaven for Inspiration*, Los Angeles Times (1992-4-24).

[544] Gunther Schuller, *Dreamscape*, Associated Music Publishers, Programme Note (2012). Also appeared in program notes (and was performed in) The Boston Symphony Orchestra concert series (spring 2015).

[545] Ann McCutchan, *The Muse that Sings: Composers Speak about the Creative Process*, USA: Oxford University Press, (1999-10-18), pp. 204-205.

[546] Anthony Shafton, Dream-Singers: The African-American Way with Dreams, John Wiley & Sons (2002-3-25), p. 135.

[547] Bede (8th century historian), *Historia ecclesiastica gentis Anglorum* book IV (circa B.C.E. 731-737), edited and translated by Bertram Colgrave; Roger Mynors, AB (1969). *Bede's Ecclesiastical History of the English People*. Oxford Medieval Texts. Oxford: Clarendon Press (1992-6-11).

[548] Kemp Malone, *Modern Language Notes*, The Johns Hopkins University Press (1961), p. 194.

[549] Hermanns, p. 103.

[550] Karen Ralls, Ph. D., *Music and The Celtic Otherworld*, druidry.org, section 5 (retrieved 2015-3-3).

[551] E. Gwynn, Metrical Dindshenchas III, Dublin (1913), p. 227.

[552] *Turlough O'Carolan 1670-1738*, http://english.glendale.cc.ca.us/carolan.html (retrieved 2015-11-14).

[553] Corey Christiansen & Neil Hellman, Celtic Songs and Slow Airs for the Mountain Dulcimer, Mel Bay Publications (2004-5-19), p. 22.

[554] Henri-Frédéric Amiel, Amiel's *Journal: The* Journal Intime Henri-Frédéric Amiel, Macmillan and Company (1885), p. 258.

[555] Marcus Tullius Cicero, Somnium Scipionis (The Dream of Scipio) (#10), De re publica, book 6 (circa 51 BC). Reprinted at: Tertullian.org (translation by W. D. Pearman).

[556] Jamie James, The Music of the Spheres: Music, Science, and the Natural Order of the Universe, Springer Science & Business Media (1995), p. 61.

[557] Mary Devlin, Medieval Music, Magical Minds, iUniverse (2001), p. 90.

[558] Carl Huffman, *Pythagoras*, The Stanford Encyclopedia of Philosophy (Summer 2014 Edition), Edward N. Zalta (ed.).

[559] George Sylvester Viereck (interviewing Albert Einstein), What Life Means to Einstein, The Saturday Evening Post (1929-10-26), p. 17.

[560] Holger Kolweit, Ph.D., Dreamtime and Inner Space: The World of the Shaman, Boston: Shambhala (1988), p. 103.

[561] Marina Roseman. Healing Sounds from the Malaysian Rainforest: Temiar music and medicine. Berkeley: University of California Press (1993), p. 9.

[562] Ann Faraday and John-Wren Lewis, *The Selling of the Senoi*, Lucidity Letter Vol. 110, No 1/2 (1991).

[563] Kolweit, p. 83.

[564] Patricia Garfield, *Creative Dreaming*, New York: Ballantine Books (1974), p. 53.

[565] William C. Sturtevant, Handbook of North American Indians: Great Basin, Government Printing Office (1978), p. 385.

[566] Bruno Nettl, The Study of Ethnomusicology: Thirty-Three Discussions, University of Illinois Press (2015-5-15), p. 299 & 385.

[567] Andrew Wiget, Handbook of Native American Literature, Taylor & Francis (1996), pp. 120-121.

[568] G. Herzog, A comparison of Pueblo and Pima musical styles, Journal of American Folklore (1936), 49, p. 318.

[569] William C. Sturtevant, Handbook of North American Indians: California, Government Printing Office (1978). p. 642.

[570] Malka Marom with Joni Mitchell, *Both Sides Now*, Gardners VI Books AMS006 / Omnibus Press (2014-11-10).

[571] Cameron Crowe, *Joni Mitchell: The 'Rolling Stone' Interview*, RollingStone Magazine (1979-7-26), p. 51. Digital copy retrieved from JoniMitchell.com

[572] Zollo, p. 7.

[573] Martin Chilton, *Patty Griffin: Servant of love - Superb Songwriting Tips for Grown-Ups*, Telegraph.co.uk (2015-9-21).

[574] Patty Griffin, shared between songs on her live 2 CD set A Kiss in Time, ATO Records (2003-10-10). Editorial Reviews transcription at: Amazon.com

[575] Julia Ward Howe, *Reminiscences: 1819-1899,* New York: Houghton, Mifflin (1899), p. 275.

[576] Thanks to radio host Paul Eno, a distant cousin of Julia Ward Howe, who mentioned this story to me when interviewing me on air.

[577] Louis F. Benson, Classic Hymn Stories: Inspiring Stories Behind Our Best-loved Hymns, Xulon Press (2007-3-1), pp. 11-12.

[578] Easy Programs For Christmas, Baker's Plays (1945), p. 24.

[579] *About This Recording*, The History of Siamese Classical Music, Vol. 5: The Mahori Orchestra.

[580] Simon Broughton & Mark Ellingham, *World Music: Latin and North America, Caribbean, India, Asia and Pacific, Volume 2*, Rough Guides (2000), p. 191.

[581] Theodore Levin, liner notes to Huun-Huur-Tu's CD Sixty Horses in my Herd, Shanachie (1993), and a paraphrased translation of Valentina Suzukei's Tuvan Traditional Musical Instruments, from oral recitation of Kombu Oorzhak (born circa 1917).

[582] Ralph Leighton, Deep in the Heart of Tuva: Cowboy Music from the Wild East, Publishing Group West (1996-5-1). Reprinted at: http://www.alashensemble.com/Instruments/igil/igil_folktale.htm

[583] Theodore Levin.

[584] *Music from Mongolia*, University of Oxford Social Sciences Dept. web site, SocSci.Ox.ac.uk, RESEARCH tab.

[585] or its predecessor, the 'huqin' or '**erhu**' from China's Song Dynasty (960-1279 CE), which is reported as the first such string instrument to be bowed with horse hair. Ref: edited by Marvelene C. Moore & Philip Ewell, Kaleidoscope of Cultures: A Celebration of Multicultural Research and Practice, R&L Education (2009-12-16), p. 64.

[586] In addition to the many striking parallels between the two stories, and even before taking into account how names can easily vary when passed down through generations of oral tradition, the beginning of the first horse-owner's name in the Tuvan tale, 'Öskus', seems to bear some resemblance to the Mongolian tale's 'Suho'

(with alternate spelling/pronunciation 'Sükhe'), and interestingly becomes surprisingly close when spoken or spelled backwards.

[587] Cathy Spagnoli, World Of Asian Stories: A Teaching Resource, Tulika Books (2008-3-1), pp. 49-51.

[588] Edited by Ivy A. Corfis, Al-Andalus, Sepharad and Medieval Iberia: Cultural Contact and Diffusion, BRILL (2009), pp. 247-249.

[589] (see: 'erhu' reference above, and also:) Sarah Wallin, Tuvan Throat Singing and the Legend of the Horse Head Fiddle (June 2005), published at: SarahWallinHuff.com

[590] Lira, Encyclopaedia Brittanica Online, Brittanica.com (2009).

[591] Op. Cit (Grace, Bulkeley).

[592] Shawn Colvin, from the WUMB Member Concert, Boston, MA (1989-10-2).

[593] Shawn Colvin, interview in The Performing Songwriter magazine (September/October 1993).

[594] Shawn Colvin, Happy Birthday, Shawn Colvin! by Lydia Hutchison, The Performing Songwriter (2011-1-10 reprint from above reference).

[595] Lenny Kravitz' dream inspiration, ElleCanada.com (2011-8-10).

[596] Lenny Kravitz, Lenny Kravitz Says He Wrote 'Raise Vibration' Album in Dreams, Out of The Box Show with Jonathan Clarke, Q1043 channel, YouTube.com (2018-9-13). At time: 1min0sec.

[597] Lenny Kravitz, Lenny Kravitz talks about his connection with Johnny Cash and his song with the namesake. SiriusXM channel, YouTube.com (2018-10-21). At time: 15sec.

[598] Op. Cit. (Lenny Kravitz, Q1043). At time: 5min0sec

[599] Janelle Monae: Dreaming In Science Fiction, All Things Considered, NPR.org (2010-5-14). Comments about dreams starting around time: 3min58sec.

[600] My LP came in a dream, The Sun, TheSun.co.uk (2010).

[601] In Search of Mona Lisa, Santana.com (circa 2019-1-25).

[602] List of Billboard 200 number-one albums of 1972, Wikipedia.org (retrieved 2015-4-7).

[603] Mark Hughes Cobb, 'American Pie' line by line, TuscloosaNews.com (2009-2-6).

[604] Paul Grein, liner notes for American Pie 2003 re-issue, Capitol Records (2003).

[605] Michael Martin Murphey, interviewed by Lynn Neary. The Lingering Mystery of 'Wildfire'. NPR Weekend Edition (2007-4-29).

[606] Gary James, Gary James' Interview with Michael Martin Murphey, ClassicBands.com.

[607] Joseph Murrell, The Book of Golden Discs (2nd ed.), London: Barrie and Jenkins Ltd. (1978), p. 361.

[608] Michael Martin Murphey, Wikipedia.org (retrieved 2015-1-17), section: "Wildfire" and the Epic Years.

[609] Paul Zollo, Closer to the Light with Bruce Cockburn, SongTalk, vol. 4, issue 2 (1994).

[610] All The Diamonds songbook, edited by Arthur McGregor, OFC Publications (1986).

[611] Zollo (SongTalk).

[612] Wondering Where the Lions Are, Wikipedia.org (retrieved 2015-4-18).

[613] Rick Henry, Horizon (1975), TheCarpentersOnline.com (formerly active website).

[614] Martin Chilton, *'You Win Again': The Story of the Bee Gees Hit*, Udiscovermusic.com (2025-9-7).

[615] Robin Gibb & Barry Gibb, Interview with the Bee Gees, The Larry King Show (2002-2-22). Transcribed at: CNN.com

[616] *Bee Gees*, Wikipedia.org (retrieved 2015-9-15), in section: Awards and nominations.

[617] *PRO MOTION Interviews Graham Russell of Air Supply*, PRO MOTION channel, YouTube.com (2014-4-10), at time: 1min30sec.

[618] RJ Carter, *Graham Russell: Taking Air Supply from Dreams to Stardom*, CriticalBlast.com (2010-6-10).

[619] Gary James, *Interview with Russell Hitchcock of Air Supply*, ClassicBands.com.

[620] Op. cit. (Carter)

[621] Kevin Cronin, KEVIN CRONIN OF REO SPEEDWAGON TALKS ABOUT HIS CLASSIC HITS AND HIS SONGWRITING, REOSpeedwagon.com (2016-1-22).

[622] James Henke, *Interview: The B-52's*, Rolling Stone Magazine (1980-12-11).

[623] 'Leap of Faith': Loggins' album, tour intensely personal, The Milwaukee Sentinel (1992-3-6), p. 1C.

[624] amy.volume, *GOOD (Canadian) MUSIC: Jonathan Roy talks blues*, wine & women (2015-10-6).

[625] Future Star of the Month, 1073koolfm.com (retrieved 2015-11-14).

[626] Henry Wadsworth Longfellow, Outre-Mer, Houghton (1883), p. 197.

[627] Tori Amos, AOL Chat, AOL.com (1999-9-29). Reprinted at: http://thedent.com/chataol0999.html / Also reprinted with other 1000-Oceans-related interviews at: http://www.yessaid.com/talk/111000oceans.html

[628] Jay S. Jacobs, Pretty Good Year: A Biography of Tori Amos, Hal Leonard Corp. (2006), pp. 92-93.

[629] Elvis Costello, liner notes for Punch The Clock 2003 reissue, Rhino Records (2003). Reprinted at www.ElvisCostello.info

[630] Elvis Costello, Girls Girls Girls (cassette edition) liner notes, Demon records: UK (1989). Reprinted at: www.ElvisCostello.info

[631] Elvis Costello, Blood & Chocolate (2002) liner notes, Rhino / Edsel reissue (2002). Reprinted at: www.ElvisCostello.info

[632] Zollo, p. 183.

[633] *P.F.Sloan*, Wikipedia.org (retrieved 2015-2-7), in section: Hits and charted songs as a songwriter

[634] Carly Simon, Let The River Run, from the Working Girl movie soundtrack, directed by Mike Nichols (1988).

[635] Nicole Atkins, interview with Eric Ginsberg, *SongStory SO.E4 - Nicole Atkins - Girl You Look Amazing*, SongStory Show, SoundCloud.com (2015-4-15), at time: 1min20sec.

[636] Zoe Atlas, *Effortless: Dan Wilson*, SoundOfBoston.com (2015-3-3).

[637] *Dan Wilson (musician)*, Wikipedia.org (retrieved 2015-11-19).

[638] Rickie Lee Jones, *The Other Side of Desire album trailer*, RickieLJonesOfficial channel, YouTube.com (2015-4-13), at time: 1min47sec.

[639] Robert Hilburn, Captivating pop veteran Tom Waits resurfaces, Los Angeles Times (1999-6-27). Reprinted in The Daily Gazette, Schenectady, New York, p. G2.

[640] Tom Waits, *'Fish in the Jailhouse'*, RollingStone.com (2014-5-12).

[641] Zollo (Songwriters), p. 559.

[642] Ibid.

[643] Ibid, p. 560.

[644] *Press Releases*, Sanandamaitreya.com (2009-6-18).

[645] Johnny Black, Where Are They Now?, Q Magazine, issue #180 (summer 2001).

[646] *Sign Your Name by Terence Trent D'Arby*, SongFacts.com (2005).

[647] *Sign Your Name*, Wikipedia.org (retrieved 2015-1-20).

[648] KT Tunstall, *KT Tunstall - My Recurring Tiger Dream*, Fonic channel, Vimeo.com (2010-11-18).

[649] Tom Sowerby, *KT Tunstall Interview - Tiger Suit*, Virgin.com (retrieved 2016-3-3).

[650] KT Tunstall, *KT Tunstall*, HollywoodForever.TicketFly.com (2013-10).

[651] *KT Tunstall*, 'Bio' tab, JamBase.com

[652] *Third Eye Blind*, Wikipedia.org (retrieved 2015-6-17).

[653] Laura Antonelli, *Stephan Jenkins of Third Eye Blind*, SongFacts.com (2015-6-16).

[654] Martin Halo, *Third Eye Blind 11.09.2013 The Wellmont Theater*, TheWaster.com (2014-06-20).

[655] Tom Lanham, *Owl City inspired by dreams*, San Francisco Examiner (2012-7-18).

[656] Tom Lanham, *Owl City Talks Nightmares and Dreams*, PureVolume.com (2012-7-19).

[657] Vengeance is Ours!, NME Magazine (November 2001).

[658] *Here Today, Here Tomorrow: Interview with Daniel Johns*, press release on Chairpage.com (1996-01-17).

[659] *Daniel Johns*, Enough Rope with Andrew Denton, ABC.com.au (2004-6-7).

[660] Triple J interview with Daniel Johns, Triple J radio. (Reprinted transcript)

[661] Henry David Thoreau, A Week on the Concord and Merrimack Rivers, J. R. Osgood (1873), p. 314.

[662] Dave Matthews Band, DreamGirl music video (2005).

[663] Nothing But Thieves, If I Get High music video, NBTVEVO YouTube channel (2016-2-8).

[664] from a student enrolled in my Dream Interpretation, Lucid Dreaming & Lucid Living course (1996).

[665] Stephen LaBerge & Howard Rheingold, Exploring the World of Lucid Dreaming, New York: Ballantine Books (1991-11-13), pp. 83-84.

[666] Stephen LaBerge & William Dement. Lateralization of alpha activity for dreamed singing and counting during REM sleep, Psychophysiology, 19 (1982b), pp. 331-332.

[667] Jorge Luis Borges, *Tlön, Uqbar, Orbis Tertius* (1940), (short story in) Labyrinths: Selected Stories & Other Writings, New Directions Publishing (1964), p. 10.

[668] Gavin Edwards, *Sea of Fire*, Spin magazine (September 2000). Reprinted at CreedFeed.com

[669] Joel Whitburn, *The Billboard Book of Top 40 Hits*, 8th Edition, Billboard Publications (2004), p. 514.

[670] Chris DeGarmo, Kerrang (June 1990).

[671] Chris DeGarmo, Empire, Japanese album edition (1990). / Also: Metal Edge (December 1990). / Also: RIP (October 1991). / Also: Queensryche *Interview in a Jar* CD (March 1997).

[672] Chris DeGarmo, RIP (October 1991).

[673] Tim Wade, *Susskind Hotel*, Phish.net (2011-12-11).

[674] Mary Colurso, *Phish Bassist Mike Gordon Hooked on Dreams as Inspiration for his Solo CD, "The Green Sparrow"*, AL.com (2009-9-18).

[675] Jan Phillips, Marry Your Muse: Making a Lasting Commitment to Your Creativity (1997), p. 176.

[676] DreamStates: Mike Gordon, SunDance TV (2011).

[677] Lauren LaRocca, *Another Lucid Dream*, Frederick News Post (2008-7-10).

[678] Pete Stergion, *Interview: Mike Gordon*, BandsThatJam.com (2011-1-25).

[679] Mike Gordon, *ORIGINAL DEMO* (after passing first step of html game), Mike-Gordon.com/andelmans/

[680] Scott Bernstein, *Interview: Mike Gordon's Solo Story*, GlideMagazine.com (2008-8-13).

[681] Kevin O'Donnell, *Q&A: How Mike Gordon Got His Groove Back*, RollingStone.com (2008-6-27).

[682] Op. cit. (SunDance TV).

[683] Stergion (Interview: Mike Gordon).

[684] Zollo (Songwriters), p. 421.

[685] Jas Morgan, Morgan Russell & Steve Ananda, Beyond Hacker Machismo: An Interview with Todd Rundgren. Mondo 2000 #7 (fall 1989), p. 104.

[686] Zollo (Songwriters), pp. 421-422.

[687] *Bang the Drum All Day*,, Wikipedia.org (retrieved 2015-6-26), section: In popular culture.

[688] Scott Mathews, in a private email interview (2015-8-1).

[689] Prince, during performance at Paisley Park, MN (2016/1/21), referred to by: Jeremiah Freed, CNN Interview (2016-4-22), at time: 2min05sec.

[690] *Interview: SOJA*, ArtistDirect.com (2014-7-21).

[691] Michael J. Gelb & Sarah Miller Caldicott, Innovate Like Edison: The Five-Step System for Breakthrough Business Success, Penguin (2007-10-25). p. ~165.

[692] Hugo, directed by Martin Scorsese, screenplay by John Logan (2011), based on book: The Invention of Hugo Cabret by Brian Selznick.

[693] Writer/director James Cameron told me directly that Avatar incorporated two dreams, and the concept for The Terminator grew directly from one of his nightmares, Coast to Coast radio (2010-8-23), hour 1.

[694] Ibid.

[695] Stephenie Meyer, *The Story of Twilight & Getting Published*, StephenieMeyer.com (retrieved 2025-11-14).

[696] The Extreme Makeover TV show was inspired by a dream of show creator Howard Schultz from Lighthearted Entertainment, according to his work colleague Mike Miller who told me that directly in 2005.

[697] Andy Gensler, *Howard Shore, Billboard/THR Maestro Award Honoree, Talks Legendary Film Scores (and Naps)*, Billboard.com (2014-11-6).

[698] Op. cit. (Andy Gensler)

[699] Steve Allen, interviewed on The Merv Griffin Show (1974-8-4).

[700] Vernon Scott, Steve Allen composed 19 songs 'Alice in Wonderland' mini-series, St. Petersburg Times (1985-7-11), p. 19D.

[701] Steve Allen (Merv Griffin Show)

[702] IMDB.com reports the show's release as Dec. 12th, 1978, so it may have aired on NBC multiple times.

[703] What a Dream!, Spartanburg Herald-Journal, South Carolina (1978-12-16), p. 10.

[704] Sam Kennedy, *Radical Dreamer | Inside the mind of gaming brilliant composer Yasunori Mitsuda*, 1up.com (2008-1-28), p. 2.

[705] Kevin Gifford, *Yasunori Mitsuda on Chrono Trigger DS: 'Finally!'*, 1up.com (2008-7-9).

[706] Yasunori Mitsuda, *Chrono Trigger DS Interview With Yasunori Mitsuda (Part 1 of 2)*, GamingMedley.com channel, YouTube.com (uploaded 2008-12-10), at time: 2min35sec

[707] *Yasunori Mitsuda*, Wikipedia.com, in section: Legacy.

[708] Gino Castaldo, *Nel blu di Modugno l'Italia si mise a cantare*, La Repubblica Spettacoli, LaRepubblica.it (1999-11-19).

[709] Salvatore Di Vita, *Domenico Modugno: It Came In a Dream*, ItaloAmericano.org (2013-12-5).

[710] *Grammy Rewind: 1st Annual Grammy Awards*, Grammy.com (retrieved 2015-11-16).

[711] Interview with Louis Armstrong: 'They Cross Iron Curtain to Hear American Jazz', US News & World Report (1955-12-2), p. 57.

[712] Chick Corea, interview #8 by Guy Rodgers for The Montreal International Jazz Festival (2004), at time: 1hr24min50sec.

[713] *Musical Minds*, NOVA television special, PBS (2009-6-30), at time: 43min17sec.

[714] Oliver Sacks, *A Neurologist's Notebook: A Bolt from the Blue*, The New Yorker (2007-07-23).

[715] Sacks (Musicophilia), p. 5.

[716] Anthony Cicoria, live presentation at the 40th Annual SSF-IIIHS International Conference in Montréal (2015-8-14).

[717] Edgar Allan Poe, (in Eleonora chapter of) Poetry and Tales, Library of America (1984), p. 468.

[718] *Land's End*, Billboard.com (2006-2-13).

[719] Grammy.com (retrieved 2015-7-28).

[720] Peter Guralnick, Dream Boogie: The Triumph of Sam Cooke, Little Brown (2005-12-1), p. 112.

[721] Tom Aswell, Louisiana Rocks!: The True Genesis of Rock and Roll, Pelican Publishing (2013-4-22), p. 64.

[722] *Experience the Music: One Hit Wonders and the Songs That Shaped Rock and Roll*, RockHall.com (retrieved 2016-3-3)

[723] Sean Rowley, Doo Wop Ballads, TheNearestFarAwayPlace.co.uk/doo-wop-ballads (retrieved 2016-3-3)

[724] Harriet Menken, National Contest Won With Songs She Heard in Her Sleep, Milwaukee Journal (1934-9-9), p. F-5.

[725] John Dunning, On the Air: The Encyclopedia of Old-Time Radio, Oxford University Press, USA, 1998-5-7), p. 323.

[726] Rebecca Goodman & Barrett J. Brunsman, This Day In Ohio History, Emmis Books (2005), p. 367.

[727] Clifford E. Olstrom, Undaunted by Blindness, 2nd edition, eBookIt.com (2012-7-10).

[728] Jeffrey Himes, *Rahsaan Roland Kirk: The Cult of Kirk*, JazzTimes.com (2008).

[729] William Saunders, Jimi Hendrix: London, Roaring Forties Press (2010), p. 103.

[730] Jeff Coffin, *About: Jeff Coffin*, JeffCoffinMusic.com/about/

[731] Op. cit. (Olstrom)

[732] Op. cit. (Himes)

[733] *Taj Mahal*, Clash Magazine / ClashMusic.com (2009-6-4).

[734] Martin Charles Strong, The Great Rock Discography, Canongate U.S. (2004), pp. 493-494.

[735] Barry Cleveland, *John McLaughlin's 4th Dimension*, GuitarPlayer.com (2014-1-30).

[736] Appointment with the Wise Old Dog, dream artwork and narration by David Blum, DVD available only directly from Sarah Blum, P.O. Box 104, Medina, WA 98039-0104 (1998).

[737] David Blum, The Healing Power of Music, BBC Music Magazine, 4 (1996), p. 30.

[738] Audrey M. Ashley, Famous People Players - A Dream Come True, Ottawa Citizen (1977-4-30), p. 31.

[739] *Famous People Players*, Wikipedia.org (retrieved 2015-10-24), section: Productions.

[740] Michelle Dawn Mooney, Craig Webb interview, Middays with Michelle on WPG 1450AM radio (2015-9-3).

[741] As told to me directly by Stephen Powers (circa 2011).

[742] *Russ Regan*, Wikipedia.org (retrieved 2015-7-22).

[743] Robert Polito, liner notes for The Big Gundown: John Zorn Plays the Music of Ennio Morricone, Nonesuch/Icon (1985).

[744] Ennio Morricone, *The Big Gundown: John Zorn Plays the Music of Ennio Morricone 15th Anniversary Edition,* New York: Tzadik (2000).

[745] Chrissie Hynde, Everything you'd rather not have known about Brian Eno, New Musical Express (1974-2-2), pp. 24 & 29. Reprinted at TheQuietus.com

[746] Sleep Concerts (interview of Robert Rich), FACT Webszine. Reprinted at RobertRich.com (September 2013).

[747] Robert Rich, *Musical lucid dream - Robert Rich interview* (interview by the author), Lucid Living channel, YouTube.com (2016-10-16).

[748] Lester, Paul, *Tank Boy*, The Guardian, London: Guardian Media Group (2001-10-5). Archived on 2008-6-10 from original article.

[749] Rob Young, Lucid Dreaming (cover feature article that includes Richard David James interview), The Wire magazine, Issue 134 (April 1995).

[750] *Albums Revisited: Aphex Twin Selected Ambient Works Volume II Turns 20*, SmellsLikeInfiniteSadness.com (2014-3-2).

[751] Karlheinz Stockhausen, *Helikopter-Streichquartett*, Grand Street 14, no. 4 (Grand Street 56: Dreams, (Spring 1996)), p. 214.

[752] Paul Dirmeikis, Le Souffle du temps: Quodlibet pour Karlheinz Stockhausen. La Seyne-sur-Mer: Éditions Telo Martius (1999), pp. 21-22.

[753] Karlheinz Stockhausen, transcription of premiere, translated by Ian Stuart (previously available at www.stockhausen.org/video_helicopter.html, 2014).

[754] Stockhausen (*Helikopter-Streichquartett*).

[755] Vivien Schweitzer, *Fulfilling a Dream With Strings and Rotors*, New York Times (2008-7-13).

[756] Stockhausen (*Helikopter-Streichquartett*), pp. 213–225.

[757] Karlheinz Stockhausen, *Interview I: Gespräch mit holländischem Kunstkreis* in his *Texte zur Musik* 4. Edited by Christoph von Blumröder / DuMont Dokumente, Cologne:DuMont Buchverlag (1973), p. 511.

[758] Jonathan Cott. *Stockhausen: Conversations with the Composer*, New York: Simon and Schuster (1973), pp. 53-55.

[759] Karlheinz Stockhausen, *Music im Bauch / Music in the Belly / Musique dans le ventre, für 6 Schlagzeuger und Spieluhren* (score), Kürten: Stockhausen-Verlag (1980), p. XIV.

[760] Joan Brunskill, Works embrace sound of music, The Argus Press, Michigan (1994-12-4), p. D1.

[761] Richard Steinitz, György Ligeti: Music of the Imagination. London: Faber and Faber (2003), p. 7. / Also: Boston: Northeastern University Press.

[762] Kaija Saariaho, Grammaire des Rêves, Helsinki: Edition Wilhelm Hansen (1988).

[763] André Breton, *The Manifesto of Surrealism* (1924; 2nd edition: 1929).

[764] Brandon Stosuy, *Current 93*, Pitchfork.com (2006-9-11).

[765] Liner notes for Earth Covers Earth CD, song #12 (1992).

[766] Chris Rice Cooper, *Composer Wendy Mae Chambers: Dreams, Death, Music & Marie Laveau*, ChrisRiceCooper.com (2013-11-1).

[767] Susan Borey, Spin Magazine (August 1984).

[768] Wendy Mae Chambers, *Car Horn Organ: A Brief History*, WendyMaeChambers.com (retrieved 2015-4-4).

[769] Wendy Mae Chambers, *Original Music of Wendy Mae Chambers*, WendyMaeChambers.com (retrieved 2015-4-4).

[770] Leon Hendrix, Jimi Hendrix: A Brother's Story, Macmillan (2012-5-8), p.~175.

[771] Marc Engel, 'Spitfire' Leann Rimes Lets Loose, Fox News Magazine (2013-6-4).

[772] Mark Oldman, Oldman's Brave New World of Wine: Pleasure, Value, and Adventure Beyond Wine's Usual Suspects, W. W. Norton & Company (2010-9-6), p. 244.

[773] As told to me 2010-8-9 by Neil Hedley, radio host at EZRock 99.7 FM, Ottawa since Bublé shared that with him on-air a couple days earlier.

[774] *New To The Top 30: Cam*, CountryCountdownUSA.com (2015-8-8).

[775] CD liner notes for Beautiful As The Moon, Cafe Con Bagels Music (2012-7-9).

[776] Robert Trujillo (interview), *Annecy 2014 - Robert Trujillo - Metallica*, annecyfestival channel, YouTube.com (posted 2014-10-20), at time: 2min01sec.

[777] Michael D. Ayers, *Scarlett Johannsen, Pete Yorn Ready 'Break Up'*, Billboard.com (2009-5-26).

[778] Rolling Stone Encyclopedia of Rock & Roll, Simon & Schuster (2001), p. 757.

[779] Shelly Peiken, *Writing By Committee*, ShellyPeiken.com (2015-9-23).

[780] Jon Matsumoto, Vanessa Carlton, MusicWorld, (2002-4-30). Reprinted at BMI.com

[781] The Voice, episode 2, season 10, NBC (2016-3-1) / [Written summary: Théoden Janes, *Could Two Charlotte-area natives find fame on 'The Voice'?*, The Charlotte Observer (2016-3-9)]

[782] Laurie Poulter, La Voix Junior, TVA (2017-10-8). At time: 1h35min.

[783] Amina Mireille, La Voix Junior, TVA (2017-10-15).

[784] This heartwarming story was shared with me directly by Shirley Lawrence who called in during an interview I did on Coast to Coast radio (2016-11-1).

[785] The Answer is You (DVD) by Rev. Michael Beckwith, Los Angeles: Agape Media International (2009).

[786] *Bill Callahan: "I feel like it's my duty to earn the air I breathe everyday"*, Uncut.co.uk (2014-2-7).

[787] Backstrom, Season 1, Episode 2, FOX Television (2015-1-29).

[788] Road show revives country legend, Lawrence Journal-World, Kansas (1976-5-5), p. 43.

[789] Mike Boehm, *A Match Made for a Folk Ballad*, Los Angeles Times / latimes.com (1999-2-16).

790 Richard Hawley, *Time Has Made A Change: Richard Hawley on Late Night Final*, QTheMusic.com (2014-10-29)

[791] Rupert Hughes, *Contemporary American Composers*, Project Gutenberg eBook #23800 (2007-12-10). [Note: when using the preceding link, an additional click is required on "Read this book online: HTML"]

[792] William B. Irvine, Aha!: The Moments of Insight That Shape Our World, Oxford University Press (2015-1-2), p. 269.

[793] Ann McCutchan, *The Muse that Sings : Composers Speak about the Creative Process*, USA: Oxford University Press (1999-10-18), p. 193.

[794] John D. Luerssen, Fleshtones Celebrate 'Hipster Heaven' Song Premiere, RollingStone.com (2014-2-3).

[795] Jake Shears, interview with Jools Holland on Holland's show *Later*, BBC2, Series 28, Episode 6 (2006-12-8).

[796] Reverend Horton Heat (interview), National Public Radio, Weekend Edition (1998-05-02).

[797] Laura Studaras, *Melody's Echo Chamber, Location, Location, Location*, www.UnderTheRadarMag.com (2012-9-7).

[798] Elsianne Caplette, shared with me in a live and email interview (2015-7-29).

[799] M. Miller, Musician's reputation began to spread only when he was 62. Toronto Globe and Mail (1987-07-17). p. D11.

[800] Carol Banks Weber, *What Dreams May Come: Songwriters Muse on Nocturnal Inspirations*, AXS.com (2015-1-2).

[801] Thomas F. Sheehan, Unexplained Piano Playing Ability Astounding – Woman dreams original music; plays pieces spontaneously, Bangor Daily News (1989-11-16), p. 23.

[802] Curtiss Hoffman, The Gilgamesh Cantata: A Personal Exploration of Dreams and Music, Dream Network Journal, Vol. 30, No. 4 (Winter 2011-2012).

[803] Nightwatcher, *Interview with Kevin Godley of 10cc*, RockNRollUniverse.com (2007-4-7).

[804] Jaguares biography, ArtistDirect.com (retrieved 2016-3-3)

[805] Simon Jeffes, PenguinCafe.com/original/simon.htm (retrieved 2015-3-2).

[806] John Diliberto, *Echo Location: Qntal's Medieval Electronica*, Echoes.org (2009-8-5).

[807] Adam Bychawski, *Two Door Cinema Club reveal 'Sleep Alone' was inspired by drug-induced dreams*, NME.com (2012-8-7).

[808] Barrett, p. 77.

[809] *Little Horn*, www.mansonwiki.com (retrieved 2015-3-2).

[810] *Tourniquet (Marilyn Manson Song)*, Wikipedia.org (retrieved 2015-3-2).

[811] *The Cramps Luc Interior RIP*, NME.com (2009-3-23).

[812] John Gentile, *Tech N9ne Puts a 'Hiccup' in Evildoers' Plans - Premiere*, RollingStone.com (2013-11-25).

[813] Richie Unterberger, liner notes for The Wackers Wackering Heights, Elektra Entertainment (1971). Reprinted at: RichieUnterberger.com/wackering.html

[814] *Maids of Gravity*, ArtistDirect.com (retrieved 2016-3-3)

[815] Michael Roberts, *Give The People a Hand*, WestWord.com (2000-3-16).

[816] *Wolf Gang Biography*, ArtistDirect.com (retrieved 2016-3-3)

[817] Fred Dellar, Ask Fred (interview with Thea Gilmore), Mojo Magazine issue #230 (January 2013).

[818] John Hicks, (press release:) Valentine's tribute to Elvis at The Academy Basingstoke, HeadlineManagement.Blogspot.ca (2008-1-1).

[819] Hudost's Secret Weapon Against 'Boring' Music, Shutter 16 Magazine review (2012-4-21). Reprinted at: Hudost.com

[820] Mark Jordan, No idle time for 'Idol' contestant Dave Archuleta, Memphis' Commerical Appeal (2010-9-9).

[821] Michael Hochanadel, Rogers ready to be inspired by himself, fans at Eighth Step, The Daily Gazette, Schenectady, New York (2002-3-21), p. D5.

[822] John Law, Dream turns into reality for local singer, Niagara Falls Review (2007-10-5).

[823] David Renshaw, *Gerard Way reveals lyrics to new solo song 'Millions'*, NME.com (2013-7-30).

[824] Austen Diamond, Liner Notes: Burnell Washburn, CityWeekly.net (2012-4-5).

[825] Kate Mossman, *Ben Gibbard: 'We've got a superhero in Seattle. I'm not making this up'*, TheGuardian.com (2012-11-14).

[826] Mew Biography, ArtistDirect.com (retrieved 2016-3-3)

[827] Rosalind Cartwright, Elizabeth Butters, Martin Weinstein & Leonard Kroeker, *The Effects of Presleep Stimuli of Different Sources and Types on REM Sleep*, Psychophysiology, Volume 14, Issue 4 (July 1977), pp. 388–392.

[828] Ed Tick, *The Practice of Dream Healing: Bringing Ancient Greek Mysteries into Modern Medicine*, Quest Books (2001).

[829] Corinne Heline, Music: the keynote of human evolution, J. F. Rowny Press (1965), p. C-66.

[830] A.W. Snyder & D.J. Mitchell, Is integer arithmetic fundamental to mental processing? The mind's secret arithmetic, Proceedings of the Royal Society of London B (1999), 266, pp. 587–592.

[831] Craig Copetas, *Beat Godfather Meets Glitter Mainman: William Burroughs Interviews David Bowie*, Rolling Stone Magazine (1974-2-28).

[832] Garry Abrams, Millionaire culled Riches from Land of Dreams, The Bulletin, Bend Oregon (1987-5-31), p. B3.

[833] Rodney R. Dietert & Janice Dietert, Science Sifting: Tools for Innovation in Science and Technology, World Scientific (2013-5-20), p. 172.

[834] Stampi & Broughton, *Why We Nap*: *Evolution, Chronobiology, and Functions of Polyphasic and Ultrashort Sleep*, Springer Science & Business Media (2013-11-27), p. 184.

[835] both drawings are from the Codex Atlanticus, stored at the Ambrosiana Library in Milan Italy.

[836] Mario Taddei, Edoardo Zanon & Domenico Laurenza, Leonardo's Machines: Secrets and Inventions in the Da Vinci Codices, Taylor & Francis (2005), pp. 207-208.

[837] Zollo (Songwriters), p. 373.

[838] Arthur M. Abell, Talks with Great Composers: Candid Conversations with Brahms, Puccini, Strauss, and Others, New York: Carol Publishing Group, Citadel Press (1994); (c) 1955, 1987 by Philosophical Library, Inc.

[839] Jorge Luis Borges, *Tlön, Uqbar, Orbis Tertius* (1940), (short story in) Labyrinths: Selected Stories & Other Writings, New Directions Publishing (1964), p. 10.

[840] Salvador Dali, 50 Secrets of Craftsmanship, Dover Publications; Reprint edition (1992-6-4). Also published by Courier Corporation (2013-6-3), pp. 36-37.

[841] Jessica Nye, PhD, *Morning Dream Recall: These Are the Factors That Influence It*, www.NeurologyAdvisor.com (2025-3-28).

www.ingramcontent.com/pod-product-compliance
Lightning Source LLC
Chambersburg PA
CBHW060457090426
42735CB00011B/2012